HUGO'S SIMP

FRENCH
IN THREE MONTHS

HUGO'S LANGUAGE BOOKS LTD
LONDON

ISBN 0 85285 025 5

*Revised and rewritten by
John and Yvonne Hetherington*

PRINTED IN GREAT BRITAIN BY
HAZELL WATSON AND VINEY LTD,
AYLESBURY, BUCKS

PREFACE

In preparing Part I of this Grammar, we have assumed that the reader wants to learn French from a practical angle and have accordingly set out those rules that will be of most use to him in this respect. The order in which they are given also takes the need for rapid progress into consideration. This order is combined with exercises containing sentences of as practical a nature as is possible within the limitations of the concurrent vocabulary, so that you will be able to put your knowledge of the language to use at an early stage. The Verbs have been simplified as much as possible; for detailed reference (complete conjugation tables and so forth) we recommend our "French Verbs Simplified". The Hugo system of Imitated Pronunciation is used throughout.

In Part II we progress to the use of idiom and common colloquial expressions, and then to reading practice. Any serious student of the language will need to have a thorough grasp of such things, and the less dedicated will find that the business of language learning takes on a new (and much brighter) light when the living idiomatic language is displayed. With an eye to the needs of the visitor to France, we have included specialized vocabularies on such subjects as travel, household articles, shops, health and so on. These lists do not merely constitute a sort of phrase book; use them together with the words and constructions already learnt in Part I, interchange them, and thus consolidate your knowledge of the language.

Part III consists of the answers to the grammar exercises in Part I. To begin with, you may prefer to check each sentence individually, despite the risk of glimpsing in advance the answer to the following one. This is preferable to making the same mistake unchecked throughout the whole exercise.

CONTENTS

PART I

PART II

PART III

FRENCH
IN THREE MONTHS

I

GRAMMAR SIMPLIFIED
EXERCISES AND VOCABULARIES
CONVERSATION

INTRODUCTION

The following few pages deal mainly with pronunciation and grammatical terms; there is no need to learn them by heart, and after reading them through you should start the first lesson. By referring back to the rules on pronunciation frequently you will soon know them.

In studying the lessons, first read each rule carefully, comparing with the examples underneath. Then translate and re-translate (preferably in writing) the exercise which follows, until you can put every sentence readily and correctly into French. The conversational sentences should be read aloud and their construction carefully noted. As the book progresses, so do these sentences become more advanced, introducing idioms and words commonly used in colloquial French.

PRONUNCIATION

In our Imitated Pronunciation we represent French sounds in English syllables; this is not very easy because there are some which have no English counterpart, and these can only be imitated approximately. However, that is better than nothing, and we have assumed the student to be working on his own. If he can get to hear the actual sounds spoken in conversation, so much the better.

French words are usually stressed very slightly on the last vowel pronounced, but beginners should pronounce all syllables with equal emphasis. As far as the notation of the Imitated Pronunciation is concerned, always bear in mind that:

ăh   must always be pronounced very short and sharp.

ng   (*italics*) must never be pronounced; these letters merely indicate that the preceding vowel has a nasal sound.

r   (*italics*) must never be pronounced; we insert it to ensure the correct pronunciation of the preceding vowel.

sh   (**bold type**) always sounds like 's' in 'leisure'.

e*r*   is the sound of 'u' in 'fur'.

er   is the same 'u' sound, but longer, with the r sounded.

EE or E (sometimes I) represents the sound of the French **u**, the exact equivalent of which does not occur in English. Say 'tree' with the lips rounded as if you were whistling, and the terminal sound is exactly that of the French **u**.

The general rules of pronunciation now follow.

Consonants are pronounced as in English, except:

c   before **e, i** or **y** sounds like 's', otherwise like 'k'.
ç   (ç cedilla) always sounds like 's'.
g   before **e, i** or **y** sounds like 's' in 'measure', otherwise like 'g' in 'go'.
h   is generally silent.
j   always sounds like 's' in 'measure'.
r   is stronger than in English.
s   between two vowels sounds like 'z'.

Important: consonants are not pronounced when they form the last letter of a word, except **c, f, l** and **r**, which *are pronounced*

Vowels are nearly always pronounced short, unless there is a circumflex accent (^) over them.

a   is like 'ah', but very short.
         case, cas, kăh; jackal, chacal, shăh-kăhll.
e   in the middle of a syllable is like 'ai' in 'fair'.
         sea, mer, mair; iron, fer, fair.
e   at the end of a syllable is like 'u' in 'fur'.
         horse, cheval, sher-văhll; mattress, matelas, măh-ter-lăh.
e   is mute at the end of a word of more than one syllable.
         cup, tasse, tăhss; ill, malade, măh-lăhdd.
é   (acute accent) is like the interjection 'eh!'.
         been, été, eh-teh*; coffee, café, kăh-feh.
è   (grave accent) and **ê** (circumflex) are like 'ay'.
         father, père, pair; dream, rêve, raiv.
i or **y** is like 'ee' in 'seen' if long, like 'i' in 'ill' if short.
         empty, vide, veed; syllable, syllabe, sil-ăhb.
o   is somewhat like 'o' in 'not'.
         thing, chose, shohz; to sleep, dormir, dor-meer.
u   is the tricky 'ee' pronounced with rounded lips.
         street, rue, rE; future, futur, fE-tEEr.
ai, ei are both similar to 'ay'.
         but, mais, may; queen, reine, rain.
au, eau are like 'oh'.
         warm, chaud, shoh; present, cadeau, kăh-doh.
eu, oeu are like 'u' in 'fur'.
         nine, neuf, nerf; sister, soeur, ser. ✳
oi   is like 'wah' or 'o'ah'.
         king, roi, ro'ăh; month, mois, mo'ăh.
ou   is like 'oo'.
         wheel, roue, roo; knife, couteau, koo-toh.

---

* In the Imitated Pronunciation, the sound of **é** is shown by 'eh' and that of **è** by 'ai' or 'ay', though in English 'eh' and 'ay' have practically the same sound.

7

Nasal sounds: Any vowel before **m** or **n** is pronounced nasally. We imitate their sounds by putting *ng* after the vowel; this *ng* must on no account be sounded.

o before **m** or **n** = 'ong' in 'song'; **om** and **on** sound alike.
  long, long, lo*ng*; name, nom, no*ng*.
u before **m** or **n** = 'ung' in 'lung'; **um** and **un** sound alike.
  perfume, parfum, pah**r**-fu*ng*; one, un, u*ng*.
a or **e** before **m** or **n** = 'ahng', similar to 'au' in 'aunt'; **am**, **an**, **em** and **en** all sound alike.
  child, enfant, ah*ng*-fah*ng*; time, temps, tah*ng*; field, champ, shah*ng*.
i before **m** or **n** = 'ang' in 'sang'; **im** and **in** sound alike.
  wine, vin, va*ng*; simple, simple, sa*ng*-pl.

The nasal sound of **i** is always used if there is an **i** or **y** in the syllable; therefore **im**, **in**, **ym**, **yn**, **aim**, **ain**, **eim** and **ein** are all pronounced alike. At the end of a syllable, **ien** is pronounced as if spelt i-en. Note that there is no nasal sound if **m** or **n** is followed by a vowel, or if there are two **m**'s or two **n**'s.

  dog, chien, she-a*ng*; well, bien, be-a*ng*.
  one (*fem.*), une, ᴇn; man, homme, omm.

Liquid sounds: **il** and **ill**, if liquid, are like 'ee-e'.

il is only liquid if at the end of words and following a vowel.
  work, travail, tră-vă-văh'e; sun, soleil, so-lay'e.
ill is always liquid, except in words beginning ill-, mill- and vill-.
  ticket, billet, bee-yay; family, famille, făh-mee-ye.
gn is like 'ni' in 'companion', **gne** if final sounds like 'ing'—but many natives will pronounce this ending as 'n-yer'.
  signal, signal, seen-yăhl; lamb, agneau, ăhn-yoh;
  country, campagne, kah*ng*-păh'ing or kah*ng*-pahn-ye**r**.

Other variations:

er at the end of words of more than one syllable is like **é** ('eh').
  to speak, parler, pah**r**-leh; to smoke, fumer, fᴇ-meh.
ez at the end of a word is also sounded 'eh', as if acute **é**.
  nose, nez, neh; shut, fermez, fai**r**-meh.
y between two vowels is equal to 'i-i' or 'i-y'.
  royal, royal, ro'ah-yăhl; to pay, payer, pay-yeh.
ti unless beginning a word is usually pronounced 'si', especially if between two vowels.
  diplomacy, diplomatie, de-plo-măh-se.

But: in the terminations **stion**, **xtion**, **tié**, **tier**, **tière** and **tième**, the **t** is pronounced as in English.
  question, question, kess-te-o*ng*; litter, litière, lee-te-ai**r**

8

If a word beginning with a vowel or an h mute follows a final consonant, this consonant (even if otherwise mute) is joined to the second word *whenever no pause could be made between the two vowels*. When thus linked to the following word, s and x sound like z, d like t, and f like v. This is called the 'liaison'.

you are, vous êtes, voo z'ate; two men, deux hommes, der z'omm

The French Alphabet: When spelling out names, remember that the pronunciation of individual letters differs from the English in many cases. K and W do not occur in real French words, and are sometimes omitted from the alphabet.

A, ah B, beh C, seh D, deh E, eh F, eff G, sheh H, ahsh I, ee
J, shee K, kah L, ell M, emm N, en O, o P, peh Q, kEE R, airr
S, ess T, teh U, EE V, veh W, doohble-veh X, eks Y, ee-greck
Z, zaid

Accents: These aren't an optional feature of written French. They are a guide to pronunciation and must always be put in. There are five kinds: (1) the acute (é), which is only found on the e; (2) the grave (à), which is found on the a, e, and u; (3) the circumflex (î), which can come on any vowel; (4) the cedilla (ç), which softens the c; (5) the diaresis or tréma (ü), which can go on the e, i, or u. Accents on capital letters are optional, though generally left out except when the whole words are printed in capitals.

GRAMMATICAL TERMS

It is impossible to describe the workings of another language without occasionally using rather daunting-looking grammatical terms, some of which may be unfamiliar to readers who have never tackled a foreign language before and whose knowledge of English grammar may be sketchy. However, don't be put off; the most forbidding jargon only boils down to our everyday experience of our own language, and we are only unfamiliar with the names of things, not the things themselves. So for the benefit of those who may need it, there follow some notes about the terms used in this book, with some comments on the main differences between English and French.

9

Gender

Means masculine or feminine. We still keep the gender distinction in such pairs as actor/actress, but on the whole gender has disappeared from English. In French, however, all nouns are either masculine or feminine and affect the endings (or terminations) of the words surrounding them accordingly. Gender isn't too troublesome when we are concerned with *natural* gender—that is, things that are male and female in nature. *Le père* (the father) is masculine, *la mère* (the mother) feminine. But *grammatical* gender is a different matter. Look at this pair of sentences:

> The beautiful French villages they visited
> The beautiful French towns they visited

A difference of one word. Now look at the French translations:

> Les be*aux* villages franç*ais* qu'ils ont visit*és*
> Les be*lles* villes franç*aises* qu'ils ont visit*ées*

The fact that *village* is a masculine noun and *ville* a feminine noun (and this is a good example of the arbitrariness of grammatical gender) makes for important differences in the endings of the other words in the sentences. There *are* rough-and-ready guides for determining gender, some of which we mention in the book, but none are foolproof, and sorting out the various agreements of French nouns and adjectives is one of the main difficulties of learning the language.

Number

Simply means singular or plural. Singular nouns must have singular agreements, plural nouns plural agreements.

> The open window *La* fenêtre ouver*te*
> The open windows *Les* fenêtres ouver*tes*

Tense

Like the Latin on which it is based, French is a highly *inflected* language—which means that the relations to one another of words in a sentence are made clear by word-endings, not by word-order. English isn't (though it used to be), and the main

10

difficulty for English people learning French is to understand the importance of different endings to words in different circumstances. This applies particularly to gender and *tense*. The tense of a verb places it in time, whether present, past, or future. There are distinctions within these categories, but they are the main ones. English has a very simple tense-structure. French has a very complicated one. Look at these examples:

PRESENT		FUTURE	
I give	je donne	I will give	je donnerai
you give	tu donnes	you will give	tu donneras
he gives	il donne	he will give	il donnera
we give	nous donnons	we will give	nous donnerons
you give	vous donnez	you will give	vous donnerez
they give	ils donnent	they will give	ils donneront

IMPERFECT	
I used to give	je donnais
you used to give	tu donnais
he used to give	il donnait
we used to give	nous donnions
you used to give	vous donniez
they used to give	ils donnaient

Here are 18 different varieties of 'giving' rendered by 11 words in English and 22 in French. The reason is that English has a number of highly useful little *auxiliary* verbs (will, would, should, was, used to, have, has, had etc.) that do the work borne by the French terminations (or inflexions). Typically, an English verb has only four or five terminations—give, gives, giving, given, gave—while the French verb *donner* has 39. Most of them have to be learned before you can have a good grasp of even conversational French.

A further difficulty arises because English often disguises the true tense of a verb. We say: 'Next week I go to Paris' when in French you must say: 'La semaine prochaine j'irai (I will go) à Paris.' So it's not just a question of knowing the French verb tenses, but of sorting out the true meaning of the English sentence before deciding which one to use.

Overleaf is a table showing all the tenses of a verb and the other terms used to describe its parts. The Future Perfect (sometimes called the Future in the Past) and Pluperfect are not named as such in this book, but practice in them is of course included.

11

INFINITIVE: to give
STEM: giv-
PRESENT PARTICIPLE: giving
PAST PARTICIPLE: given (Note that some English verbs have two; French verbs have only one)

PERSON/NUMBER	PRESENT	FUTURE	IMPERFECT	PERFECT
1st Person Sing. 2nd „ „ 3rd „ „ 1st Person Plur. 2nd „ „ 3rd „ „	I give *or* I am giving *or* I do give you give he *or* she *or* it gives we give you give they give	I will give *or* I shall give *etc.*	I used to give *or* I was giving *etc.*	I have given *or* I gave *or* I did give *etc.*

PERSON/NUMBER	FUTURE PERFECT	PLUPERFECT	CONDITIONAL	PAST HISTORIC*
1st Person Sing. *etc.*	I will have given *or* I shall have given *etc.*	I had given *etc.*	I would give (if I could) *etc.*	I gave *etc.*

* The Past Historic is a past tense used only in written French, *never* in conversation.

The INTERROGATIVE (Question) form is 'Do I give? Shall I give?' etc.
The NEGATIVE form is 'I do not *or* don't give, I won't give' etc.
The IMPERATIVE (Command) form is 'Give!' 'Let us give'.

The tenses above belong to what is known as the ACTIVE voice. The PASSIVE voice is 'I am given, I will be given, I used to be given' etc. However the Passive is usually avoided in spoken French (See Para. 145).

The SUBJUNCTIVE tenses are not included above, but a full explanation of their function and meaning is given in Lesson 26.

Regular and Irregular Verbs

A Regular verb is one that behaves predictably, regularly, in all its tenses. Knowing that *donner* is a regular -er verb, and knowing the rules about the formation of tenses in this *conjugation* (a collection of similar verbs), you can then immediately use the verb in all its possible inflexions. The main Regular con-

12

jugations end in -er, -ir, and -re. Unfortunately most of the commonest French verbs are not so helpful. They are Irregular. The *stems* vary according to tense and their participles often vary too, though luckily the terminations, with a few minor exceptions, remain regular. For example *aller* (to go) is an Irregular verb. The Future of the Regular verb *donner* is *je donnerai*. The Future of *aller* is not *j'allerai* but *j'irai*. There is nothing for it but to learn the irregularities of French verbs by constant practice.

Parts of a Sentence

I like wine

That's very simple. The Subject of 'like' is 'I' and its Object is 'wine'. However the Subject and Object in an English sentence are not always so easy to pick out, and they are parts that sometimes *must* be accurately identified before you can translate into French. Look at this sentence:

She gave the teacher an apple

At first glance the Object of 'gave' might be taken as 'the teacher', but this is in fact the *Indirect* Object, the *Direct* Object being 'an apple'. By leaving out a word '(to) the teacher' English creates a possible confusion where there can never be any in French, because French grammar is always precise. In French you would have to put the missing 'to' in, in order to make quite clear the grammatical relationships of the sentence. In the same way English sometimes likes to disguise the presence of a *Relative Clause*:

The book she bought them was the one I showed her yesterday

'(that *or* which) she bought (for) them' and '(that *or* which) I showed (to) her' are in fact Relative Clauses and must always be given in full in French.

Le livre *qu'*elle *leur* a acheté était celui *que* je *lui* ai montré hier
The book *which* she *for-them* has bought was the-one *which* I *to-her* have shown yesterday

Always make sure that you have identified the parts—particularly Subject, Direct Object, Indirect Object—and the tenses of an English sentence before you try to put it into French.

13

LESSON ONE

1. A or AN is translated **un** before a masculine noun, and **une** before a feminine noun:

a ticket	**un billet** (u*ng* bee-yay)
a mother	**une mère** (ᴇᴇn mai*r*)

Most names of things are masculine in French, except those ending in **-e**, most of which are feminine (those ending in **-te**, **-eur**, **-ion** and **-son** are also generally feminine).

2. THE is translated **le** before a masculine singular noun (*m*), **la** before a feminine singular noun (*f*):

the day	**le jour** (le*r* shoohr)
the woman	**la dame** (lăh dăhmm)

3. Before a vowel or H mute use **l'** instead of **le** or **la**. All H's are mute (that is, unaspirated) unless we indicate the contrary:

the friend	**l'ami** (lăh-me)
the man	**l'homme** (lomm)

Exercise I

1 a brother; 2 a sister; 3 a ticket; 4 a mother; 5 a day; 6 a door; 7 an hotel; 8 a railway station; 9 a friend; 10 the book; 11 the door; 12 the father; 13 the church; 14 the table; 15 the suitcase; 16 the address; 17 the day; 18 the hour; 19 the hotel; 20 the mother; 21 the friend.

VOCABULARY: brother, **frère** (frair); sister, **soeur** (ser); door, **porte** *f* (port); hotel, **hôtel** *m* (oh-tell); railway station, **gare** *f* (găhr); book; **livre** *m* (lee-vr); father, **père** (pair); church, **église** *f* (eh-gleez); table, **table** *f* (tăhbl); suitcase, **valise** *f* (văh-leez); address, **adresse** *f* (ăh-dress); hour, **heure** *f* (er).

CONVERSATIONAL SENTENCES

Où[1] est[2] la gare?	Where is the railway station?
La gare est là[3].	The railway station is there.
Qui[4] est à[5] la porte?	Who is at the door?
Un homme est à la porte.	A man is at the door.
Qui a[6] le livre.	Who has the book?

Le frère a le livre.	The brother has the book.
Où est l'hôtel?	Where is the hotel?
L'hôtel est ici.	The hotel is here.
Qui est la dame?	Who is the woman?
L'oncle[7] a un ami.	The uncle has a friend.
Où est le billet?	Where is the ticket?
La mère a une valise.	The mother has a suitcase.

IMITATED PRONUNCIATION: 1 oo, 2 ay; 3 lăh; 4 kee; 5 ăh (always very short); 6 ăh; 7 ong-kl.

In French words, the last vowel pronounced is usually stressed very slightly, but beginners should pronounce all syllables with equal emphasis.

4. THE must always be translated **les** if followed by a plural noun. The **s** which is added to form the plural of nouns is not sounded, but the **s** of **les** is sometimes linked to the noun when the noun begins with an H mute or a vowel.

the sisters	**les soeurs** (lay ser)
the friends	**les amis** (lay z'ăh-me)
the days	**les jours** (lay shoohr)
the churches	**les églises** (lay z'eh-gleez)

EXERCISE II

1 the books;   2 the fathers;   3 the tables;   4 the suitcases;
5 the hotels;   6 the addresses;   7 the tickets;   8 the hours.

5.   Present tense of TO HAVE, **avoir**

I have	**j'ai** (sheh)
you have (thou hast)*	**tu as** (tee ah)
he has, she has†	**il a, elle a** (ill ăh, ell ăh)
we have	**nous avons** (noo z'ăh-vong)
you have	**vous avez** (voo z'ăh-veh)
they (m/f) have†	**ils ont, elles ont** (ill z'ong, ell z'ong)

---

* The second person singular (**tu**) of a French verb is used only between close friends. When in doubt, use the plural form (**vous**). The same applies to the pronouns **ton, ta** and **tes** (See Para. 38).

† The third person (**a, ont**) must be used after nouns: the man has, **l'homme a**; the men have, **les hommes ont**.

15

Exercise III

1 he has bought a car;   2 we have found two suitcases;
3 they (*f*) have received a letter;   4 the brother and the sister
have bought a dog;   5 I have received two parcels;   6 you
have found the passports;   7 she has a television set.

VOCABULARY: bought, **acheté** (ăhsh-teh); car, **voiture** *f* (vo'ăh-tEEr);
found, **trouvé** (troo-veh); two, **deux** (de*r*); received, **reçu** (re*r*-SEE);
letter, **lettre** *f* (lettr); and, **et** (eh); dog, **chien** *m* (she-a*ng*); parcel,
paquet *m* (păh-kay); passport, **passeport** *m* (păhss-po*r*); television set,
télévision *f* (teh-leh-ve-ze-o*ng*).

6. OUR **notre, nos*** (notr, noh)
  YOUR **votre, vos*** (votr, voh)
  THEIR **leur, leurs*** (ler, ler)

our brother	**notre frère**	our brothers	**nos frères**
our sister	**votre soeur**	your sisters	**vos soeurs**
their friend	**leur ami**	their friends	**leurs amis**

Exercise IV

1 from our door;   2 to your hotels;   3 the doors of our
church;   4 at their table;   5 from your hotel to our door;
6 at their church;   7 of our tickets;   8 of their friends.

VOCABULARY: from *or* of, **de** (de*r*); to *or* at, **à** (ah).

CONVERSATIONAL SENTENCES

Où est votre voiture?	Where is your car?
Notre voiture est là (ici).	Our car is there (here).
Qui a trouvé les passeports?	Who has found the passports?
J'ai trouvé les passeports.	I have found the passports.
Qui a reçu les lettres?	Who has received the letters?
Ils ont reçu les paquets et[1] les lettres.	They have received the parcels and the letters.
Notre père a acheté une voiture et une télévision.	Our father has bought a car and a television set.
Elle a trouvé un chien.	She has found a dog.

PRON.: 1 eh. The t of ET is never pronounced, even if a Vowel follows.

---

* Plural forms to be used if the noun following is plural.

LESSON TWO

7. The plural of most French Nouns is formed by adding **s** to the Singular, as in English (See Rule 4). This **s** is not pronounced.

The following additional Rules apply to comparatively few words. (For further exceptions see Appendix, p. 124.)

(A) Words ending in **-s, -x, -z,** do not change in the Plural; as,

a month	un mois (u*ng* mo'ăh)	two months	deux mois (de*r* mo'ăh)
a price	un prix (u*ng* pree)	two prices	deux prix (de*r* pree)
the nose	le nez (le*r* neh)	the noses	les nez (lay neh)

(B) Most words ending in **-au** or **-eu** add **x** in the Plural; as,

a hat	un chapeau (u*ng* shăh-poh)
two hats	deux chapeaux (de*r* shăh-poh)
a nephew	un neveu (u*ng* ne*r*-ve*r*)
two nephews	deux neveux (de*r* ne*r*-ve*r*)

(c) Most words ending in **-al** change **-al** into **-aux;** as,

an animal	un animal (u*ng* ăh-ne-măhl)
two animals	deux animaux (de*r* z'ăh-ne-moh)

Exercise I

1 a knife, the knives; **2** one (= an) arm, two arms; **3** the newspaper, the newspapers; **4** the voice, the voices; **5** the fire, the fires; **6** one (= a) son, three sons.

VOCABULARY: knife, **couteau** *m* (koo-toh); arm, **bras** *m* (brăh); newspaper, **journal** *m* (shoohr-năhl); voice, **voix** *f* (vo'ăh); fire, **feu** *m* (fe*r*); son, **fils** *m* (fiss); three, **trois** (tro'ăh).

8. The INTERROGATIVE (Question) form of **j'ai,** etc., is formed as in English; but a hyphen (-) is placed between the verb and pronoun, and in the third person singular a **t** between two hyphens (-t-), thus:

have I?	ai-je? (aysh)
have you?	as-tu? (ăh-tEE)
has he? has she?	a-t-il? a-t-elle? (ăh-til, ăh-tel)
have we?	avons-nous? (ăh-vo*ng* noo)
have you?	avez-vous? (ăh-veh voo)
have they? (*m/f*)	ont-ils? ont-elles? (o*ng*-til, o*ng*-tel)

17

EXERCISE II

1 Have I met your nephews?* 2 Have they sent a postcard?
3 Have you written the address? 4 Have we received the newspapers? 5 Has he seen the animals? 6 Have they (*f*) written
to their friends? 7 They have two sons. 8 Have you seen your
friends? 9 Have they bought your house? 10 Has she
received the parcel?

VOCABULARY: met, **rencontré** (rah*ng*-ko*ng*-treh); sent, **envoyé**
(ah*ng*-vo'ăh-yeh); postcard, **carte postale** *f* (kăhrt poss-tahl); seen, **vu**
(VEE); written, **écrit** (eh-kree); house, **maison** *f* (may-zo*ng*).

CONVERSATIONAL SENTENCES

Avez vous vu notre ami?	Have you seen our friend?
Oui¹, j'ai vu votre ami.	Yes, I have seen your friend.
A-t-il acheté la maison?	Has he bought the house?
Non², il a acheté leur voiture,	No, he has bought their car.
Ont-ils reçu nos lettres?	Have they received our letters?
Oui, ils ont reçu deux lettres.	Yes, they have received two letters.
Qui a trouvé l'adresse?	Who has found the address?
Notre soeur a trouvé l'adresse.	Our sister has found the address.
Où avez-vous acheté le billet?	Where did you buy the ticket?
J'ai acheté le billet ici.	I bought the ticket here.
Leurs neveux sont là.	Their nephews are there.

PRON.: 1 we; 2 no*ng*

9. MY **mon, ma, mes** (mo*ng*, măh, may)
  HIS, HER, ITS **son, sa, ses** (so*ng*, săh, say)
  YOUR (familiar form) **ton, ta, tes** (to*ng*, tăh, tay)

mon, ton, son are used if the following Noun is	*masculine singular*
ma, ta, sa ,, ,, ,, ,, ,, ,, is	*feminine singular*
mes, tes, ses ,, ,, ,, ,, ,, ,, is	*plural*

* (or Did I meet) The three forms of the perfect tense in English—
I met, I have met, I did meet—are all translated by *j'ai rencontré*. Similarly
ai-je rencontré can be translated have I met? *or* did I meet?

18

my brother, **mon frère**	my sister, **ma soeur**
his (*or* her) sister, **sa soeur**	her (*or* his) brother, **son frère**
my brothers, **mes frères**	his (*or* her) sisters, **ses soeurs**

Remember that **son frère** means 'her brother' as well as 'his brother,' and that **sa soeur** means 'his sister' as well as 'her sister,' because these words always take the Gender of the FOLLOWING Noun.

EXERCISE III

1 my book; 2 his father; 3 my hat; 4 her mother; 5 my arms; 6 his shirts; 7 my (bed)room; 8 his mother; 9 her handbag; 10 her family; 11 his family; 12 her hats.

VOCABULARY: shirt, **chemise** *f* (sher-meez); bedroom, **chambre** *f* (shah*ng*-br)—Any other room in a house is *une pièce*; handbag, **sac à main** *m* (săhck-ăh-mă*ng*); family, **famille** *f* (făh-mee-ye).

10. **mon, ton, son** are used before words beginning with a vowel or an H mute, *even if the Noun is feminine*:

    my friend (*f*), **mon amie**   her address, **son adresse**

EXERCISE IV

1 her handwriting; 2 his school; 3 his room; 4 her uncle; 5 his street; 6 his shoulder; 7 her shoulder.

VOCABULARY: handwriting, **écriture** *f* (eh-kre-tEEr); school, **école** *f* (eh-kol); uncle, **oncle** *m* (o*ng*-kl); street, **rue** *f* (rEE); shoulder, **épaule** *f* (eh-pohl).

11. NOT is translated by the two words **ne . . . pas.**

pas always occupies the same place in the sentence as the English word *not*, and **ne** (**n'** only before a vowel) always PRECEDES THE VERB; thus,

I have not	**je n'ai pas** (sher neh păh)
you have not	**tu n'as pas** (tEE năh păh)
he has not	**il n'a pas** (ill năh păh)
we have not	**nous n'avons pas** (noo năh-vo*ng* păh)
you have not	**vous n'avez pas** (voo năh-veh păh)
they have not	**ils n'ont pas** (il no*ng* păh)

have I not?	n'ai-je pas? (naysh păh)
have you not?	n'as-tu pas? (năh-tee păh)
has he not?	n'a-t-il pas? (năh-til păh)
have we not?	n'avons-nous pas? (năh-vong noo păh)
have you not?	n'avez-vous pas? (năh-veh voo păh)
have they not?	n'ont-ils pas? (nong-til păh)

EXERCISE V

1 Have you not (or haven't you got) my book?*   2 He hasn't seen her handwriting.   3 We haven't found the gloves.   4 Haven't they written to your friends?   5 I haven't read his letter.

VOCABULARY: glove, **gant** *m* (gah*ng*); read, **lu** (lee).

CONVERSATIONAL SENTENCES

Avez-vous reçu un paquet par la poste[1]?

Have you received a parcel by (the) post?

Non, mais[2] j'ai reçu deux lettres de Paris.

No, but I have received two letters from Paris.

N'a-t-il pas rencontré sa soeur dans[3] la rue?

Didn't he meet his sister in the street?

N'avez-vous pas vu mon ami?

Haven't you seen my friend?

N'ont-ils pas trouvé mon sac à main?

Haven't they found my handbag?

Où a-t-elle acheté les chemises?

Where did she buy the shirts?

Elle n'a pas écrit à son père.

She hasn't written to her father.

N'avez-vous pas vu mes livres sur[4] la table?

Haven't you seen my books on the table?

PRON.: 1 posst (*f*); 2 may; 3 dah*ng*; 4 seer.

---

* The English idiom *I have got* is simply translated by **j'ai** (*I have*).

LESSON THREE

12. WHICH? WHAT? WHAT A are all translated:

Singular: *m* **quel** (kell), *f* **quelle** (kell)
Plural: *m* **quels** (kell), *f* **quelles** (kell)

which street? **quelle rue?**   which hats? **quels chapeaux?**

EXERCISE I

1 which school? 2 what months? 3 which rooms? 4 what a man! 5 what voices? 6 which family? 7 what station?

13. THIS, THAT *m* **ce** (ser), *f* **cette** (set);
Plural: THESE, THOSE **ces** (say)

this (*or* that) book, **ce livre**   these (*or* those) books, **ces livres**
that (*or* this) street, **cette rue**   those (*or* these) streets, **ces rues**

EXCEPTION: **cet** is used instead of **ce** if the next word begins with a vowel or an H mute; as,

this (*or* that) friend **cet ami**   that (*or* this) man **cet homme**
            cet is never used instead of **cette** or **ces**.

EXERCISE II

1 this car; 2 that flower; 3 these knives; 4 those forks;
5 this child; 6 that restaurant; 7 this hour; 8 those days;
9 this hotel; 10 these gardens; 11 this shop.

VOCABULARY: flower, **fleur** *f* (fler); fork, **fourchette** *f* (foohr-shett); child, **enfant** *m* (ahng-fahng); restaurant, **restaurant** *m* (ress-toh-rahng); garden, **jardin** *m* (shähr-dang); shop, **magasin** *m* (măh-găh-zang).

14. Constructions like the following must be changed thus:

my father's hat *into* the hat of my father; your sister's husband *into* the husband of your sister; the girls' friends *into* the friends of the girls.

EXERCISE III

1 my sister's husband; 2 your father's car; 3 this flower's colour; 4 my sister's address; 5 which girl's dress? 6 those travellers' suitcases; 7 your friend's mother; 8 Have you found this woman's gloves? 9 Her husband has written to his

21

brother's friend.   10 Their nieces haven't read this woman's letter.   11 Our neighbours' windows.

VOCABULARY: husband, **mari** *m* (măh-re); colour, **couleur** *f* (koo-ler); girl, **fille** *f* (fee-ye); dress, **robe** *f* (rob); traveller, **voyageur** *m* (vo'ah-yăh-**sher**); niece, **nièce** *f* (ne-ess); neighbour, **voisin** *m* (vo'ăh-za*ng*); window, **fenêtre** *f* (fe*r*-nay-tr).

CONVERSATIONAL SENTENCES

Où est la voiture de votre père?	Where is your father's car?
Elle est là (ici).	It (=she) is there (here).
Quel est le prix de cette robe?	What is the price of this dress?
Qui est cet homme?	Who is that man?
N'avez-vous pas lu ce livre?	Haven't you read this book?
Quelle est la date[1]?	What is the date?
Je n'ai pas acheté un journal.	I haven't bought a newspaper.
Elle a envoyé son fils à l'hôtel.	She has sent her son to the hotel.
Avez-vous trouvé l'adresse de cet homme?	Have you found that man's address?

PRON.: 1 daht.

15.   Present Tense of (TO) BE, **être**

I am	**je suis** (sher swe)
you are	**tu es** (TEE ay)
he is	**il est** (ill ay)
she is	**elle est** (ell ay)
we are	**nous sommes** (noo somm)
you are	**vous êtes** (voo z'ate)
they (*m*) are	**ils sont** (ill so*ng*)
they (*f*) are	**elles sont** (ell so*ng*)

EXERCISE IV

1 Who is there?   2 Where are our friends?   3 I am very tired.   4 He is very rich.   5 She is at (the) church.   6 We are at his hotel.   7 You are late (in delay).   8 The book is on the table.   9 Who are these men?   10 Where are our newspapers?   11 Your friends are at the station.

VOCABULARY: very, **très** (tray); tired, **fatigué** (făh-te-gay); rich, **riche** (reesh); late, **en retard** (ah*ng*-re*r*-tăhr).

16. Adjectives generally form the Feminine by adding **e** (those ending in **e** do not change). **s** is generally added in the Plural. (For further exceptions see Para. 7 and Appendix, p. 124.)

	MASCULINE			FEMININE		
	Singular	*Plural*		*Singular*	*Plural*	
right	droit	droits	(dro'ăh)	droite	droites	(dro'ăht)
left	gauche	gauches	(gohsh)	gauche	gauches	(gohsh)
large	grand	grands	(grahng)	grande	grandes	(grahngd)
small	petit	petits	(per-te)	petite	petites	(per-teet)

17. Adjectives generally take the Gender and Number of the word to which they refer, as:

The man is tall (= large)	L'homme est grand
The woman is tall	La dame est grande
The men are tall	Les hommes sont grands
The women are tall	Les dames sont grandes

EXERCISE V

1 Our friends are absent. 2 These men are rich. 3 His house is too small. 4 We are tired. 5 This water is hot. 6 That apple is bad. 7 You are very kind. 8 I am ill. 9 This room is very cold. 10 My car is very small.

VOCABULARY: absent, **absent** (ăhb-sahng); water, **eau** *f* (oh); too, **trop** (tro); hot, **chaud** (shoh); apple, **pomme** *f* (pomm); bad, **mauvais** (moh-vay); kind, **aimable** (ay-măh-bl); ill, **malade** (măh-lăhd); cold, **froid** (froh'ăh).

LESSON FOUR

18. The INTERROGATIVE of **je suis**, etc., is formed as in English, but a hyphen (-) is placed between the Verb and the Pronoun:

am I?	**suis-je?** (sweesh)
is he?	**est-il?** (ay-t'ill)
are we?	**sommes-nous?** (somm noo)
are you?	**êtes-vous?** (ate voo)

19. The NEGATIVE is always formed as explained in Rule 11:

I am not	je ne suis pas	am I not?	ne suis-je pas?
she is not	elle n'est pas	are we not?	ne sommes-nous pas?
they are not	ils ne sont pas	are you not?	n'êtes-vous pas?

Exercise I

1 She isn't young. 2 This lamp isn't very pretty. 3 Aren't you (*fam.*) satisfied? 4 Isn't he too old? 5 Am I not late? 6 We (*f*) aren't tired. 7 Those gloves are too small. 8 My coat isn't dirty. 9 Your neighbours are very rich.

VOCABULARY: young, jeune (shern); lamp, lampe *f* (lahngp); pretty, joli (sho-le); satisfied, satisfait (săh-tiss-fay); old, vieux (masc. sing. and plur. ve–er); coat, manteau *m* (mahng-toh); dirty, sale (săhl).

20. QUESTIONS must be changed when translating, as follows:

Has THE MAN a coat? = THE MAN has HE a coat?
L'homme a-t-il un manteau?
Have THE MEN the tickets? = THE MEN have THEY the tickets?
Les hommes ont-ils les billets?
Is THE LAMP on the table? = THE LAMP is SHE on the table?
la lampe est-elle sur la table?

The above construction is only used when the SUBJECT in questions is a Noun. The Subject, which comes immediately after the Verb in English questions, is printed above in CAPITALS.

Exercise II

1 Has the postman brought a letter? 2 Has that woman bought your coat? 3 Are these flowers very pretty? 4 Is your daughter at school? 5 Has that man two sons or three? 6 Has the doctor seen your foot? 7 Aren't the newspapers on the table? 8 Isn't the waiter here? 9 Is his house large?

VOCABULARY: brought, apporté (ăh-por-teh); daughter (or girl), fille *f* (fee-ye); doctor, docteur *m* (dock-ter); or, ou (oo); foot, pied *m* (pe-eh); waiter (or boy), garçon *m* (găhr-song).

CONVERSATIONAL SENTENCES

Monsieur[1] S. est-il à la maison?	Is Mr. S. at home?
Oui, il est dans le salon.[2]	Yes, he is in the sitting-room.
Les enfants sont-ils en haut[3]?	Are the children upstairs?
Non, ils sont en bas[4].	No, they are downstairs.
Où avez-vous été[5] aujourd-'hui?[6]	Where have you been today?
Nous avons été au théâtre[7].	We have been to the theatre.
N'êtes-vous pas fatigués?	Aren't you (*plur.*) tired?

24

Si[8], nous sommes bien[9] fatigués.	Yes, we are very tired.
Voulez-vous une tasse[10] de café?[11]	Will you (have) a cup of coffee?
Oui, s'il vous plaît[12].	Yes, please.

PRON.: 1 mer-se-er; 2 săh-long; 3 ahng oh; 4 ahng băh; 5 eh-teh; 6 oh-**shoohr**-dwe; 7 teh-äh-tr; 8 se (YES is translated by **si**, in answering a negative question); 9 be-ang (**bien** is often used instead of **très**); 10 tăhss; 11 kăh-feh; 12 sill voo play.

21. The PAST TENSE is generally changed into the PERFECT TENSE when translating; as,

PAST:	The man saw: *into*	} **L'homme a vu**
PERFECT:	The man HAS SEEN	
PAST:	Did* you speak? *into*	} **Avez-vous parlé?**
PERFECT:	HAVE you SPOKEN?	
PAST:	We did* not buy: *into*	} **Nous n'avons pas acheté**
PERFECT:	We HAVE not BOUGHT	
PAST	Did* they not find? *into*	} **N'ont-ils pas trouve?**
PERFECT:	HAVE they not FOUND?	

* *did* must be changed into *have*, *has* or *had* (Note carefully that the PAST PARTICIPLE can only be used after *have*, *has* or *had*. **Je reçu, nous trouvé**, etc. is impossible French, just as 'she written, they spoken', is bad English.)

EXERCISE III

1 I received (=I have received).   2 My friend broke the glass.   3 Did you hear the noise?   4 She lost her lighter. 5 Did the doctor read my letter?   6 He didn't open the parcel. 7 Didn't they see the fire?   8 We didn't open the door.

VOCABULARY: broke (past participle), **brisé** (bree-zeh); glass, **verre** (*m*. vair, exception to rule); hear (past participle), **entendu** (ahng-tahng-dEE); noise, **bruit** *m* (brwee); lost (past participle), **perdu** (pair-dEE); lighter, **briquet** *m* (bre-kay); open (past participle), **ouvert** (oo-vair); fire **incendie** (*m* exception to rule) (ang-sahng-de).

22. OF THE, FROM THE are generally translated **du** (dEE) before masculine singular nouns (not 'de le'), and **de la** before feminine singular nouns.

TO THE, AT THE are generally translated **au** (oh) before masculine singular nouns (not 'à le'), and **à la** before feminine singular nouns.

EXCEPTION: When the noun begins with a vowel or an H mute, **de l'** and **à l'** must be used instead of du, au, de la and à la.

of the father, **du** père	to the father, **au** père
of the car, **de la** voiture	to the car, **à la** voiture
of the hotel, **de l'**hôtel	to the hotel, **à l'**hôtel
of the child, **de l'**enfant	to the child, **à l'**enfant

EXERCISE IV

1 from the garden;   2 to the doctor;   3 of the knife; 4 to the boat;   5 from the house;   6 at the hotel.   7 Did you receive the manager's message?   8 The first day of the week. 9 The last day of the month.   10 Did you see the doctor's car?

VOCABULARY: boat, **bateau** *m* (băh-toh); manager, **directeur** *m* (de-reck-**ter**); message, **message** *m* (mess-ăh**sh**); first, **premier** (pre*r*-me-eh); week, **semaine** *f* (se*r*-main); last, **dernier** (dair-ne-eh).

CONVERSATIONAL SENTENCES

Avez-vous pris[1] une tasse de café?	Did you have (take) a cup of coffee?
Non, j'ai pris une tasse de thé[2].	No, I had (=took) a cup of tea.
Un garçon a apporté le petit déjeuner[3] à ma chambre.	A waiter brought breakfast to my room.
Le garçon a-t-il apporté une lettre pour[4] vous?	Did the waiter bring a letter for you?
Non, mais il a apporté un paquet pour ma femme[5].	No, but he brought a parcel for my wife.
Quel est le nom[6] du directeur?	What is the manager's name?
Nous n'avons pas bien dormi[7] cette nuit[8].	We didn't sleep well last night.
Pourquoi[9] n'avez-vous pas ouvert les fenêtres de la chambre?	Why didn't you open the bedroom windows?
Ce matin l'eau était froide.	This morning the water was cold.

PRON.: 1 pree; 2 teh; 3 pe*r*-te deh-**sher**-neh; 4 poohr; 5 făhmm; 6 no*ng*; 7 dor-me; 8 nwee; 9 poohr-ko'ăh.

26

LESSON FIVE

23. IT is translated by **il** if referring to a Masculine Noun mentioned just previously, and **elle** if referring to a Feminine Noun:

Where is your ticket?	Où est votre billet?
It is in my handbag	**Il** est dans mon sac à main
Where is her dress?	Où est sa robe?
It is in the case	**Elle** est dans la valise

24. THEY is translated **ils** or **elles**, according to the gender of the Noun just previously mentioned; as,

I have seen your flowers	J'ai vu vos fleurs
They are on the table	**Elles** sont sur la table

EXERCISE I

1 Have you heard his voice? Yes, it is very loud.   2 I read his letter; it is very short.   3 We bought this novel; it is very interesting.   4 Have you bought the house? No; it is sold. 5 Where are the apples? They aren't good.

VOCABULARY: loud, **fort** (for); short, **court** (koohr); novel, **roman** *m* (ro-mah*ng*); interesting, **intéressant** (a*ng*-teh-ress-ah*ng*); sold, **vendu** (vah*ng*-DEE); good, **bon** *m* (bo*ng*) **bonne** (bonn) (an irregular feminine form).

25. OF THE, FROM THE are translated **des** (day) instead of **'de les'**.

TO THE, AT THE are translated **aux** (oh) instead of **'à les.'**

des, aux are the only forms used in the Plural; as,

of the boats, **des** bateaux	to the boats, **aux** bateaux
from the houses, **des** maisons	at the houses, **aux** maisons
from the girls, **des** filles	to the girls, **aux** filles
from the men, **des** hommes	to the men, **aux** hommes

27

EXERCISE II

1 the pages of the books; 2 the feathers of the birds; 3 the boys' trousers; 4 the girls' shoes; 5 We gave the money to the children; 6 They spoke to the workmen's wives. 7 I wrote to our friend's dentist. 8 We sent the parcel to your father's friends. 9 They saw the headlights from the windows of our house.

VOCABULARY: page, **page** *f* (păhsh); feather, **plume** *f* (plEEm); bird, **oiseau** *m* (wăh-zoh); trousers (pair of), **pantalon** *m* (pahng-tăhlong); shoe, **chaussure** *f* (shohss-EER); gave, **donné** (donn-eh); money, **argent** *m* (ăhr-shahng); spoke, **parlé** (parh-leh); workman, **ouvrier** *m* (oov-re-eh); dentist, **dentiste** *m* (dahng-tisst); headlight, **phare** *m* (făhr).

CONVERSATIONAL SENTENCES

Ce parfum[1] est-il anglais[2]?	Is that perfume English?
Non, il est français[3].	No, it's French.
Mon manteau est-il là?	Is my coat there?
Oui, il est dans l'entrée.	Yes, it's in the hall.
Sa robe est-elle prête[4]?	Is her dress ready?
Non, elle est encore[5] chez[6] le teinturier[7].	No, it's still at the cleaner's.
Elle a acheté cette jupe[8] en[9] Angleterre[10].	She bought that skirt in England.
Avez-vous vu sa montre?[11]	Did you see her watch?
Oui, elle est très jolie.	Yes, it is very nice.
Elle a acheté cette montre en Suisse.[12]	She bought that watch in Switzerland.
Elle a passé[13] ses vacances[14] à Zurich.[15]	She spent her holidays in Zurich.
J'ai acheté ces sandales[16], mais malheureusement[17] elles sont trop petites.	I bought these sandals, but unfortunately they are too small.

PRON.: 1 păhr-fung; 2 ahng-glay; 3 frahng-say; 4 praytt; 5 ahng-kor; 6 sheh; 7 tang-tEE-re-eh; 8 shEEp; 9 ahng; 10 ahng-gler-tair; 11 mong-tr; 12 sweess; 13 păhss-eh; 14 văh-kahngss (*f* generally used in the plural); 15 zEE-rick; 16 sahng-dahl; 17 măhl-er-rerz-mahng.

26. SOME (or ANY) is translated the same as OF THE:

some bread, **du** pain (DEE pa*ng*)

any money, **de l'argent** (de*r* lăhr-shah*ng*)

some meat, **de la** viande (de*r* lăh ve-ahngd)

some friends, **des** amis (day z'ăh-me)

Have you *any* bread? = Have you *of the* bread?
Avez-vous du pain?

They have bought *some* books = They have bought *of the* books.
Ils ont acheté des livres

SOME is only translated as above if a Noun follows—see Paragraphs 103, 111.

EXERCISE III

1 some beer; 2 any milk; 3 some fish; 4 any glasses; 5 some butter; 6 any salt; 7 some salad; 8 any water; 9 some flowers; 10 He has bought some cheese and (some) wine. 11 Did you find any money on the table? 12 They (have) had some soup. 13 Did you hear any noise? 14 I have some change.

VOCABULARY: beer, **bière** *f* (be-air); milk, **lait** *m* (lay); fish, **poisson** *m* (po'ăhss-o*ng*); butter, **beurre** *m* (ber); salt, **sel** *m* (sell); salad, **salade** *f* (săh-lăhd); cheese, **fromage** *m* (from-ăh**sh**); wine, **vin** *m* (va*ng*); had, **eu** (EE) (this is an exception to the rules of pronunciation, **eu** being usually pronounced 'er' in French); soup, **soupe** *f* (soop); change, **monnaie** *f* (monn-ay).

27. ANY after NOT is simply translated **de** or **d'**; as,

We haven't any bread

Haven't you any friends?

Nous n'avons pas **de** pain

N'avez-vous pas **d'**amis?

28. NO before a Noun is translated the same as NOT ANY; as,

They have no soup

Have they no money?

Ils n'ont pas **de** soupe

N'ont-ils pas **d'**argent?

29. SOME or ANY must be expressed in French, even if omitted in English; as,

He had bread and water

Il a eu **du** pain et de l'eau

29

1 We haven't any money. 2 Hasn't he any matches? 3 Have you no change? 4 I haven't any time. 5 She has no ticket. 6 Haven't we any sugar? 7 This room has no windows. 8 Haven't they any beer? 9 They haven't received any letters. 10 The men had bread, cheese and wine. 11 Have you friends in (à) Paris?

VOCABULARY: match, **allumette** f (ăh-lEE-mett); time, **temps**, m (tahng); sugar, **sucre** m (sEEkr); room (not bedroom), **pièce** f (pe-ess); Paris, **Paris** (păh-ree).

CONVERSATIONAL SENTENCES

Avez-vous de la bière?	Have you any beer?
Oui, j'ai un verre de bière.	Yes, I have a glass of beer.
Est-elle assez[1] glacée[2]?	Is it chilled enough?
Non, ils n'ont pas de frigidaire.[3]	No, they have no refrigerator.
N'ont-ils pas acheté un frigidaire la semaine dernière?	Didn't they buy a refrigerator last week?
Non, ils n'ont pas assez d'argent.	No, they don't have enough money.
A-t-il des amis à Paris?	Has he any friends in Paris.
Je ne sais[4] pas.	I don't know.
Son frère n'est-il pas en haut?	Isn't his brother upstairs?
Il a des soeurs mais il n'a pas de frères.	He has sisters but he has no brothers.
N'avez-vous pas de sel ici?	Haven't you any salt here?
Si, il est là.	Yes, it is there.
Qui a ouvert la porte?	Who opened the door?
Pourquoi n'avez-vous pas écrit à votre frère?	Why haven't you written to your brother?
Parce que[5] je n'ai pas de timbres[6].	Because I have no stamps.

PRON.: 1 ăhss-eh; 2 glăhss-eh; 3 fre-she-dair; 4 say; 5 păhrser-ker; 6 tang-br.

LESSON SIX

Most French Verbs end in the Infinitive in -er. This -er is called the TERMINATION; the rest of the word is called the STEM, thus:

INFINITIVE		STEM	PRONUNCIATION
(to) give	donner	donn ...	donn-eh, donn
„ speak	parler	parl ...	păhr-leh, păhrl
„ thank	remercier	remerci ...	rer-mair-se-eh, rer-mair-se
„ pass	passer	pass ...	păhss-eh, păhss

Verbs with Infinitives ending in -re and -ir will be dealt with later.

30. The PRESENT TENSE of Verbs ending in -er is formed by adding to the Stem the Terminations printed in bold type below:

Present Tense of (TO) GIVE, donner

I give	je donne (sher donn)
you give	tu donnes (tEE donn)
he gives	il donne (il donn)
she gives	elle donne (ell donn)
we give	nous donnons (noo donn-ong)
you give	vous donnez (voo donn-eh)
they m give	ils donnent (ill donn)
they f give	elles donnent (ell donn)

EXERCISE I

1 he speaks; 2 we thank; 3 you pass; 4 they accept; 5 I visit; 6 he shuts; 7 they (f) close; 8 we speak; 9 she thanks; 10 they pass; 11 I* accept; 12 she visits.

VOCABULARY: to accept, accepter (ăhck-sep-teh); to visit, visiter (ve-ze-teh); to shut or close, fermer (fair-meh).

---

* j, le, ne, and other words where the final e is the only vowel, become j', l', n', etc., if the next word begins with a vowel or an H mute: as, I accept, j'accepte, instead of je accepte.

31

The Third Person Singular or Plural must be used after a Noun.

| The **man** speaks | L'homme parl**e** |
| The **days** pass | Les jours pass**ent** |

EXERCISE II

1 She gives some bread and (some) butter to the children.
2 The men speak to their wives. 3 Her husband thanks the manager. 4 We speak to the men. 5 You accept his money. 6 They visit the house. 7 She shuts the door. 8 The men pass before the house. 9 We give (some) bread to the birds. 10 They close the windows. 11 He visits this school. 12 They thank their friends.

VOCABULARY: before, **devant** (de*r*-vah*ng*).

CONVERSATIONAL SENTENCES

Quels sont les jours de la semaine?	What are the days of the week?
Les jours de la semaine sont: lundi[1], mardi[2], mercredi[3], jeudi[4], vendredi[5], samedi[6], dimanche[7].	The days of the week are: Monday, Tuesday, Wednesday, Thursday, Friday, Saturday, Sunday.
Quelle heure est-il?	What time (= hour) is it?
Il est une heure.	It is one o'clock.
Est-il deux heures?	Is it two o'clock?
Il n'est pas encore[8] trois heures.	It is not yet three o'clock.
N'est il pas quatre[9] heures?	Is it not four o'clock?
Il est huit[10] heures et demie[11].	It is half past eight.
Il est neuf[12] heures moins[13] le quart[14].	It is a quarter to nine.
Le film[15] commence[16] à deux heures un quart.	The film starts at quarter past two.
Nous n'avons pas de monnaie pour le cinéma[17].	We have no change for the cinema.
Avez-vous vu ce film?	Have you seen this film?
Ce restaurant ferme à onze heures.	This restaurant shuts at eleven o'clock.

Les magasins dans cet arrondissement[18] ne ferment pas le dimanche.	The shops in this district don't shut on Sunday.
Ils restent ouverts tard[19] le mercredi.	They stay open late on Wednesday.
Nous dînons[20] d'habitude[21] à huit heures et demie.	We usually dine at half past eight.
Nous invitons[22] souvent[23] nos amis le samedi soir[24].	We often invite our friends on Saturday evening.

PRON.: 1 lu*ng*-de; 2 mahr-de; 3 mair-kre*r*-de; 4 **sher**-de; 5 vah*ng*-dre*r*-de; 6 săhm-de; 7 de-mah*ng*sh; 8 ah*ng*-kor; 9 kăhtr; 10 wit; 11 de*r*-me; 12 ne*r*f; 13 mwa*ng*; 14 kăhr; 15 feelm; 16 komm-ah*ng*ss; 17 se-neh-mah; 18 ăh-ro*ng*-diss-mah*ng*; 19 tahr; 20 de-no*ng*; 21 d'ăh-be-tEEd; 22 a*ng*-ve-to*ng*; 23 soo-vah*ng*; 24 so'ahr.

31. 'I am giving', 'she is speaking', 'they are passing,' and similar constructions are all translated by the Present tense in French.

The flower is growing = the flower grows **La fleur pousse**
The men are speaking = the men speak **Les hommes parlent**

EXERCISE III

1 He is smoking his pipe. 2 We are cutting the grass. 3 She is looking for the address. 4 They are lighting the fire. 5 I am carrying the luggage. 6 You are eating too much. 7 He is wearing a coat. 8 I am arriving tomorrow morning. 9 She is giving some money to my brother.

VOCABULARY: to smoke, **fumer** (fEE-meh); pipe, **pipe** *f* (peep); to cut, **couper** (koo-peh); grass, **herbe** *f* (airb); to look for *or* fetch, **chercher** (shair-sheh); to light, **allumer** (ăh-lEE-meh); to carry *or* wear, **porter** (por-teh): luggage, **bagage** *m* (băh-gahsh) generally used in the plural; to eat, **manger** (mahng-sheh); too much, **trop** (tro); to arrive, **arriver** (ăh-re-veh); tomorrow, **demain** (der-ma*ng*); morning, **matin** *m* (măh-ta*ng*).

32. Questions are formed by putting the Pronoun after the Verb.

does he give? *or* is he giving? *into* **gives he?**
do they speak? *or* are they speaking? *into* **speak they?**
do you visit? *or* are you visiting? *into* **visit you?**

Note that DO and DOES are not translated at all.

The Verb and the Pronoun are connected by a hyphen, and -t- is inserted in the Third Person Singular; as,

does he give?	donne-t-il?	(donn-till)
does she smoke?	fume-t-elle?	(fEEm-tell)
do you close?	fermez-vous?	(fair-meh-voo)
do they speak?	parlent-ils?	(păhrl-till)
do we light?	allumons-nous?	(ăh-lEE-mong noo)
do I give?	donné-je?*	(donn-aish)

* Notice that an acute accent is placed on the **e** in the First Person Singular; but this form is never used in conversation. The correct question form is **Est-ce que je donne?** (See Para. 51.)

Is your friend arriving = Your friend arrives he? **Votre ami arrive-t-il?**

EXERCISE IV

1 Are they smoking cigars or cigarettes? 2 Is she looking for a flat? 3 Does he arrive (in) the morning or evening? 4 Are you lighting your pipe? 5 Are those men eating cheese? 6 Are they (*f*) closing their doors? 7 Do they accept those presents? 8 Are you looking for your lighter? 9 Does your friend speak to his neighbour?

VOCABULARY: cigar, **cigare** *m* (se-găhr); cigarette, **cigarette** *f* (se-găh-rett); flat, **appartement** *m* (ăh-pahr-ter-mahng); present, **cadeau** *m* (kăh-doh).

CONVERSATIONAL SENTENCES

Fumez-vous des cigares?	Do you smoke cigars?
Quelquefois,[1] mais générale-ment[2] je fume des cigarettes.	Sometimes, but generally I smoke cigarettes.
Je fume vingt[3] cigarettes par[4] jour.	I smoke twenty cigarettes a day.
Vous dépensez[5] trop d'argent pour le tabac[6].	You spend too much money on tobacco.
J'aime les cigares aussi[7].	I like cigars too.
Ne fumez-vous pas?	Don't you smoke?
Non, j'ai arrêté[8] de fumer.	No, I've stopped smoking.
Maintenant[9] je mange trop.	Now I'm eating too much.
Avez-vous du feu?	Have you a light?
Non, nous n'avons pas d'allu-mettes.	No, we have no matches.
Ils marchent[10] vite[11].	They are walking quickly.
Le soleil[12] brille[13] aujourd'hui.	The sun is shining today.
Portez-vous toujours[14] un im-perméable[15]?	Do you always wear a rain-coat?
Je porte quelquefois un para-pluie[16].	I sometimes carry an umbrella.
Que[17] cherchent-ils?	What are they looking for?
Qui a allumé les feux?	Who has lit the fires?
Nous allumons toujours le feu à cette heure.	We always light the fire at this hour.
Porte-elle cette jupe?	Is she wearing that skirt?
Elle est beaucoup trop[18] courte[19].	It is much too short.
Ne préfèrent[20]-elles pas des robes longues[21] le soir?	Don't they prefer long dresses in the evening?
Elle arrive toujours en retard.	She always arrives late.

PRON.: 1 kell-ker-fo'ah; 2 sheh-neh-răhl-mah*ng*; 3 va*ng*; 4 păhr; 5 deh-pah*ng*ss-eh; 6 tăh-bă*k*; 7 ohss-e; 8 ăh-ray-teh; 9 ma*ng*t-nah*ng*; 10 măhrsh; 11 veet; 12 soll-ay'e; 13 bree-ye; 14 too-shoohr; 15 a*ng*-pair-meh-ăh-bl; 16 păh-răh-plwee; 17 ker; 18 boh-koo tro; 19 koohrt; 20 preh-fayr; 21 lo*ng*-gh.

35

LESSON SEVEN

33. The NEGATIVE of all French Verbs is formed in the same way (See Para. 11), DO and DOES not being translated.

In translating, the English construction is therefore changed thus:

I do not give *or* I am not giving *into* **I give not.**

Does he not accept? *or* Is he not accepting? *into* **Accepts he not?**

Your friend does not speak (*or* is not speaking) } Votre ami **ne** parle **pas.**

Are not those men smoking? = Those men smoke they not? } Ces hommes **ne** fument-ils **pas?**

EXERCISE I

1 He doesn't find the way. 2 They don't pay their debts. 3 Aren't you living in this house? 4 Doesn't she often work? 5 Aren't they looking for their shoes? 6 Why don't you cut this string? 7 He isn't living there. 8 Don't I sing well? 9 He doesn't travel by plane. 10 Why don't you look at the menu?

VOCABULARY: to find, **trouver** (troo-veh); way, **chemin** *m* (sher-ma*ng*); to pay, **payer** (pay-yeh); debt, **dette** *f* (dett); to live, **habiter** (ăh-be-teh); to work, **travailler** (trăh-văh'e-yeh); string, **ficelle** *f* (fe-sell); to sing, **chanter** (shah*ng*-teh); well, **bien** (be-a*ng*); to travel, **voyager** (vo'ah-yah-sheh); by plane, **par avion** *m* (păhr ăh-ve-o*ng*); why, **pourquoi** (poohr-kwah); to look at, **regarder** (rer-găhr-deh); menu, **menu** *m* (mer-nEE).

34. WHO? WHOM? **qui** (kee)   WHAT? **que** (ke*r*)

que before a vowel or an H mute becomes **qu'.**

Who is speaking to the manager?   **Qui** parle au directeur?
Whom did you see there?   **Qui** avez-vous vu là?
What are you looking for?   **Que** cherchez-vous?
What have they bought?   **Qu'**ont-ils acheté?

WHAT? is translated by **quel?** etc. before a Noun, or before any part of the Verb *to be* (**être**) followed by a Noun—see Paras. 12, 59. WHAT? is translated by **que?** before any other verb—see also Paras. 39, 143.

Exercise II

1 Who is shutting the door? 2 Who has put the matches on the table? 3 What are you looking at? 4 What did she accept? 5 Whom are they looking for? 6 Who opened the window? 7 What did you say? 8 What is he carrying? 9 Who travelled by boat? 10 What did we pay? 11 What is he giving to the policeman? 13 To whom did you write?

VOCABULARY: put, **mis** (past participle, mee); say, **dit** (past participle, dee); pay, **payé** (past participle, pay-yeh); policeman, **agent** *m* (äh-shah*ng*).

CONVERSATIONAL SENTENCES

Avez-vous appris[1] les nombres[2] depuis[3] un jusqu'à[4] quatre?

Have you learnt the numbers from (= since) one to (= till) four?

Prononcez[5] après[6] moi[7]: cinq[8], six, sept, huit, neuf, dix.[8]

Pronounce after me: five, six, seven, eight, nine, ten.

Il est cinq heures.

It is five o'clock.

Est-il six heures?

Is it six o'clock?

Il n'est pas sept heures.

It is not seven o'clock.

N'est-il pas huit heures?

Is it not eight o'clock?

Est-il neuf heures ou dix heures?

Is it nine or ten o'clock?

A quelle heure rentrez[9]-vous?

At what time do you go home?

Je travaille d'habitude jusqu'à six heures et demie.

I usually work until half past six.

Qu'a-t-elle dit à votre femme?

What did she say to your wife?

Combien[10] ont-ils payé pour leur repas[11]?

How much did they pay for their meal?

Ils ont payé dix francs[12].

They paid ten francs.

Nous avons passé trois jours à Paris.

We spent three days in Paris.

Qu'avez-vous vu là?

What did you see there?

Qui vous a rencontré[13] à l'aéroport[14]?

Who met you at the airport?

37

Qu'avez-vous porté hier[15]?	What did you wear (= carry) yesterday?
Qui a laissé[16] ses clefs*[17] ici?	Who has left his keys here?
J'ai quitté[18] ma maison à huit heures.	I left my house at eight o'clock.

PRON.: 1 ah-pree; 2 no*ng*-br; 3 de*r*-pwe; 4 shEES-kah; 5 pro-no*ng*-seh; 6 ah-pray; 7 mo'ah; 8 sa*ng*kt†, siss, sett, wit, ne*r*f, disst†; 9 rah*ng*-treh; 10 ko*ng*-be-a*ng*; 11 re*r*-pah; 12 frah*ng*; 13 rah*ng*-ko*ng*-treh; 14 ah-eh-ro-po**r**; 15 e-ai**r**; 16 layss-eh; 17 kleh; 18 ke-teh.

35. Some useful PREPOSITIONS are

FOR, **pour** (poohr); IN, **dans** *or* **en*** (dah*ng*, ah*ng*); ON, **sur** (SEEr); UNDER, **sous** (soo); WITH, **avec** (ah-veck); WITHOUT, **sans** (sah*ng*); AFTER, **après** (ah-pray); AGAINST, **contre** (ko*ng*tr).

***Dans** defines a situation more precisely. It is generally used before an article, either definite or indefinite (*the* or *a, an*). Otherwise **en** is used:

In the North of France	**Dans le nord de la France**
In France	**En France**
He is travelling about	**Il est en voyage**
He is in the train	**Il est dans le train**

The difference in meaning is also used to make distinctions such as:

In a year's time	**Dans un an**
During the space of a year	**En un an**

EXERCISE III

1 for her son; 2 in the fire; 3 on the boat; 4 under the table; 5 with your knife; 6 without that money.

---

* *Key* can also be spelled **clé** but **clef** is much more common.

† The final Consonant in **cinq, six, huit, dix** is NOT pronounced if the next word in the phrase begins with a pronounced Consonant. Thus, **six pages** = see pǎhsh; **cinq dames** (five women) = sa*ng* dǎhm. But: **cinq hommes** (five men), sa*ng* k'omm, because the H is not pronounced.

36. The PAST PARTICIPLE of Verbs ending in **-er** is formed by changing the **-er** into **-é**; as,

> (to) give, **donner**; PAST PARTICIPLE: given, **donné**.

Both these two words are pronounced in the same way (donn-eh).

We spoke *or* we have spoken	Nous AVONS **parlé**
She accepted *or* she has accepted	Elle A **accepté**
Did they carry? *or* have they carried?	ONT-ils **porté**?
He didn't close *or* he hasn't closed	Il n'A pas **fermé**

The PAST PARTICIPLE can only be used after the Auxiliary Verbs 'to have' and 'to be' (see Paragraph 21).

EXERCISE IV

1 I paid = I have paid; 2 we visited; 3 she gave; 4 he did not find; 5 did they pass? 6 did you not accept? 7 He looked for his coat; 8 They closed the door. 9 We didn't speak to the doctor. 10 Didn't I give money to the boy?

37. Distinguish carefully between the *Present* and the *Past Tense* in English.

DO, DOES, AM, IS and ARE are *Present*; DID is *Past* as,

they pass *or* they are passing	ils passent
they passed *is translated* they HAVE passed	ils ont passé
I DO not give *or* I am not giving	je ne donne pas
I DID not give *is translated* I HAVE not given	je n'ai pas donné
he DOES not find *or* he is not finding	il ne trouve pas.
DID he not find? *is translated* HAS he not found?	n'a-t-il pas trouvé?
We DO not carry *or* we are not carrying	nous ne portons pas
We DID not carry *is translated* we HAVE not carried	nous n'avons pas porté

EXERCISE V

1 He doesn't light the fire. 2 Didn't they light the fire? 3 We don't like this room. 4 Didn't they look for your watch? 5 Aren't you looking at the paper? 6 I paid your bill.

VOCABULARY: to like, **aimer** (ay-meh); bill, **addition*** *f* (ăh-de-se-*ong*).

---

* This is a restaurant or café bill; any other sort of bill is **une note** (not), or **un compte** (ko*ngt*), or **une facture** (făhck-tEER).

39

CONVERSATIONAL SENTENCES

Quels sont les noms des mois ?

What are the names of the months?

Les noms des mois sont: janvier[1], février, mars, avril[1], mai[2], juin, juillet, août[2], septembre[3], octobre, novembre, décembre[3].

The names of the months are: January, February, March, April, May, June, July, August, September, October, November, December.

Il est une heure et demie.

It is half past one (o'clock).

Cherchez-vous un restaurant ?

Are you looking for a restaurant?

Il n'a pas apporté l'addition avec le café.

He didn't bring the bill with the coffee.

Nous avons trouvé la rue sur la carte[4].

We found the street on the map.

Aiment-ils ce pays[5] ?

Do they like this country?

N'avez-vous pas envoyé un message à votre femme ?

Didn't you send a message to your wife?

Elle n'envoie pas de lettres.

She doesn't send any letters.

L'Angleterre joue[6] quelquefois contre la France en février.

England sometimes plays against France in February.

Nous visitons d'habitude nos amis en juillet.

We usually visit our friends in July.

Avez-vous vu la mer[7] ?

Did you see the sea?

Il a attrapé plusieurs[8] poissons.

He caught several fish.

Ont-ils quitté l'Angleterre à temps[9] ?

Did they leave England in time?

PRON.: 1 sha*ng*-ve-eh, feh-vre-eh, măhrss, ăh-vreel; 2 may, shwa*ng*, shwe-yay, oo; 3 sep-tah*ng*-br, ok-to-br, no-vah*ng*-br, deh-sah*ng*-br; 4 kahrt; 5 pay-ee; 6 shoo; 7 mair; 8 plEE-ze-er; 9 ah tah*ng*.

38. MINE, **le mien, la mienne** (me-ang, me-enn)
THINE, **le tien, la tienne** (te-ang, te-enn)
HIS, HERS, **le sien, la sienne** (se-a-ng, se-enn)
OURS **le** (or **la**) **nôtre** (noh-tr)
YOURS **le** (or **la**) **vôtre** (voh-tr)
THEIRS **le** (or **la**) **leur** (ler)

The above POSSESSIVE PRONOUNS take the Gender and
Number of the word they stand for; the Plural is formed by
changing **le** or **la** into **les**, and adding an **s** to the Singular:

Your house and *his*	Votre maison et **la sienne**
Our hats and *yours*	Nos chapeaux et **les vôtres**
His brother and *hers*	Son frère et **le sien**
He didn't find his letters, but *mine*	Il n'a pas trouvé ses lettres, mais **les miennes**

EXERCISE I

1 I have your address and you have mine.   2 Has she taken
my ticket. or hers?   3 We have their keys and they have ours.
4 He hasn't brought my bill but theirs.   5 Did you meet my
sons or his?   6 I lost her watch and mine.   7 They didn't buy
my pictures but hers.   8 Hasn't he spent his money and yours?

VOCABULARY: picture, **tableau**, *m* (tah-bloh).

39. WHAT? after a Preposition is translated **quoi** (kwah) as,

Of what are you speaking?	**De quoi parlez-vous?**
What did he pay with?	**Avec quoi a-t-il payé?**

Prepositions always come before their Object in French.

WHAT! in exclamations is also translated **quoi!** as,

What! you are here!	**Quoi! vous êtes ici!**

1 What have you written the address on? 2 What did you say? 3 Which picture did they buy? 4 Whom did he meet at the airport? 5 What did she send the things in? 6 Why do you sing? 7 What did he find in the book?

VOCABULARY: thing, **chose** *f* (shohz).

CONVERSATIONAL SENTENCES

Avec quoi avez-vous attrapé ce poisson?	What did you catch that fish with?
J'ai passé la journée[1] sur la plage[2].	I spent (=passed) the day on the beach.
Nous n'aimons pas rester[3] à la maison.	We don't like staying (=to stay) at home (=at the house).
Quelquefois la mer est calme[4], et quelquefois elle est agitée[5].	The sea is sometimes calm, and sometimes rough.
Dans quel magasin avez-vous acheté ce maillot de bain[6]?	In which shop did you buy that bathing costume?
Est-ce que c'est ma serviette[7] ou la vôtre?	Is this my towel or yours?
Avez-vous apporté[8] votre déjeuner[9]?	Have you brought your lunch?
Non, nous mangeons* d'habitude à l'hôtel.	No, we usually eat at the hotel.
Avez-vous nagé[10] ce matin?	Did you swim this morning?
Qu'avez-vous trouvé là?	What did you find there?
J'ai vu nos enfants et les vôtres à la piscine[11].	I saw our children and yours at the swimming pool.

PRON.: 1 **shoohr**-neh; 2 plahsh; 3 ress-teh; 4 kahlm; 5 ah-she-teh; 6 mah'e-yo de*r* ba*ng*; 7 sair-ve-ett; 8 ăh-por-teh; 9 deh-**sher**-neh; 10 nah-**sheh**; 11 pee-seen.

---

* See para. 134 for this slight irregularity in **-ger** verbs.

42

40. ADJECTIVES generally follow the Noun in French; as,

our *absent* friends = our friends *absent*

nos amis absents
(noh z'ăh-me z'ahb-sah*ng*)

these *black* cows = these cows *black*

ces vaches noires
(say văhsh no'ăhr)

EXERCISE III

1 an English town; 2 (some) German cars; 3 (some) French ships; 4 this round table; 5 those rich men; 6 my right hand; 7 his electric razor; 8 Did they bring these yellow flowers? 9 Did you drink red wine?

VOCABULARY: town, **ville** *f* (veel); German, **allemand** *m* (ăhl-mah*ng*) allemande *f* (ăhl-mah*ng*d); ship, **vaisseau** *m* (vayss-oh); round, **rond** (ro*ng*); electric, **électrique** (eh-leck-trick); razor, **rasoir** *m* (răh-zo'ăhr); yellow, **jaune** (shohn); drink, **bu** (past participle) (bEE): red, **rouge** (roosh).

41. PAST PARTICIPLES used as adjectives follow the same rules.

A *broken* window = a window *broken*

Une fenêtre cassée
(kăhss-eh)

The letter is *lost*

La lettre est perdue

The pictures are *sold*

Les tableaux sont vendus

PAST PARTICIPLES are invariable if coming after 'to have' (unless the direct object precedes the verb—see Paragraph 64).

Our wives have *eaten* their meals

Nos femmes ont mangé leurs repas

EXERCISE IV

1 a closed door; 2 two lost children. 3 The string is cut. 4 His debts are paid. 5 Are the windows open(ed)? 6 The children are not yet found. 7 Has he sold his horses? 8 His horses are not yet sold. 9 Have they drunk the water?

VOCABULARY: horse, **cheval** *m* (sher-văhl),

CONVERSATIONAL SENTENCES

Comment[1] prononce-t-on[2] les nombres cinq, six, huit et dix suivis[3] d'une consonne[4]?	How does one pronounce the numbers five, six, eight, and ten followed by a consonant?
Dans ce cas[5] on[6] ne prononce pas la consonne finale[7].	In this case one doesn't pronounce the final consonant.
Par exemple[8]; cinq francs, six pommes, huit livres, dix centimes[9].	For example, five francs, six apples, eight books, ten centimes.
Cent[10] centimes font[11] un franc.	A hundred centimes make a franc.
Les fenêtres sont cassées.	The windows are broken.
Une fenêtre cassée est dangereuse[12].	A broken window is dangerous.
Elle a cassé plusieurs assiettes[13].	She broke several plates.
Sa femme n'a-t-elle pas ouvert la porte?	Didn't his wife open the door?
Elle a toujours aimé les roses[14] rouges.	She has always liked red roses.
Dans quoi avez-vous mis ces fleurs jaunes?	What did you put those yellow flowers in?
Elle a emprunté[15] ma montre parce que la sienne est cassée	She borrowed my watch because hers is broken.
A quelle ville anglaise avez-vous envoyé la lettre?	Which English town did you send the letter to?
Avez-vous vu une prise[16] pour un rasoir électrique?	Have you seen a point for an electric razor?
Ils ont apporté du vin rouge et du vin blanc[17].	They brought red and white wine.
Cette place[18] est-elle réservée[19]?	Is this seat reserved?

PRON.: 1 komm-ah*ng*; 2 pro-no*ng*ss-to*ng*; 3 swe-ve; 4 ko*ng*-sonn; 5 kah; 6 o*ng*; 7 fe-nahl; 8 păhr egg-zah*ng*-pl, sa*ng* frah*ng*, see pomm, wee lee-vr *f*; 9 dee sah*ng*-teem; 10 sah*ng*; 11 fo*ng*; 12 dah*ng*-sher-rerz; 13 ăhss-e-ett; 14 rohz; 15 ah*ng*-pru*ng*-teh; 16 preez; 17 blah*ng*; 18 plahss; 19 reh-zair-veh.

LESSON NINE

42. PERSONAL PRONOUNS, as below, are placed in French **immediately before** the verb of which they are the object (in English they follow this verb).

ME, TO ME **me** (me*r*)	US, TO US **nous** (noo)
THEE, TO THEE **te** (te*r*)	YOU, TO YOU **vous** (voo)
HIM, IT *m* **le** (le*r*)	
HER, IT *f* **la** (lah)	THEM *m & f* **les** (lay)
TO HIM, TO HER **lui** (lwe)	TO THEM *m & f* **leur** (le*r*)

They break *them*	Ils **les** brisent
The man speaks *to-us*	L'homme **nous** parle
We are carrying *it*	Nous **le** (*or* **la**) portons

EXERCISE I

1 They carry it. 2 We give (to-) them the flowers. 3 I am-smoking* it (*f*). 4 She is-looking-for* us. 5 You find them. 6 He meets you. 7 The women are-speaking to-us. 8 The doctor is-speaking to-him. 9 The girl is-singing to-her.†

43. me, te, le, la before a vowel (or an H mute) become **m', t', l', l'**; as,

The man brings *it* (*f*)	L'homme **l'**apporte (lom lăh-port)
His neighbours like *him*	Ses voisins **l'**aiment (say vo'ahza*ng* layme)

EXERCISE II

1 We invite him. 2 I invite her. 3 She forgets us. 4 They forget me. 5 We accept it. 6 They accept them. 7 The boy brings it. 8 The children are-speaking to them. 9 They find it (*f*). 10 Your sister is-looking-at it. 11 He likes it. 12 We like them. 13 He brings us some bread and butter. 14 Your friends are-looking-for you. 15 We meet them. 16 My mother is-speaking to-her. 17 You forget them. 18 Where is the letter? 19 He is writing it. 20 Do your sons wear them?

VOCABULARY: to invite, **inviter** (a*ng*-vee-teh); to forget, **oublier** (oo-ble-eh).

---

* English words connected by hyphens are rendered in French by one word.

† In French, an object must follow, such as: *a song*, une chanson (shah*ng*-sa*ng*).

CONVERSATIONAL SENTENCES

Apprenez[1] par[2] coeur[2] les nombres suivants[3].

Learn by heart the following numbers:

Onze[4], douze, treize, quatorze, quinze, seize, dix-sept, dix-huit, dix-neuf[4], vingt.

Eleven, twelve, thirteen, fourteen, fifteen, sixteen, seventeen, eighteen, nineteen, twenty.

Fermez la porte s'il vous plaît.

Shut the door (if you) please.

Où habitez-vous?

Where do you live?

Nous habitons à Londres[5].

We live in (=at) London.

Qui est cet homme là-bas[6]?

Who is that man over there?

Mon mari lui parle.

My husband is speaking to him.

Le connaissez[7]-vous?

Do you know him?

Oui, je le connais bien.

Yes, I know him well.

Il nous apporte nos journaux.

He brings us our papers.

Il nous cherche.

He is looking for us.

Elle nous regarde.

She is looking at us.

Notre voiture est tombée en panne[8].

Our car has broken down.

Le mécanicien[9] la répare[10].

The mechanic is mending it.

Nous avons quitté le village[11] à une heure et demie.

We left the village at half past one.

Ils ont tourné[12] à gauche.

They turned left.

Les rues sont très étroites[13].

The roads are very narrow.

Je l'aime bien, je l'invite souvent.

I like him (well), I often invite him.

J'ai oublié[14] qui a voyagé[15] avec nous.

I've forgotten who travelled with us.

Ils lui donnent beaucoup d'argent.

They give her plenty (=a lot) of money.

PRON.: 1 äh-pre*r*-neh; 2 par ke*r*; 3 swee-vah*ng*; 4 o*ng*z, dooz, trayz, kah-torz, ka*ng*z, sayz, deez-sett, deez-witt, deez-ne*r*f; 5 lo*ng*-d*r*; 6 läh-bäh; 7 kon-ess-eh; 8 to*ng*-beh ah*ng* pahn; 9 meh-kah-ne-se-a*ng*; 10 reh-pähr; 11 vee-läh**sh**; 12 tooh*r*-neh; 13 eh-tro'äht; 14 oo-blee-yeh; 15 vo'äh-yäh-**sheh**.

44. The rule in Paragraph 42 of course applies to QUESTIONS also, as the following examples show.

Does he speak *to them?*	**Leur** parle-t-ils?
Do they thank *us?*	**Nous** remercient-ils?
Are you forgetting *him?*	**L'**oubliez-vous?
Does she invite *you?*	**Vous** invite-elle?

(By Rule 42, **me, te, le** etc. *always* come immediately before the Verb.)

EXERCISE III

1 Does he speak to you? 2 We do not like her. 3 Do you thank them? 4 Is he looking-at us? 5 Do they bring them? 6 Are you looking-at me? 7 We thank you. 8 Is your friend looking-for us? 9 They are-breaking it (*f*). 10 Why do you hide them? 11 Have you (got)* it? 12 We have them.

VOCABULARY: to hide, **cacher** (kăh-sheh).

45. The rule in Paragraph 42 also applies to Negations, thus:

I haven't (got) *it*	Je ne **l'**ai pas
She isn't speaking *to him*	Elle ne **lui** parle pas
Don't you like *them?*	Ne **les** aimez-vous pas?
Don't they (*f*) invite *her?*	Ne **l'**invitent-elles pas?

As **me, te, le** etc. must always *immediately* precede the Verb, the **ne** comes before these Pronouns.

EXERCISE IV

1 He doesn't find it† 2 Don't you thank us? 3 Aren't you speaking to him? 4 We don't give (to) them the books. 5 Why don't you look-at me? 6 He doesn't hide it (*f*). 7 Why doesn't she bring the menu to us? 8 My friend doesn't like them. 9 Why don't you show (to) me his letter? 10 Don't you meet them every day? 11 Why doesn't he smoke French cigarettes? 12 He doesn't like them. 13 Why isn't this window shut? 14 I am closing it (*f*).

VOCABULARY: to show, **montrer** (mo*ng*-treh); every day = all the days, **tous les jours** (too lay **shoohr**).

---

* In such phrases 'got' is not to be translated.
† IT is to be translated by **le** unless marked to the contrary, or referring to a Feminine Noun.

CONVERSATIONAL SENTENCES

Est-il midi[1]?

Is it midday?

Il est minuit[2].

It is midnight.

Il est une heure cinq.

It is five past one.

Est-il deux heures dix?

Is it ten past two?

Comment s'appelle[3] cette ville?

What is the name of this town?

Est-ce que c'est ma place ou la vôtre?

Is this my seat or yours?

A quelle heure commence[4] le match[5]?

What time does the match begin?

Nous avons passé nos vacances en Bretagne[6].

We spent our holidays in Brittany.

Où a-t-elle habité l'année[7] dernière?

Where did she live last year?

Elle a habité en Espagne[8].

She lived in Spain.

Pourquoi ne le mangez-vous pas?

Why don't you eat it?

Parce que je déteste[9] l'ail[10].

Because I hate garlic.

Il leur envoie[11] de l'argent tous les mois.

He sends them money every month.

Comment le dépensent-ils?

How do they spent it?

Ils lui donnent beaucoup de cadeaux.

They give her a lot of presents.

Vous ne nous aidez[12] pas.

You aren't helping us.

Pourquoi ne réserve-t-il pas une place aujourd'hui?

Why doesn't he book a seat today?

PRON.: 1 me-de; 2 me-nwe; 3 săh-pehl; 4 komm-ah*ng*ss; 5 maht-ch; 6 bre*r*-tahn-ye*r*; 7 ah-neh; 8 ess-pahn-ye*r*; 9 deh-tesst; 10 ăh'e; 11 ah*ng*-vo'äh; 12 ay-deh.

LESSON TEN

Besides the Verbs ending in the Infinitive in **-er**, of which there are more than 4,000, there are about 50 Verbs ending in **-re**, and 300 ending in **-ir**, both belonging to what are known as the Regular Conjugations.

EXAMPLES OF VERBS ending in **-re**.

to SELL, **vendre** (vah*ng*-de) to LOSE, **perdre** (pair-de)
to REPLY, **répondre** (reh-po*ng*-dr) to GIVE BACK, **rendre** (rah*ng*-dr)
to EXPECT *or* to WAIT-FOR, **attendre** (ăh-tah*ng*-dr)

46. The PRESENT TENSE of Verbs ending in **-re** is formed by adding to the Stem the **terminations** printed in bold type below.

Present Tense of TO SELL, **vendre**

I sell	je vend**s** (vah*ng*)
you sell (familiar form)	tu vend**s** (vah*ng*)
he sells	il vend (vah*ng*)
we sell	nous vend**ons** (vah*ng*-do*ng*)
you sell	vous vend**ez** (vah*ng*-deh)
they sell	ils vend**ent** (vah*ng*d)

There is no termination in the Third Person Singular, which consists of the Stem only. The Stem of these Verbs consists of the part preceding **-re**.

EXERCISE I

1 he loses; 2 we give-back; 3 you are-selling; 4 they reply; 5 I am-expecting; 6 she is-selling; 7 they lose; 8 we are-replying; 9 you are-waiting for; 10 your friend is-giving back; 11 she replies; 12 these men are-losing; 13 They always reply to us by return of (the) post. 14 Have you seen his house? Yes, he is-selling it. 15 He expects us at five o'clock.

VOCABULARY: by return of (the) post, **par retour du courrier** (păh**r** re**r**-toohr dEE koohr-e-eh).

49

47. NEGATIONS and QUESTIONS are of course formed in the same way with all Verbs, as explained in paragraphs 31, 32 and 33:

are you selling? *or* do you sell?	vendez-vous?
he doesn't lose *or* he isn't losing	il **ne** perd **pas**
don't they give back? *or* aren't they giving back?	**ne** rendent-ils **pas**?
does he wait for? *or* is he waiting for?	attend-il?*

* No **-t-** is used in the 3rd person, because the Verb does not end in a vowel. However the **d** is pronounced as a **t**.

EXERCISE II

1 does she sell?   2 are you losing?   3 are they replying?
4 I don't give-back;   5 she doesn't expect;   6 don't we sell?
7 isn't she giving-back?   8 why don't you reply?   9 I am-waiting for the train.   10 Don't they sell stamps?   11 I often lend him my books but he doesn't return them.   12 I met your brother today; don't you expect him this evening?

VOCABULARY: train, **train** *m* (tra*n*g); to lend, **prêter** (pray-teh).

CONVERSATIONAL SENTENCES

Il est six heures moins cinq.	It is five to six. (=six hours less five).
N'est-il pas neuf heures[1] moins vingt.	Isn't it twenty to nine?
Il est dix heures moins vingt-cinq.	It is twenty five to ten.
Pourquoi ne les vendez-vous pas?	Why don't you sell them?
A quelle heure nous attendent-ils?	At what time are they expecting us?
Je le lui rends demain.	I am giving it back to him tomorrow.
Vous perdez[2] votre temps.	You are wasting (=losing) your time.
Il les attend depuis plusieurs jours.	He has been waiting for them for several days†.
Ils lui rendent l'argent.	They are giving her back the money.

† Note that in French the Present Tense is always used in such constructions.

Nous leur vendons notre voiture le mois prochain[3].	We are selling them our car next month.
Combien vous payent-ils?	How much are they paying you?
Ne pouvez-vous pas entendre ce bruit?	Can't you hear that noise?
Oui, je l'entends.	Yes, I hear it.

PRON.: 1 ner ver; 2 pair-deh; 3 prosh-ang

48. The PAST PARTICIPLE of verbs ending in **-re** is formed by changing **-re** into **-u**; as,

to sell, **vendre**   PAST PARTICIPLE: sold, **vendu**

| they lost *or* they have lost | **ils ont perdu** |
| didn't he wait? | **n'a-t-il pas attendu?** |

EXERCISE III

1 She heard his voice. 2 They sold their car. 3 Does he return it? 4 Did he give back the money? 5 Aren't you waiting for me? 6 Didn't you expect your wife yesterday? 7 Doesn't the chemist sell it? 8 We went down (descended) the stairs.

VOCABULARY: chemist, **pharmacien** *m* (făhr-măh-se-ang); to descend, **descendre** (dess-ahng-dr); stairs, **escaliers** *m pl* (ess-kăh-le-eh).

CONVERSATIONAL SENTENCES

Vous avez appris les nombres depuis un jusqu'à vingt, n'est-ce pas[1]?	You have learnt the numbers from one to twenty, haven't you?
Apprenez par coeur les nombres suivants:	Learn by heart the following numbers:
Vingt et un[2], vingt-deux, vingt-trois, vingt-quatre, vingt-cinq, vingt-six, vingt-sept, vingt-huit, vingt-neuf[2].	Twenty-one, twenty-two, twenty-three, twenty-four twenty-five, twenty-six, twenty-seven, twenty-eight, twenty-nine.
N'a-t-elle pas encore descendu les escaliers?	Hasn't she come down the stairs yet?

51

Il est déjà dix heures vingt-cinq.	It is already twenty-five past ten.
Le bruit de la circulation[3] la réveille[4] d'habitude.	The noise of the traffic usually wakes her up.
A quelle heure est le petit déjeuner?	What time is breakfast?
De huit heures à neuf heures et demie.	From eight to half past nine.
A quelle heure est le déjeuner?	What time is lunch?
Elle n'a pas entendu quand j'ai frappé[5] à sa porte.	She didn't hear when I knocked at her door.
Je vais rester au lit aujourd'hui.	I'm going to stay in bed today.
J'ai mal[6] à la tête[7].	I have a headache.
Ils ont entendu claquer[8] les volets[9].	They heard the shutters banging.
J'ai perdu votre numéro de téléphone[10].	I've lost your telephone number.
J'ai perdu tout mon argent hier soir.	I lost all my money last night.
Je vous attends depuis deux heures.	I've been waiting for you for two hours.
Il est défendu[11] de fumer.	It is forbidden to smoke.

PRON.: 1 literally: is it not? ness-păh; 2 vang-t'eh-ung, vangt-der, etc. (the t of *vingt* is sounded in the number 21 to 29 inclusive); 3 seer-KEE-lah-se-ong; 4 reh-vay-e; 5 frăh-peh; 6 mahl; 7 tayt; 8 klăh-keh; 9 voll-ay; 10 teh-leh-fon; 11 deh-fahng-DEE.

LESSON ELEVEN

49. The Pronouns **me, le, lui,** etc. always come before the Verb; in COMPOUND TENSES they are placed before the FIRST Verb.

A COMPOUND TENSE in French consists of a PAST PARTICIPLE preceded by part of *to have* or *to be*.

He *has* written **to us**	Il no**us** a écrit.
Have they spoken to **him**?	Lui ônt-ils parlé?
We *haven't* replied ⎱ to them	Nous ne **leur** avons pas répondu.
or We did not reply ⎰	
Haven't you sent ⎱ to me?	Ne m'avez-vous pas envoyé?
or Didn't you send ⎰	

EXERCISE I

1 They haven't written to you.   2 Have you spoken to her?
3 We haven't replied to them.   4 Haven't they found him?
5 I have brought (to-) him the letters.   6 We have seen him
today.   7 She didn't give me her telephone number.   8 They
haven't lost it.

EXAMPLES OF VERBS ending in -ir

to FINISH, **finir** (fe-neer);   to FILL, **remplir** (rahng-pleer);
to CHOOSE, **choisir** (sho'äh-zeer);   to PUNISH, **punir** (pEE-neer);
   to SUCCEED, BE SUCCESSFUL, MANAGE TO, **réussir** (reh-EESS-eer).

50. The PRESENT TENSE of Verbs ending in **-ir** is formed by
adding to the Stem the terminations printed in bold type
below.

Present Tense of (to) FINISH, **finir**

I finish	je fin**is** (fe-nee)
you finish (familiar form)	tu fin**is** (fe-nee)
he finishes	il fin**it** (fe-nee)
we finish	nous fin**issons** (fe-niss-o*ng*)
you finish	vous fin**issez** (fe-niss-eh)
they finish	ils fin**issent** (fe-niss)

Paragraphs 31, 32, 33 also apply to -ir Verbs

EXERCISE II

1. They don't finish their meal.   2 Are they filling it?
3 We don't choose these colours.   4 Don't you punish your
dog?   5 Why doesn't she fill the glass?   6 Why do you choose
the difficult jobs?   7 He is finishing your suit today.   8 She
usually succeeds.

VOCABULARY: difficult, **difficile** (de-fe-sill); job, **tâche** *f* (tahsh);
suit, **costume** *m* kos-tEEm.

53

CONVERSATIONAL SENTENCES

Continuez[1] à apprendre[2] les nombres suivants:

Continue to learn the following numbers:

Trentè[3], trente et un[3], trente-deux, etc. quarante[4], quarante et un, quarante-trois, etc. cinquante[5], cinquante et un, cinquante-quatre, etc. soixante[6], soixante et un, soixante cinq, etc. soixante-dix[7].

Thirty, thirty-one, thirty-two, etc. forty, forty-one, forty-three, etc. fifty, fifty-one, fifty-four, etc. sixty, sixty-one, sixty-five, etc. seventy.

Lui avez-vous déjà parlé?

Have you already spoken to her?

Non, je ne l'ai pas vue depuis mercredi dernier.

No, I haven't seen her since last Wednesday.

Quand[8] je passe des examens[9], d'habitude je réussis.

When I take (= pass) exams, I usually pass.

Quelquefois elle réussit à arriver à l'heure.

Sometimes she manages to arrive on time.

Je lui ai envoyé les documents[10] le mois dernier.

I sent him the documents last month.

Remplit-elle les formulaires[11]?

Is she filling in the forms?

Ils choisissent toujours les mauvaises[12] rues.

They always choose the wrong (= bad) roads.

Je punis mon chien quand il ne m'obéit[13] pas.

I punish my dog when he doesn't obey me.

Pourquoi ne le cherchez-vous pas?

Why don't you look for it?

Parce que je suis sûr[14] qu'il est perdu.

Because I am sure it is lost.

Sa maison est vendue; la mienne est trop vieille.

His house is sold; mine is too old.

L'avez-vous entendu entrer?

Did you hear him come in?

Il a rempli le réservoir[15] d'essence[16].

He filled the tank with petrol.

PRON.: 1 kong-te-nEE-eh; 2 däh-prehng-dr; 3 trahngt, trahngt-eh ung; 4 käh-rahngt; 5 sang-kahngt; 6 so'ähss-ahngt; 7 so'ähss-ahngt-diss; 8 kahng; 9 egg-zah-mang; 10 dockEE-mahng m; 11 formEE-lair m; 12 moh-vayz; 13 m'ob-eh-yee; 14 sEEr; 15 reh-zair-vo'ahr; 16 d'eh-sahngss.

51. The PAST PARTICIPLE of Verbs ending in **-ir** is formed by changing **-ir** into **-i**, thus:

to FINISH, **finir**; Past Participle: FINISHED, **fini** (fe-ne)

They have *obeyed* (to) him	**Ils lui ont obéi**
I haven't *chosen* it } I didn't choose it }	**Je ne l'ai pas choisi**
Haven't you *finished* it? } Didn't you finish it? }	**Ne l'avez-vous pas fini**

EXERCISE III

1 Why haven't you filled the bottle?   2 They haven't yet finished their work.   3 We didn't choose this wine.   4 Has she chosen a ring?   5 Do you obey (to) his orders?   6 Haven't they punished him too much?   7 We tried and we succeeded.   8 Did they choose?

VOCABULARY: bottle, **bouteille** *f* (boo-tay'e); work, **travail**, *m* (trăh-vah'e); ring, **bague** *f* (băhg); order, **ordre** *m* (ordr); to try, **essayer** (eh-say-yeh).

The Interrogative of French Verbs can be formed in two ways: either by placing the Pronoun after the Verb (See para. 32), or by prefixing **est-ce que?** (is it that?). **Est-ce que?** (ess-ke*r*) corresponds to the English *do, does, did,* and should nearly always be used in the FIRST PERSON SINGULAR.

Do you smoke?	Fumez-vous? *or* Est-ce que vous fumez?
Did they win?	Ont-ils gagné? *or* Est-ce qu'ils ont gagné (gahn-yeh)
Do I speak?	Est-ce que je parle? (*better than* parlé-je?)
Do I sell?	Est-ce que je vends? (*not* vends-je?)

52. Interrogative words (HOW? WHEN? WHERE? WHY? etc.) always begin sentences like those in Paragraph 20, thus:

Pourquoi l'homme a-t-il un manteau? NOT L'homme pourquoi a-t-il un manteau?

EXCEPTION: If the sentence begins with **que**, the Verb comes next, thus:

What is the man looking at? *or* What is that the man is looking at?	Que regarde l'homme? *or* Qu'est-ce que l'homme regarde?

The Verb is also often placed immediately after **où** (WHERE?)

1 Why did the man speak to you? 2 Where does your brother live? 3 How did the policeman find you? 4 What did your friend send (to) you? 5 Where are my cases? 6 What did your wife hear? 7 What does that shop sell?

CONVERSATIONAL SENTENCES

Finissons par les nombres de soixante et onze[1] jusqu'à cent.	Let us finish with (= by) the numbers, from seventy-one, to a hundred.
Soixante et onze, soixante-douze, soixante-treize, soixante-dix-sept, soixante-dix-neuf.	Seventy-one, seventy-two, seventy-three, seventy-seven, seventy-nine.
quatre-vingts[2], quatre-vingt-un[3], quatre-vingt-deux, quatre-vingt-dix, quatre-vingt-onze, quatre-vingt-dix-neuf, cent.	eighty, eighty-one, eighty-two, ninety-, ninety-one, ninety-nine, a hundred.
Nous avons fini une bouteille et nous en avons commandé une autre[4].	We finished one bottle and ordered another.
Ont-ils réussi à gagner le match?	Did they manage to win the match?
Est-ce que je parle bien français?	Do I speak French well?
Oui, mais vous avez un fort[5] accent[6] anglais.	Yes, but you have a strong English accent.
Pourquoi ne m'avez-vous pas cherché?	Why didn't you look for me?
Ne l'avez-vous pas encore fini?	Haven't you finished it yet?
Est-ce que ce magasin vend des bonbons?[7]	Does this shop sell sweets?
Pourquoi n'avez-vous pas réservé les places plus tôt[8]?	Why didn't you reserve the seats earlier?
Il ne m'a pas donné de monnaie.	He didn't give me any change.
Où l'avez-vous vu?	Where did you see it?

Quand rentrez-vous?	When are you going back?
Nous rentrons le quinze juillet.	We are going back on July the fifteenth.
Je ne l'ai pas oublié[9].	I didn't forget him.
L'avez-vous mis dans le placard[10]?	Did you put it in the cupboard?
Non, je l'ai laissé en bas.	No, I left it downstairs.

PRON.: 1 so'ahss-ah*ng*t-eh-o*ng*z; 2 kah-tre*r*-va*ng*; 3 kah-tre*r*-va*ng*-u*ng*; 4 oh-tr; 5 fo*r*; 6 ahck-sah*ng*; 7 bo*ng*-bo*ng* *m*; 8 plEE-toh; 9 oo-blee-yeh; 10 plah-kah*r* *m*.

LESSON TWELVE

53. Contrary to Paragraph 40, the following Adjectives nearly always come **before** the Noun in French:

good, **bon** (bo*ng*); bad, **mauvais** (moh-vay); wicked, horrid, **méchant** (meh-shah*ng*); new (or different), **nouveau*** (noo-voh); young, **jeune** (she*r*n); old, **vieux*** (ve-e*r*) big, fat, **gros** (groh); tall, large, **grand** (grah*ng*); small, little, **petit** (pe*r*-te); beautiful, fine, handsome, **beau*** (boh); pretty, nice, **joli** (sHo-le); naughty, nasty, **vilain** (ve-la*ng*).

IRREGULAR FEMININES: good **bonne** (bonn); new, **nouvelle** (noo-vell), **vieille** (ve-ay'e); big, fat, **grosse** (grohss); beautiful, etc. **belle** (bell).

EXERCISE I

1 a good thing; 2 these fine apples; 3 this little cat; 4 a pretty flower; 5 what (a) small foot! 6 an old friend; 7 those large rivers; 8 her beautiful ring; 9 a bad opinion; 10 these wicked men; 11 that big bird; 12 a new car.

VOCABULARY: cat, **chat** *m* (shăh); river, **fleuve** *m* (fle*r*v); opinion, **opinion** *f* (o-pe-ne-o*ng*).

54. When the Adjective comes before the Noun, *some* or *any* is usually translated **de**.

They have some fine pictures	Ils ont **de** beaux tableaux.
He sells good wine	Il vend **de** bon vin.

This is the strict grammatical construction but *before singular adjectives* the words **du** and **de la** are used more and more frequently nowadays, as: J'ai du bon vin; il vend de la bonne viande.

*** Before Masculine Singular words beginning with a Vowel or an H mute, **nouvel**, **vieil**, **bel** must be used as: a handsome man, **un bel homme**.

Remember that *some* must be expressed in French, even if not in English.

EXERCISE II

1 Here is some old wine. 2 Here are some beautiful flowers.
3 There is a big aeroplane. 4 There are some big mountains.
5 Here is a good spot. 6 There are some small lakes. 7 Here are some young animals. 8 There is some good butter and (good) cheese. 9 They gave us good meat but bad wine.

VOCABULARY: 1 Here is *or* here are, **voici** (vo'ăh-se); there is *or* there are, **voilà** (vo'ăh-lăh); mountain, **montagne** *f* (mong-tahn-yer); spot, **endroit** *m* (ahng-dro'ah); lake, **lac** *m* (lăhck).

EXERCISE III

1 Have you any good butter? 2 We drank some old wine.
3 They have bought some beautiful rings. 4 We have a bad opinion of you. 5 She wears a new hat every day.

CONVERSATIONAL SENTENCES

Voici le reste[1] des nombres cardinaux[2]: cent un, cent dix, deux cents, quatre cents, huit cent[3] soixante, mille[4], deux mille francs, en[5] mil[6] neuf cent soixante-dix, cent mille[7], un million[8], un milliard[9].

Here are the rest of the cardinal numbers: one hundred and one, one hundred and ten, two hundred, four hundred, eight hundred and sixty, a thousand, two thousand francs, in the year one thousand nine hundred and seventy, a hundred thousand, a million, a milliard.

Il nous a donné du (*or* de) très vieux cognac[10].

He gave us some very old brandy.

Ils nous ont invité dans leur belle maison à la campagne[11].

They invited us to their beautiful house in the country.

En juillet de grosses fraises[12] poussent dans son petit jardin.

In July big strawberries grow in his little garden.

Est-ce qu'il achète une nouvelle voiture tous les ans?	Does he buy a new car every year?
Il a de grandes mains[13] et de petits pieds.	He has big hands and small feet.
Que pensez-vous de sa nouvelle amie?	What do you think of her new friend?
Je pense qu'elle est trop grosse.	I think she is too fat.
Il y a une grosse différence[14] entre votre climat et le nôtre.	There is a big difference between your climate and ours.
Voici une vue[15] magnifique[16].	Here is a magnificient view.
Ont-ils de jeunes enfants?	Have they any young children?
Non, ils ont un gros chien à la place[17].	No, they have a big dog instead.
Il gagne dix mille livres par an.	He earns ten thousand pounds a year.

NOTES & PRON.: 1 resst; 2 kahr-de-noh; 3 *cent* (sah*ng*) does not take an s in the Plural—(a) if followed by another number; (b) in dates, as *en quinze cent*; (c) if used instead of the ordinal number as, *page deux cent*. *Quatre vingts* follows the same rules. 4 *mille* (pronounced 'mill') never takes an s, and becomes *mil* in dates after Christ. 5 en (ah*ng*) = in the year. 6 mill; 7 A, AN, ONE before 100 to 1,000 are not translated in French; hyphens (-) are inserted in numbers 17 to 99, except 21, 31, 41, 51, 61, 71, where *et* is used. 8 mill-e-o*ng*; 9 mill-e-ar; 10 kon-yahck; 11 kah*ng*-păhn-yer; 12 frayz; 13 ma*ng*; 14 de-feh-rah*ng*ss; 15 VEE; 16 mahn-yee-fick; 17 ăh-lăh-plăhss.

55. RICHER, TALLER, etc. must be translated by *more rich, more tall*, etc.; RICHEST, TALLEST, by *the more rich, the more tall.* THAN is rendered by **que.**

He is *taller* than you	Il est **plus** grand **que** vous
They are *younger* than we	Ils sont **plus** jeunes **que** nous
She is *smaller* than her sister	Elle est **plus** petite **que** sa soeur
She is *the tallest*	Elle est **la plus** grande
They (*f*) are *the smallest*	Elles sont **les plus petites**

59

Note that IN after a Superlative* is translated as *of*; and that THAN before a Number is also translated as *of*:

The *richest*† man *in* the world	L'homme **le plus** riche du monde
He has more *than six* farms	Il a plus **de six** fermes (fai**r**m) *f*

EXERCISE IV

1 Our bedroom is bigger than yours. 2 Your garden is smaller than ours. 3 Is that tree the highest in the garden? 4 The twins are the youngest of the family. 5 Her foot is smaller than his. 6 Isn't she prettier than her sister? 7 The poorest woman in the town lives there.

VOCABULARY: tree, **arbre** *m* (ăh**r**-b**r**); twins, **jumeaux** *m pl.*, **jumelles** *f pl* (shEE-moh, shEE-mell); poor, **pauvre** (poh-v**r**); high, **haut** (oh).

56. Learn the following words:

good, **bon**; better, **meilleur**, **meilleure** (may'e-y e**r**); the best, **le meilleur**, **la meilleure**; less, **moins** (mo'a*n*g); the least, **le** *or* **la moins**; as ... as, **aussi ... que** (oh-se ... ke**r**); so ... as, **si ... que** (see ... ke**r**).

She is *less* pretty than her sister	Elle est **moins** jolie que sa soeur
This month is *the least* cold	Ce mois est **le moins** froid
He is *as* tall *as* you	Il est **aussi** grand **que** vous
These flowers aren't *so* beautiful *as* yours	Ces fleurs ne sont pas **si** belles **que** les vôtres

EXERCISE V

1 My car is as fast as his. 2 He is less intelligent than his brother. 3 This beach is the best in the district. 4 My hands aren't so dirty as yours. 5 Her ring is the least beautiful. 6 The highest mountain in the world. 7 Isn't he the best pianist in Europe? 8 My cooking is as good as hers. 9 He earned less than ten francs today. 10 I gave her more than eight thousand francs.

VOCABULARY: fast, **rapide** (răh-peed); intelligent, **intelligent** (*a*ng-tell-le-shah*n*g); district, **région** *f* (reh-she-o*n*g); world, **monde** *m* (mo*n*gd); pianist, **pianiste** *m* or *f* (pe-ăh-nisst); Europe, **Europe** (e*r*-**r**op); cooking, **cuisine** *f* (kwee-zeen).

---

* Forms like *largest, most serious* are called Superlatives.

† **plus, le plus** before an Adjective do not alter its position (Paras. 40, 53).

CONVERSATIONAL SENTENCES

Quel sont les nombres ordinaux[1]*? Ce sont les suivants:

Which are the ordinal numbers? They are the following:

Le premier[2], le deuxième[3] *or* le second[4], le troisième[5], le quatrième, le cinquième, le sixième, le septième, le huitième, le neuvième, le dixième, le onzième, le vingtième, le vingt et unième[5], etc.

The first, the second, the third, the fourth, the fifth, the sixth, the seventh, the eighth, the ninth, the tenth, the eleventh, the twentieth, the twenty-first. etc.

Les jours les plus heureux[6] de ma vie.

The happiest days of my life.

La journée la plus chaude de l'année.

The hottest day of the year.

La plus grande cité[7] du pays.

The largest city in the country.

L'homme le plus célèbre[8] de son temps.

The most famous man of his time.

Ils lui ont acheté une motocyclette[9] pour son dix-huitième anniversaire[10].

They bought him a motor-bike for his eighteenth birthday.

Il a passé plus de trois semaines là.

He spent more than three weeks there.

L'Angleterre n'est pas aussi grande que la France.

England is not as big as France.

Cette route[11] est presque[12] aussi longue que l'autre.

This route is nearly as long as the other.

Voici un meilleur endroit pour un pique-nique[13].

Here is a better spot for a picnic.

PRON.: 1 or-de-noh; 2 ler prer-me-eh; 3 ler der-ze-ame; 4 ler ser-gong; 5 ler tro'ăh-ze-ame, ler kăh-tre-ame, ler sang-ke-ame, ler se-ze-ame, ler sett-e-ame, ler wit-e-ame, ler ner-ve-ame, ler de-ze-ame, ler ong-ze-ame, ler vang-te-ame, ler vang-t'eh-EE-ne-ame; 6 er-rer; 7 se-teh; 8 seh-leh-br; 9 mo-toss-e-klett; 10 ăh-ne-vair-sair; 11 root; 12 press-ker; 13 peek-neek.

---

* The ORDINAL NUMBERS are formed from the cardinal numbers by adding **-ième**; if the cardinal number ends in **-e**, the **-e** is omitted in adding **-ième**. **Premier** and **second** are irregular, and 5th and 9th slightly change the spelling.

LESSON THIRTEEN

57. The FUTURE of **all** verbs is formed by adding to the IN-FINITIVE the following terminations: **-ai, -as, -a, -ons, -ez, -ont** (same terminations as in **j'ai, tu as,** etc.)

I will give	**je donnerai** (she*r* donner-e*r*-reh)
you will (familiar) give	**tu donneras** (tEE donn-e*r*-rah)
he will give	**il donnera** (ill donn-e*r*-rah)
we will give	**nous donnerons** (noo donn-e*r*-ro*ng*)
you will give	**vous donnerez** (voo donn-e*r*-reh)
they will give	**ils donneront** (ils donn-e*r*-ro*ng*)

The final **-e** of **-re** Verbs is omitted when adding these terminations; **avoir** adds them to **aur-**, and **être** to **ser-**, as,

I will sell	**je vendrai**	I will have	**j'aurai**
I will finish	**je finirai**	I will be	**je serai**

QUESTIONS and NEGATIONS are formed as in the other Tenses:

will he speak?	**parlera-t-il?**
will we finish?	**finirons-nous?**
they won't have	**ils n'auront pas**
won't she be?	**ne sera-t-elle pas?**

Exercise I

1 He will be here tomorrow.   2 We will be there.   3 I will speak to his father.   4 He will sell his house.   5 Will you have (the) time tomorrow?   6 The programme will finish at eight o'clock.   7 They will reply to our letter by return of (the) post. 8 Will you have some money next week?   9 I won't give him the money.   10 Where will they live?   11 Won't they be late?

VOCABULARY: programme, **programme** *m* (prog-răhm).

Exercise II

1 I will speak to him tomorrow.   2 We will give the book back to them.   3 He won't finish it before this evening.   4 Won't they look for us if we are late?   5 They won't reply to her. 6 Won't she expect you?   7 You will have it.   8 We won't find him at home.   9 Won't they accept it?

VOCABULARY: before, **avant** (ăh-vah*ng*); at home, **à la maison** (ăh lăh may-zo*ng*).

CONVERSATIONAL SENTENCES

C'est aujourd'hui le premier (1er) mars, n'est-ce pas?
Today is the first of* March, isn't it?

Quel jour était[1]-il ici?
On* what day was he here?

Il était ici lundi.
He was here on Monday.

Quand lui avez-vous écrit?
When did you write to him?

Le 15 (quinze†) septembre.
On the 15th of September.

Quand l'avez-vous vu?
When did you see him?

Vendredi, le 2 (deux) juin.
On Friday, the 2nd of June.

Quel jour de la semaine est-ce?
What day of the week is this?

Lundi, le 25 (vingt-cinq) mai.
Monday, the 25th of May.

Ils arriveront à deux heures le premier juin.
They will arrive at two o'clock on the first of June.

Dans ce cas ils ne me trouveront pas ici.
In that case they won't find me here.

Je rentrerai avant la fin[2] du mois de mai.
I will go back before the end of (the month of) may.

Demain nous commencerons à emballer[3].
Tomorrow we will begin packing.

Le jour suivant ils ont commencé à déballer[4].
The next day they began unpacking.

La semaine dernière il a coupé l'herbe[5] et il la coupera encore la semaine prochaine.
Last week he cut the grass and he will cut it again next week.

L'année dernière ma fille a appris à nager.
Last year my daughter learned to swim.

L'année prochaine nous passerons plus de quinze jours à la mer.
Next year we will spend more than a fortnight at the seaside.

J'ai depensé plus de mille francs hier.
I spent more than a thousand francs yesterday.

PRON.: 1 eh-tay; 2 fang; 3 ahng-bah-leh; 4 deh-băh-leh; 5 airb.

---

* of and on are not translated before DAYS, MONTHS and DATES.
† In dates, TWO, THREE, etc., are used instead of 2nd, 3rd, etc., the 1st (le premier) being the only exception. It is not customary to begin names of days and months with a capital letter in French.

58. The IMPERATIVE is the same as the PRESENT, except that the Pronouns **vous, nous, tu** are omitted, thus:

speak, **parlez**	do not speak, **ne parlez pas**
sell, **vendez**	do not sell, **ne vendez pas**
let us speak, **parlons**	don't let us speak, **ne parlons pas**
let us finish, **finissons**	don't let us finish, **ne finissons pas**

Familiar forms : speak, parle*; do not sell, ne vends pas; finish, finis.

The Imperative of to HAVE and to BE is:

have	**ayez** (ay-yeh)
be	**soyez** (so'ah-yeh)
have (familiar)	**aie** (ay)
be (familiar)	**sois** (so'ăh)
let us have	**ayons** (ay-yong)
let us be	**soyons** (so'ăh-yong)

The Imperative has only the above forms; *let him speak* and *let them speak* are translated by the Subjunctive Present. (See Lesson 26).

EXERCISE III

1 Don't be late.   2 Reply to his letter by return (of post). 3 Let's ask for the menu.   4 Fill the glasses.   5 Don't smoke here.   6 Look-at these pictures.   7 Don't eat that food.   8 Don't sell your books.   9 Shut the window.   10 Don't let's spend that money.   11 Cut some bread.   12 Be reasonable.

VOCABULARY: to fill, **remplir** (rah*ng*-pleer); food, **nourriture** *f* (noo-re-tEEr); reasonable, **raisonnable** (ray-zonn-ăh-bl).

59. WHAT? WHICH? are translated **quel?** etc. if followed by the Verb **être** (*to be*) and a Noun (See also paras. 34 and 39); as,

What **is** your OPINION?	Quelle **est** votre OPINION?
Which **are** their FRIENDS?	Quels **sont** leurs AMIS?
What **will be** the PRICE?	Quel **sera** le PRIX?

60. WHICH? WHICH ONE (or ONES)? followed by OF are translated *the which* (**lequel, laquelle, lesquels, lesquelles**):

Which (one) of these girls?	**Laquelle** de ces filles?
Which (ones) of these men smoke?	**Lesquels** de ces hommes fument?

* The final **s** of **-er** Verbs is omitted in the Imperative Singular.

1 What will his salary be? 2 What is her name? 3 Which is your house? 4 Which are your friends? 5 What is his address? 6 Which is his sister? 7 What is your size? 8 Which of these children is the youngest? 9 Which of these rooms is the most expensive? 10 Which newspaper did you buy?

VOCABULARY: salary, **salaire**, *m* (săh-lair); size, **taille** *f* (tăh'e); expensive, **cher** *m* (shair), **chère** *f*.

CONVERSATIONAL SENTENCES

Avez-vous faim[1]?

Are you hungry? (= have you hunger).

Pas encore, mais j'ai très soif[2].

Not yet, but I am very thirsty.

J'aurai bientôt[3] faim.

I will be hungry soon.

Attachez[4] vos ceintures[5].

Fasten your seatbelts.

Eteignez[6] les lumières[7].

Put the lights out.

Quel âge[8] aurez-vous l'année prochaine?

What age will you be (=have) next year?

Quel est notre train?

Which is our train?

Ne soyez pas impatient[9].

Don't be impatient.

Cherchons une autre plage.

Let's look for another beach.

Regardez cette vue!

Look at that view!

Lequel de ces autobus[10] va à l'aérogare[11]?

Which of these buses goes to the air terminal?

Parlez doucement[12].

Speak softly.

N'oubliez pas de m'écrire.

Don't forget to write to me.

Essayez de venir[13] demain.

Try to come tomorrow.

N'ayez pas peur[14].

Don't be frightened (have fear).

Je serai là à l'heure du déjeuner.

I'll be there at lunchtime.

Vous aurez besoin d'un pneu[15] neuf[16].

You will need (have need of) a new tyre.

Ouvrez la bouche[17] et fermez les[18] yeux[18].

Open your mouth (= the mouth) and close your eyes (= the eyes).

PRON.: 1 fa*ng*; 2 so'ăhf; 3 be-a*ng*-toh; 4 ăh-tăh-sheh; 5 sa*ng*-teer *f*; 6 eh-teh-ne-yeh; 7 lee-me-air; 8 ăhsh; 9 a*ng*-păh-sse-ah*ng*; 10 oh-toh-bees; 11 ăh-eh-ro-gahr *f*; 12 dooss-mah*ng*; 13 ver-neer; 14 per; 15 pner; 16 nerf; 17 boosh; 18 lay z'e-er.

LESSON FOURTEEN

61. The CONDITIONAL of **all** Verbs is formed by changing the terminations of the FUTURE to **-ais, -ais, -ait; -ions, -iez, -aient.** The Stems of the Future and Conditional are therefore always the same.

I would give	**je donnerais** (she*r* donn-e*r*-ray)
you would give (familiar)	**tu donnerais** (TEE donn-e*r*-ray)
he would give	**il donnerait** (ill donn-e*r*-ray)
we would give	**nous donnerions** (noo donn-e*r*-re-o*ng*)
you would give	**vous donneriez** (voo donn-e*r*-re-eh)
they would give	**ils donneraient** (ill donn-e*r*-ray)

QUESTIONS and NEGATIONS are formed in the usual way:

he would not be	il ne serait pas
would they have?	auraient-ils?
would he not sell?	ne vendrait-il pas?
would we finish?	finirions-nous?

EXERCISE I

1 You wouldn't be happy there.   2 He wouldn't be there in time.   3 I would like a glass of wine.   4 They wouldn't lose the way.   5 They wouldn't have the time.   6 She would be alone. 7 We would spend too much money.   8 They wouldn't be at home.   9 Would you have paid the bill?

VOCABULARY: alone, **seul** (se*r*l).

62. WHO, WHOM, WHICH, THAT, when referring to a preceding word, are called RELATIVE PRONOUNS; thus,

Subject	—*who, which, that*	**qui**
Object	—*whom, which, that*	**que** (**qu'** before a vowel or a mute H)

qui is used if the Verb comes immediately after these words in English; in this case it will always be the SUBJECT of its clause.

que is used if there is another word between; in this case it will always be the OBJECT of its clause.

The children who live here	= **Les enfants qui habitent ici**
The price that we pay	= **Le prix que nous payons**
The train that he is waiting for	= **Le train qu'il attend**

In the first sentence the relative pronoun is the subject; in the other two the object. Note that *qui* is **never** abbreviated to *qu'*.

1 The man who spoke to us.   **2** The coffee that we drank this morning.   **3** A house that gives on (to) the sea.   **4** The letter that is on the table is for your friend.   **5** The newspapers that are here are French.   **6** We don't like the food that they eat.   **7** The film that we saw yesterday.

63. WHOM, WHICH, THAT are often left out but must always be expressed in French; as,

| The books you are looking for are here | Les livres que vous cherchez sont ici |

EXERCISE III

1 The hotel we chose is full.   **2** The noise I heard.   **3** Where is the money I gave you?   **4** There is the man I met yesterday.

VOCABULARY: full, **plein** (pla*ng*).

CONVERSATIONAL SENTENCES

avoir raison[1], tort[2], peur, honte[3], chaud, froid.
(to) be right, wrong, afraid, ashamed, warm (hot), cold.

Qui a raison?
Who is right?

Vous avez tort.
You are wrong.

Il fait très froid aujourd'hui.
It is (makes) very cold today.

Mais pas aussi froid qu'hier.
But not as cold as yesterday.

N'a-t-il pas froid?
Isn't he cold?

Non, au contraire[4], il a chaud.
No, on the contrary, he is warm (hot).

J'aurais honte.
I would be ashamed.

N'aurait-elle pas peur?
Wouldn't she be afraid?

Ne seraient-ils pas plus heureux ensemble[5]?
Wouldn't they be happier together?

Aimeriez-vous une tasse de thé?
Would you like a cup of tea?

Les vêtements[6] que nous lui achetons seraient moins chers à Londres.
The clothes we buy (for) her would be less expensive in London.

Les gens[7] qui habitent dans ces appartements.
The people who live in those flats.

67

Combien coûterait[8] cette voiture en Angleterre?	How much would that car cost in England?
Nous serions obliges[9] de payer un droit[10] d'entrée.[10].	We would have to (be obliged to) pay an import duty.
La première[11] fois[11] que je l'ai vu.	The first time I saw him.
La dernière[12] fois[12] que j'ai visité la France.	The last time I visited France.

PRON.: 1 ray-zo*ng*; 2 to**r**; 3 o*ng*t; 4 ko*ng*-trai**r**; 5 ah*ng*-sah*ng*-bl; 6 vaytt-mah*ng*; 7 **sh**ah*ng*; 8 koo-ter-ray; 9 ob-le-**sh**eh; 10 dro'äh d'ah*ng*-treh; 11 pre**r**-me-ai**r** fo'äh; 12 dai**r**-ne-ai**r** fo'äh.

64. The PAST PARTICIPLE of verbs using *avoir* to form their past tenses (some use *être*—see para. 116) always takes the same Gender and Number as its *Direct Object* when it FOLLOWS the Object in French. This occurs in three kinds of sentences:

(a) In Questions beginning with WHICH, WHAT, followed by a Noun.

WHICH HOUSE have you bought?	QUELLE MAISON avez-vous achetée?
WHICH CHILDREN did you meet?	QUELS ENFANTS avez-vous rencontrés ?
WHAT TOWNS did you visit?	QUELLES VILLES avez-vous visitées?

(b) after the Relative Pronoun **que (qu')**

The dress THAT I bought	La robe QUE j'ai achetée
The boys WHOM you saw	Les garçons QUE vous avez vus
The flowers THAT I gave her	Les fleurs QUE je lui ai données

(c) After the Personal Pronouns given in Paragraph 42, unless they mean: TO ME, TO US, TO HIM, etc.

We met HER in the street	Nous L'avons rencontrée dans la rue
Didn't they expect YOU (*m plur*)?	Ne VOUS ont-ils pas attendus?
I didn't see YOU (*f. sing.*)	Je ne VOUS ai pas vue
Didn't you lose THEM (*f.*)?	Ne LES avez-vous pas perdues?
She saw US (*m*) yesterday	Elle NOUS a vus hier
BUT:—He gave (to) us the money	Il nous a *donné* l'argent

In the above examples, the Object is printed in SMALL CAPITALS. In the last sentence (*to*) us is of course an INDIRECT Object, and there is no agreement in French.

1 Which page have you read? 2 I have found the stamps
(that) you lost. 3 The postman brought three letters for you;
have you received them? 4 What animals did you see? 5 Is
the water (which) he brought you hot? 6 Their house is very
big; have you seen it?

CONVERSATIONAL SENTENCES

En été[1], en automne, en hiver, au printemps[1], à Noël[2], à Paques[2].	In Summer, in Autumn, in Winter, in Spring, at Christmas, at Easter.
Il y a une semaine, il y a un mois.	A week ago, a month ago.
Quel âge avez-vous?	How old are you?
J'ai vingt ans.	I am twenty.
Quel âge a son fils?	How old is his son?
Il a dix ans.	He is ten.
Quel est votre âge?	What is your age?
J'ai quarante ans.	I am forty.
Quel est l'âge de votre fille?	What is the age of your daughter?
Elle aura onze ans au mois de juin prochain.	She will be eleven next June.
Elle a des cheveux[3] blonds[4] et des yeux bleus[5].	She has blond hair and blue eyes.
Les chaussures que nous avons achetées étaient trop grandes.	The shoes we bought were too big.
Quelles personnes[6] auriez-vous invitées?	Which people would you have invited?
Les places que nous avons réservées il y a trois jours.	The seats we reserved three days ago.
Les endroits que nous avons visités.	The places we visited.
Où est l'eau qu'il a apportée?	Where's the water he brought?
Je l'ai bue.	I've drunk it.

PRON.: 1 eh-teh, oh-tonn, e-vair, prang-tah*ng*; 2 no-ell, pahk; 3 sher-
ve*r*, 4 blo*ng*, 5 ble*r*; 6 pair-sonn.

LESSON FIFTEEN

65. The IMPERFECT TENSE of all Verbs is formed by adding to the *Stem*:

-ais, -ais, -ait; -ions, -iez, -aient.

I was giving	**je donnais** (donn-ay)
you were giving (familiar)	**tu donnais** (donn-ay)
he was giving	**il donnait** (donn-ay)
we were giving	**nous donnions** (donn-e-o*ng*)
you were giving	**vous donniez** (donn-e-eh)
they were giving	**ils donnaient** (donn-ay)

Verbs ending in **-ir** take **-iss-** before the above terminations; **avoir** adds them to **av-**, and **être** to **ét-**. Examples:

I was selling	**je vendais** (she*r* vah*ng*-day)
I was finishing	**je finissais** (she*r* fe-niss-say)
I had	**j'avais** (shăh-vay)
I was	**j'étais** (sheh-tay)

EXERCISE I (on the Imperfect)

1 I was-giving (to) him a lesson.   2 She had† two sisters.
3 They were† alone.   4 She was-playing the piano.   5 They were-listening-to the music.   6 We were-waiting-for her plane.
7 She was-speaking to us.   8 I was-smoking a cigarette.   9 He had† a headache.   10 We were† at home.   11 You were (= had) wrong; I was (= had) right.

VOCABULARY: lesson, **leçon** *f* (le*r*-so*ng*); to play the piano, **jouer du piano** (shoo-eh DEE pe-ăh-no); to listen, **écouter** (eh-koo-teh); music, **musique** *f* (mEE-zick); to have a headache, **avoir mal à la tête** (ăh-vo' ăh*r* măhl ăh lăh tayt); at home, **à la maison** (ăh lăh may-zo*ng*).

---

† *had, was, were* are generally translated by the Imperfect, and must be so translated in these exercises.

66. The Imperfect Tense means 'I used to give', 'he used to sell' etc. as well as 'I was giving', 'he was selling'. Therefore, 'I gave, he sold', etc., when meaning 'I used to give', 'he used to sell' etc., must be translated by the Imperfect Tense.

She used to speak to me.	Elle me parlait.
They (*f*) used to visit us.	Elles nous rendaient visite*.

EXERCISE II (on the Imperfect)

1 They used to play every day.   2 He used to earn a lot of money.   3 We used to study (the) French together.   4 They were going to the market with their baskets.   5 Weren't they playing (at the) cards yesterday evening?   6 She always won, and I always lost.   7 He was finishing his meal.   8 They weren't here.   9 We had† a little house.   10 They hadn't† (the) time. 11 Wasn't she French?

VOCABULARY: a lot, **beaucoup** (boh-koo); to study, **étudier** (eh-tEE-de-eh); to go, **aller** (ăh-leh); market, **marché** *m* (măhr-sheh); basket, **panier** *m* (păh-ne-eh); card, **carte** *f* (kăhrt).

CONVERSATIONAL SENTENCES

Il n'avait pas peur.	He wasn't afraid.
Nous avions tort.	We were wrong.
De quoi parlait-elle?	What was she speaking about?
Vous avez bien raison.	You are quite (well) right.
Il est arrivé hier matin.	He (is) arrived yesterday morning.
Nous ne serions pas à temps.	We wouldn't be in time.
Qu'a-t-il dit cette fois?	What did he say this time?
Nous passions nos vacances avec des amis en Italie[1].	We used to spend our holidays with friends in Italy.

---

* To visit a place is *visiter*; to visit a person is *rendre visite à*.

† *had, was, were* are generally translated by the Imperfect, and must be so translated in these exercises.

Je nageais* tous les matins avant le petit déjeuner.	I swam every morning before breakfast.
La mer était dangereuse² à cause³ des courants⁴.	The sea was dangerous because of currents.
Nous plongions⁵ dans l'eau des rochers⁶.	We used to dive into the water from the rocks.
Les vagues⁷ étaient très grosses et effrayantes⁸.	The waves were very big and frightening.
Aviez-vous perdu pied?	Were you out of your depth? (= Had you lost foot)
Quand elle était jeune elle habitait⁹ seule dans une grande maison.	When she was young she lived alone in a big house.
Elle aimait les contes¹⁰ de fées¹⁰.	She liked fairy stories.
Je n'avais pas d'argent.	I had no money.
Je ne dormais pas quand le réveil¹¹ a sonné¹².	I wasn't asleep (sleeping) when the alarm went.
Il était sept heures un quart.	It was quarter past seven.
J'avais la gueule¹³ de bois¹³.	I had a hangover (the mouth of wood).

PRON.: 1 e-tăh-lee; 2 dah*ng*-sher-rerz; 3 ah kohz; 4 koo-rah*ng*; 5 plo*ng*-sheo*ng*; 6 rosh-eh; 7 vahg; 8 eh-fray-yah*ng*t; 9 ăh-be-tay; 10 ko*ng*t der feh; 11 reh-**vay**'e; 12 sonn-eh; 13 gherl der bo'ah.

67. WHICH and WHOM after a PREPOSITION (see Paragraph 35) are translated by THE WHICH, thus:

lequel, laquelle, lesquels, lesquelles (ler-kell, etc.)

WHOM and WHICH are in such cases RELATIVE pronouns, as they do not ask a question.

the house *in which* we live	la maison **dans laquelle** nous habitons
the man *with whom she was dancing*	l'homme **avec lequel** (*or* avec qui) elle dansait (dah*ng*-say)

After a Preposition, WHOM can also be translated by **qui**.

---

* See Para. 134.

1 The train in which he was travelling was late. 2 The means by which he earned his living. 3 The man with whom I discussed the matter yesterday is not here. 4 The girl for whom you bought the shoes. 5 The envelope on which he wrote the address. 6 The man by whom he sent the money.

VOCABULARY: means, **moyens** *m pl* (mo'ăh-ya*ng*); living, **vie** *f* (vee); to discuss, **discuter** (diss-KEE-teh); matter, **affaire** *f* (ăh-fair); envelope, **enveloppe** *f* (ah*ng*v-lop).

68. OF WHOM, OF WHICH (when Relative) are often translated by **dont** instead of **de qui,** or **duquel,* de laquelle, desquels,** etc.

the people *of whom* you were speaking	les personnes **dont** (*or* de qui *or* desquelles) vous parliez
the book *of which* he forgot the title	le livre **dont** il a oublié le titre (tee-tr)

EXERCISE IV

(In many cases the English sentence has to be given in a rather stilted form to help with the construction of the French sentence)

1 Have you let the rooms of which we were speaking? 2 Where is the list from which he was copying the names? 3 There is the man to whom I gave it. 4 The fire of which we heard was very serious. 5 We were speaking of our son and not of yours. 6 We lent it to our friends and not to theirs. 7 To which one of these men did you send it? 8 Of which (*pl*) of these girls were you speaking? 9 Did they hear it from my daughter or from hers?

VOCABULARY: to let, **louer** (loo-eh); list, **liste** *f* (list); to copy, **copier** (kop-e-eh); heard = have heard speak; serious, **grave** (grăhv); not, **non** *or* non pas (no*ng*, no*ng* pah); did they hear = did they learn, **appris** (ăh-pree).

---

* All such words beginning with **le** or **les** are contracted with **de** and **à** as usual (see paragraphs 22, 25).

Il arrivera le dix-huit août. He will arrive on the 18th of August.

Quel jour arriverons-nous? What day will we arrive?

Vendredi, le seize novembre. Friday, November 16th.

Savez-vous quelle heure il est? Do you know what time it is?

Non, la montre dont je vous ai parlé retarde[1] toujours. No, the watch I told you about is always slow.

Je crois[2] qu'il est environ[3] midi. I think that (= I believe that) it's about midday.

Où sont les musées[4] dont vous avez parlé et les cafés[5] que vous avez aimés? Where are the museums you spoke about and the cafés you liked?

La voiture que j'ai louée est tombée en panne pour la troisième fois. The car I hired has broken down for the third time.

L'homme à qui j'ai presenté[6] ma femme a disparu[7] avec elle. The man I introduced my wife to has disappeared with her.

Il aurait préféré la mienne s'il l'avait vue. He would have liked mine better (= preferred) if he had seen her.

Il avait quatre-vingt-sept ans, il était chauve[8] et il boitait[9]. He was eighty-seven, and bald, and he limped.

La voiture dans laquelle ils voyageaient* a eu[10] un accident[11]. The car they were travelling in had an accident.

A quel commissariat[12] de police[12] l'avez-vous signalé[13]? Which police station did you report it to?

Si j'étais à votre place je ne dirais rien[14]. If I were you I'd say nothing.

PRON.: 1 rer-tăhrd; 2 kro'ah; 3 ahng-ve-rong; 4 mEE-zeh; 5 kah-feh; 6 preh-zahng-teh; 7 diss-păh-rEE; 8 shohv; 9 bo'äh-tay; 10 EE; 11 ăhck-se-dahng; 12 komm-iss-săh-re-ăh der poll-iss; 13 seen-yăh-leh; 14 re-ang.

* See Para. 134.

LESSON SIXTEEN

69. The PRESENT PARTICIPLE is formed by adding **-ant** to the *stem*; Regular Verbs ending in **-ir** take **-iss-** before the **-ant**:

> giving, **donnant** (donn-ah*ng*); selling, **vendant** (vah*ng*-dah*ng*;
> finishing, **finissant** (fe-niss-ah*ng*)
> IRREGULAR: having, **ayant** (ay-yah*ng*; being, **étant** (eh-tah*ng*)

NOTE: The INFINITIVE is used in French instead of the PRESENT PARTICIPLE after any preposition *except* **en** (in, on, while); as,

without paying it	**sans le payer**
after speaking = after having spoken	**après avoir parlé**
BUT: *while crossing* the street	**en traversant la rue**
on meeting their friends	**en rencontrant leurs amis**

EXERCISE I

1 While speaking to his friend;   2 on turning the corner;
3 while visiting Athens;   4 without replying to the letter;
5 after writing (after having written);   6 I have the pleasure of
informing you;   7 for having lost the money;   8 while looking
for the street;   9 without waiting for a reply;   10 having lost
the way;   11 for having sold;   12 on hearing the noise.

VOCABULARY: to turn, **tourner** (tooh**r**neh); corner, **coin** *m* (ko-a*ng*);
Athens, **Athènes** (ăh-tayn); pleasure, **plaisir** *m* (play-zee**r**); to inform,
informer (a*ng*-for-meh); reply, **réponse** *f* (reh-po*ng*ss).

70. THIS, THAT, not followed by a Noun, are translated thus:

THIS, **ceci** (se**r**-se)   THAT, **cela** (se**r**-lah)

ça (sah) is a very commonly heard contraction of **cela. ce** (or
c' before a vowel) is generally used instead of **ceci** or **cela**, if
connected with a tense of *to be*—see Paragraphs 74, 75.

What is the price of *this*?	**Quel est le prix de ceci?**
Did you buy *that*?	**Avez-vous acheté cela?**
This will be easy	**Ce sera facile**
Isn't *that* difficult?	**N'est-ce pas difficile?**

Exercise II

1 Give this to your brother.   2 This costs more than that.
3 Why didn't you choose that?   4 This is the best colour.
5 Wasn't that stupid?   6 This is too expensive.   7 That will be
interesting.   8 Don't show (to-) him this.   9 That is too small.
10 This doesn't seem very heavy.   11 Won't that be difficult?
12 This wasn't easy.

Vocabulary: stupid, **stupide** (stEE-peed); interesting, **intéressant**
(a*ng*-teh-rayss-ah*ng*); to seem, **sembler** (sah*ng*-bleh); heavy, **lourd**
(loo*r*); difficult, **difficile** (de-fe-sill); easy, **facile** (făh-sill).

71. The PAST HISTORIC (also known as the Past Definite) is
never used in conversation but is frequently met with in
reading. You should go on translating the PAST by the *Perfect*
or *Imperfect* except for a little practice in the three exercises
below.

The PAST HISTORIC of Verbs ending in **-er** is formed by
adding to the *Stem* the terminations printed in thick type
below:

I gave	je donn**ai** (donn-ay)
you gave (familiar)	tu donn**as** (dohn-ah)
he gave	il donn**a** (donn-ah)
we gave	nous donn**âmes** (donn-ăhm)
you gave	vous donn**âtes** (donn-ăht)
they gave	ils donn**èrent** (donn-air)

Exercise III

1 he spoke;   2 I didn't look-for her;   3 we accepted;
4 you forgot;   5 they cut;   6 we found;   7 they didn't give;
8 we left the town;   9 we closed the door;   10 they didn't pay
the bill;   11 he looked at me.

72. The PAST HISTORIC of Regular Verbs in **-re** and **-ir** is
formed by adding to the Stem **-is, -is, -it; -îmes, -îtes,
-irent**, thus:

I SOLD, etc.		I FINISHED, etc.	
je vendis	(vah*ng*-dee)	je finis	(fin-ee)
tu vendis	(vah*ng*-dee)	tu finis	(fin-ee)
il vendit	(vah*ng*-dee)	il finit	(fin-ee)
nous vendîmes	(vah*ng*-deem)	nous finîmes	(fin-eem)
vous vendîtes	(vah*ng*-deet)	vous finîtes	(fin-eet)
ils vendirent	(vah*ng*-deer)	ils finirent	(fin-eer)

EXERCISE IV

1 we finished; 2 he did not sell; 3 you chose; 4 we lost;
5 they replied; 6 she gave back; 7 I filled; 8 they didn't
succeed.

73. The PAST HISTORIC of **avoir** and **être** have the same terminations as the **-re** and **-ir** Verbs, except that **i** is changed
into **u**:

I HAD, etc.		I WAS, etc.	
j'eus	(shEE)	je fus	(fEE)
tu eus	(tEE EE)	tu fus	,,
il eut	(ill EE)	il fut	,,
nous eûmes	(noo z'EEm)	nous fûmes	(fEEm)
vous eûtes	(voo z'EEt)	vous fûtes	(fEEt)
ils eurent	(ill z'EEr)	ils furent	(fEEr)

EXERCISE V

1 I was; 2 she had; 3 we were; 4 they had; 5 they (*f*)
were; 6 we had; 7 I hadn't; 8 he wasn't; 9 they weren't.

74. THIS, THAT, THESE and THOSE are all translated by **ce** (**c'**) if
connected with a tense of *to be* and a Noun or Pronoun; as,

That (or *this*) will be your room	**Ce sera votre chambre**
These (or *those*) are my friends	**Ce sont mes amis**
Isn't *this* (or *that*) my seat?	**Est-ce que ce n'est pas ma place?***
That (or *this*) was yours	**C'était le vôtre**

---

* When **ce** comes in a question it is always safer to choose the **est-ce
que** form (See Para. 51). Although it is correct to say, for example,
est-ce bon? (is it good?) in conversation such constructions are rarely
heard. French people would say **est-ce que c'est bon?** or simply **c'est
bon?** Also, the singular form **c'est** is always correct, even when followed
by a plural, so you can say either **c'est mes enfants** or **ce sont mes
enfants.** Note also that **ce sont** can only be used with a third person
plural. (For example you *can't* say **ce sont nous**).

Exercise VI

1 This is my flat.　2 Is this your seat?　3 These are my keys.
4 Those aren't his children.　5 Isn't this your ticket?　6 Was
that our bus?　7 Will that be your address?　8 That was our
train.　9 Isn't this his shop?　10 What birds were those?

75. IT is generally translated by **ce** unless referring to a Noun
just mentioned (See Para. 23). HE, SHE, THEY are also translated by **ce** if used with the Verb *to be* and a Noun and Pronoun.

It isn't easy	**Ce n'est pas facile**
Is *he* a German?	**Est-ce que c'est un Allemand?**
They are Spaniards	**Ce sont des Espagnols** (ess-păhn-yol)

Exercise VII

1 It was her husband.　2 Are they your shoes?　3 It wasn't
my opinion.　4 It is good.　5 They are Germans.　6 Is he a
Spaniard?　7 Was it expensive?　8 They aren't Frenchmen.

76. All the Pronouns mentioned in Paragraph 42 follow a Verb
in the Imperative, unless the Verb is in the Negative.

When following the Verb, these Pronouns are connected
with it by a hyphen; and **me** and **te**, when following the
Verb, are changed into **moi** and **toi**.

sell them	vendez-**les**	don't sell them	ne **les** vendez pas
accept it	acceptez-**le**	don't accept it	ne l'acceptez pas
speak to me	parlez-**moi**	don't speak to me	ne **me** parlez pas

Exercise VIII

1 Give him my address.　2 Show us the way.　3 Lend them
the money.　4 Send the letters to us.　5 Telephone me this
evening.　6 Don't accept it.　7 Let's finish it.　8 Don't give
her any wine.　9 Don't sell them.　10 Kiss me.　11 Don't disturb them.　12 Don't forget us.

VOCABULARY: to telephone, **téléphoner** (teh-leh-fon-eh); to kiss,
embrasser (an*ng*-brahss-eh); to disturb, **déranger** (deh-rah*ng*-**sh**eh).

78

CONVERSATIONAL SENTENCES

Je ne comprends[1] pas ce que vous dites[2].

I don't understand what you are saying.

Parlez plus lentement[3].

Speak more slowly.

Apportez-nous le menu.

Bring us the menu.

Il conduisait[4] sans regarder la route.

He was driving without looking at the road.

Merci pour les belles fleurs que vous m'avez envoyées.

Thank you for the beautiful flowers you sent me.

J'espère que nous n'avons pas longtemps[5] à attendre.

I hope we don't have to wait long.

Après avoir attendu plusieurs heures nous avons téléphoné à la police.

After waiting several hours we telephoned the police.

Essayez d'entrer sans faire du bruit.

Try to come in without making a noise.

Il a été arrêté pour ne pas avoir payé son addition.

He was arrested for not paying (having paid) his bill.

Il nous a quitté sans dire[6] un mot[7].

He left us without saying a word.

Cela ne vous regarde pas.

That is none of your business (= That does not look at you).

Ce n'était pas à ma femme qu'il a parlé.

It wasn't my wife he spoke to.

C'était quelqu'un[8] d'autre.

It was somebody else.

Quand est-ce que la voiture sera ici?

When will the car be here?

Elle ne sera pas longue.

It won't be long.

Je regrette[9] d'avoir de mauvaises[10] nouvelles[11] pour vous.

I'm afraid I have some bad news for you.

Ayant perdu notre chemin nous avons décidé[12] de chercher un hôtel.

Having lost our way we decided to look for a hotel.

PRON.: 1 kong-prahng; 2 deet; 3 lahngt-mahng; 4 kong-dwee-zay; 5 long-tahng; 6 deer; 7 moh; 8 kell-kung; 9 rer-graytt, 10 moh-vayz; 11 noo-vell; 12 deh-se-deh.

79

LESSON SEVENTEEN
IRREGULAR VERBS

Many of the commonest verbs in French are Irregular. Fortunately they are easy to learn, because although the stems change the terminations are quite Regular (except sometimes in the Present Tense). Example:

77.   INFINITIVE: to see, **voir** (vo'ahr)

PRES. PARTICIPLE: seeing, **voyant** (vo'ăh-yah*ng*)
PAST PARTICIPLE: seen, **vu** (VEE)
PRES. TENSE: I see, etc., je **vois,*** etc. (she*r* vo'ah)
PAST HIST.: I saw, etc., je **vis**, etc. (she*r* vee)
FUTURE: I will see, etc., je **verrai**, etc. (she*r* vair-eh)

The above is all that need be learnt, if attention is paid to the three important rules given below.

FULL CONJUGATION FOR REFERENCE

PRESENT *I see*	IMPERFECT *I was seeing*	PAST HISTORIC *I saw*	FUTURE *I will see*	CONDITIONAL *I would see*
je vois	voyais	vis	verrai	verrais
tu vois	voyais	vis	verras	verrais
il voit	voyait	vit	verra	verrait
nous voyons†	voyions	vîmes	verrons	verrions
vous voyez†	voyiez	vîtes	verrez	verriez
ils voient	voyaient	virent	verront	verraient

IMPERATIVE: *let us see*, voyons: *see* voyez; *see* (familiar) vois.

EXERCISE I

1 Do you see that man? 2 I shall see you tomorrow. 3 I saw him last week. 4 Have you seen them? 5 They saw (past hist.) the boat. 6 They don't see us. 7 On seeing that. 8 After having seen him. 9 We used-to-see them every day. 10 I would see them if they were there.

VOCABULARY: on, **en** (ah*ng*); if, **si** (se) (**s'** before **il** or **ils**, **si** before **elle**).

---

* If the first person ends in **s**, the second also ends in **s**, and the third in **t**.

† **i** is always changed to **y** before a sounded syllable.

A complete list of the irregular French verbs will be found in Hugo's "French Verbs Simplified", as well as a table showing all the irregularities tense by tense.

RULES FOR REFERENCE ONLY

1. The Terminations are always regular, except in the PRESENT TENSE.
2. The Stem of the IMPERFECT, the IMPERATIVE, and the *plural* of the PRESENT, is the same as that of the PRESENT PARTICIPLE.
3. The Stems of the FUTURE and CONDITIONAL are always alike.

From these Rules it follows that the PARTICIPLES, the PRESENT TENSE, and the FUTURE and PAST HISTORIC Stems, are all that need be learnt.

78. THIS, THAT, meaning *this one, that one,* are translated thus:

This one	**celui-ci**	**celle-ci** (se*r*-lwe-se, sell-se)
That one	**celui-là**	**celle-là** (se*r*-lwe-lăh, sell-lăh)
These	**ceux-ci**	**celles-ci** (se*r*-se, sell-se)
Those	**ceux-là**	**celles-là** (se*r*-lăh, sell-lăh)

These PRONOUNS always refer to a *noun mentioned just previously,* with which they agree in Gender; as,

This house and *that*	Cette maison-ci et **celle-là**
These books or *those*	Ces livres ou **ceux-là**
Here are two watches; will you have *this one* or *that one?*	Voici deux montres; voulez-vous **celle-ci** ou **celle-là ?**

79. -ci (*here*), -là (*there*) may be added to the Noun to make a distinction between THIS and THAT, THESE and THOSE.

This man and *that* woman.	**cet** homme-**ci** et **cette** femme-**là**
These boys or *those* girls.	**ces** garçons-**ci** ou **ces** filles-**là**

EXERCISE II

1 Did you see this film or that one? 2 What is the price of these apples? 3 These (*f*) cost two francs, and those two francs fifty. 4 This bottle is full, and that (one) is empty. 5 Here are several coins; these are English and those are French. 6 Will you have these grapes or those?

VOCABULARY: empty, **vide** (veed); coin, **pièce de monnaie** (pe-ess de*r* monn-ay); grape, **raisin** (ray-za*ng*); will you have? **voulez-vous** (voo-leh voo).

80. Expressions like 'his father's', 'their friends', must be translated by: that (*or* those) of his father, that (*or* those) of their friends.

My ticket or *my brother's*	Mon billet ou **celui de mon frère**
Your remarks and *your friends'*	Vos observations et **celles de vos amis.**

THE ONE is translated like THAT-ONE. **ci** and **là** are left off before Relative Pronouns (Paragraph 62) or before **de** meaning *of*.

This house and *the one* we rented	Cette maison et **celle** que nous avons louée
These children and *those of* whom we were speaking	Ces enfants et **ceux de** qui (*or* ceux dont) nous parlions

EXERCISE III

1 Is this your book or your sister's? 2 He brought our bill and our friends'. 3 This letter and the one (that) I received last week. 4 Our garden is smaller than our neighbour's. 5 These pictures are finer that those we saw yesterday. 6 Is this your car or your brother's?

81.   INFINITIVE: to read, **lire** (leer)

PRES. PARTICIPLE: reading, **lisant** (lee-zah*ng*)
PAST PARTICIPLE: read, **lu** (lee)
PRES. TENSE: Singular—I read, je **lis*** Plural—we read, nous **lisons**

Rule 1: The Stem of the Plural of the Present is the same as that of the Present Participle.

IMPERFECT: I was reading, je **lisais**
PAST HISTORIC: I read, je **lus**

Rule 2: The Stem of the Imperfect is the same as that of the Present Participle.

FUTURE: I will read, je **lirai**
CONDITIONAL: I would read, je **lirais**

Rule 3: The Future and Conditional always have the same stem.

IMPERATIVE: read, **lisez**; let us read, **lisons** (Familiar Form: read, **lis**)

Rule 4: The Imperative is the same as the Present, without **vous, nous**, and **tu.**

The rules in Paragraph 77 are repeated here singly. It is only necessary to learn part of the Verb printed in bold type to conjugate the Verb in full, thus:

PRESENT	IMPERFECT	PAST HISTORIC	FUTURE	CONDITIONAL
je lis*	lisais	lus	lirai	lirais
tu lis	lisais	lus	liras	lirais
il lit	lisait	lut	lira	lirait
nous lisons	lisions	lûmes	lirons	lirions
vous lisez	lisiez	lûtes	lirez	liriez
ils lisent	lisaient	lurent	liront	liraient

EXERCISE IV

1 Have you read this story? 2 Not yet, I am reading this one. 3 Will you read the one (that) I was reading? 4 Read the instructions. 5 Let's read their brochure. 6 Which book were you reading? 7 The one (that) he lent me. 8 I wouldn't read it. 9 I shall read the one that is here.

VOCABULARY: story, **histoire** f (iss-to'ăhr); not yet, **pas encore** (pah z'ahng-kor); instruction, **instruction** f (angss-trɛɛk-se-ong); brochure, **brochure** f (brosh-ɛɛr).

82. The Verbs formed from **lire** are conjugated in the same way:
    to elect, **élire**; to re-elect, **réélire**; to read again, **relire**

---

* If the first person ends in **s**, the second ends in **s**, and the third in **t.**

1 We will elect a mayor. 2 He was re-elected (as) our Member of Parliament. 3 I was reading his letter again. 4 We will not read the story again. 5 Who has been elected? 6 On reading it again. 7 Without being elected.

VOCABULARY: mayor, **maire** *m* (mair); Member of Parliament, **député** *m* (deh-PEE-teh).

CONVERSATIONAL SENTENCES

Cet hôtel-là était plein; celui-ci est presque vide.	That hotel was full; this one is nearly empty.
Quelles langues parlez-vous?	What languages do you speak?
Le français, l'allemand, l'italien et l'espagnol.	French, German, Italian and Spanish.
A travers[1] lesquelles de ces villes aimeriez-vous voyager?	Which of these towns would you like to travel through?
Celles que nous n'avons pas vues l'année dernière.	The ones we didn't see last year.
Avez-vous rempli ce verre-ci ou celui-là?	Did you fill this glass or that one?
Celui qui était à moitié[2] vide.	The one that was half empty.
Elle lisait un roman par jour.	She used to read a novel a day.
Portait-elle des lunettes?	Did she wear glasses?
Après avoir lu ma lettre.	After reading my letter.
Est-ce que c'est votre disque[3] ou celui que vous avez emprunté[4]?	Is this your record or the one you borrowed?
N'oubliez pas la roue[5] de secours[5].	Don't forget the spare tyre (wheel).
Quelles cigarettes fume-t-elle?	What cigarettes does she smoke?
Celles à bout[6] filtre[6].	The ones with a filter tip.
Nous n'avons pas trouvé l'église catholique[7] ni celle dont vous nous avez parlé.	We didn't find the Catholic church or the one you spoke to us about.

PRON.: 1 ăh trăh-vair; 2 mwăh-te-eh; 3 disk; 4 ahng-prung-teh; 5 roo der ser-koohr; 6 boo feel-tr; 7 kăh-toll-ick.

LESSON EIGHTEEN

83. THAT WHICH, and WHAT meaning THAT WHICH, are translated: **ce qui** when the Subject, and **ce que (ce qu')** when the Object of a Verb.

THAT WHICH and WHAT are generally the Object; but they are the Subject if followed immediately by the Verb in English.

I know *what* you said	Je sais **ce que** vous avez dit
This is *what* he has done	C'est **ce qu'**il a fait
That which is on the table is mine	**Ce qui** est sur la table est à moi

Exercise I

1 Did he show you what we found? 2 She gave us what she bought. 3 What you said is not true. 4 He will give you all that you ask for. 5 I know what he has done. 6 That is not what I saw. 7 I do not know what is in this box.

VOCABULARY: true, **vrai** (vray); all that, **tout ce que** (tooss ke*r*); to ask *or* ask for (de*r*-mahng-deh) **demander**; I know, **je sais** (she*r* say); done, **fait** (fay); box **boîte** *f* (bo'ăht).

Numbers will be used in future instead of the names of the Tenses, thus:
1 Infinitive. 2 Present Participle. 3 Past Participle. 4 Present. 5 Imperfect. 6 Past Historic. 7 Future. 8 Conditional. 9 Imperative.

84.   1 TO WRITE, **écrire** (eh-kree*r*)

As explained in Para. 77, if the parts printed in bold type are learned, the whole Verb can be easily learned.

2 writing, **écrivant** (eh-kre-vah*ng*)
3 written, **écrit** (eh-kree)
4 I write, etc. **j'écris** (sheh-kree) tu écris, il écrit, **nous écrivons** (noo z'eh-kree-vo*ng*), vous écrivez, ils écrivent.

85

5 I was writing, etc. j'écrivais (**sh**eh-kre-vay)
6 I wrote, etc. **j'écrivis**, etc. (**sh**eh-kre-vee)
7 I will write, etc., j'écrirai, etc. (**sh**eh-kree-ray)
8 I would write, etc., j'écrirais, etc. (**sh**eh-kree-ray)
9 write, écrivez (eh-kre-veh), let us write, écrivons (eh-kre-vo**ng**). *Familiar form:* write, écris (eh-kre)

EXERCISE II

1 I am writing what you are dictating.   2 Why did you not write to them?   3 I will write several letters after (the) lunch. 4 He wrote (*Past Historic*) his name on a piece of paper.   5 Wasn't she writing in her room?

VOCABULARY: to dictate, **dicter** (dick-teh); piece, **morceau** *m* (mor-soh); paper, **papier** *m* (pah-pe-eh).

85. If the PERSONAL PRONOUNS (Para. 42) are not the Subject or Object of a Verb, they are translated like this:

I, me **moi** (mo'ăh)	we, us **nous** (noo)
you (*fam.*) **toi** (to'ăh)	you, you **vous** (voo)
he, him **lui** (lwe)	they, them *m* **eux** (e*r*)
she, her **elle** (ell)	they, them *f* **elles** (ell)

These Pronouns are used principally—

(1) after prepositions, (2) in Comparisons, (3) if standing alone; as,

for me, **pour moi**	from him, **de lui**
you and I, **vous et moi**	he and they, **lui et eux**
he is taller than I	il est plus grand que **moi**

(4) if the Verb used in English is not expressed in French, as in the following examples:

Who is there? *I am*	Qui est là? **Moi**
Who has spoken? *They have*	Qui a parlé? **Eux**
Whom have you seen? *Him*	Qui avez-vous vu? **Lui**

86

EXERCISE III

1 Have you anything for him? 2 I have received it from you. 3 We won't continue without them. 4 Who was listening? She (was). 5 Who has bought your house? He (did). 6 Who showed the town to your friends? I (did). 7 Is he speaking about her? 8 Have you received the money from them (*m*)? 9 She isn't so old as he. 10 My friend and I. 12 He and they (*f*).

VOCABULARY: anything, **quelque chose** (kell-ker shohz); to continue, **continuer** (kong-tee-nEE-eh); old, **âgé** (ah-sheh).

86. moi, lui, eux, etc. are used after **ce** and a tense of *to be*, as:

it is *I*	c'est **moi**	it is not *we*	ce n'est pas **nous**
was it *he?*	est-ce que c'était **lui?**	was it *you?*	est-ce que c'était **vous?**
is it *they?*	est-ce que c'était **eux?**	it is *they*	**ce sont eux**

Look back at the remarks about the use of **ce** in Paragraph 74.

EXERCISE IV

1 Who's there? It is I. 2 Wasn't it you? No, it was she. 3 It will be he. 4 It isn't I. 5 It is your brother. 6 No, it wasn't he. 7 Isn't it they? 8 It is Michael. 9 Was it John? 10 Is it Mary?

VOCABULARY: Michael, **Michel** (me-shell); John, **Jean** (shahng); Mary, **Marie** (mäh-re).

87. MINE, HIS, etc. are generally translated by **à moi, à lui**, etc., after *to be*, if it has the meaning of 'to belong,' thus:

This seat is *mine* (= to me)	Cette place est **à moi**
Those suitcases are THEIRS	Ces valises sont **à eux**

à is also used in sentences like:

This record is *Mary's*	Ce disque est **à Marie**
Is this car *John's?*	Cette voiture est-elle **à Jean?**

1 This money is mine.   2 Those flowers aren't yours; they are hers.   3 Are these seats ours?   4 No, they are theirs. 5 This coat is my wife's.   6 Are these children Mary's? 7 Is this plate mine?   8 No, it is that man's.

88.   1 TO SAY, TO TELL **dire** (deer)

2 saying, **disant** (de-zah*ng*)
3 said **dit** (dee)
4 I say, etc. **je dis,** tu dis, il dit, nous **disons** (de-zo*ng*) vous **dites,** ills disent. (ditt, deez)
   5 I was saying, etc., je disais, etc. (di-zay)
   6 I said, etc., je **dis,** etc.
   7 I will say, etc., je dirai, etc. (de-ray)
   8 I would say, etc., je dirais, etc. (de-ray)
   9 say, **dites,** let us say, disons   (*Familiar*: say, dis)

EXERCISE VI

1 He used-to-say that.   2 They will say so.   3 I wouldn't say so.   4 What did you say to him?   5 Tell her what I said. 6 You don't say what they told you.   7 I will tell you something tomorrow.   8 Tell me your name.   9 He only said (Past Historic) yes.   10 What were you saying just now?

VOCABULARY: so = it, **le**; only = not ... but, **ne ... que** (ne*r*-ke*r*); just now, **tout à l'heure** (too t'äh le*r*).
Redire, to say again, is conjugated in exactly the same way.

89. All Verbs formed from **dire** are conjugated in the same way. The 2nd Person Plural Present, however, ends in **-sez.** Example:

To contradict, **contredire**; you contradict, **vous contredisez.**

Exception: curse, **maudire**, which doubles the **s** in the Present Participle (**maudissant**), and in the parts of the Verb formed from the Present Participle.

Chez le boucher[1], chez le boulanger[2], chez l'épicier[3], chez le pharmacien, chez le coiffeur[4], chez le docteur, chez le dentiste.

At *or* to the butcher's, at *or* to the baker's, at *or* to the grocer's, at *or* to the chemist's, at *or* to the hairdresser's, at *or* to the doctor's, at *or* to the dentist's.

Ecoutiez-vous ce que je disais?

Were you listening to what I was saying?

Est-ce que c'était vous qui avez téléphoné?

Was it you who telephoned?

Qu'est-ce qu'il a dit?

What did he say?

Je ne sais pas ce qu'il a dit.

I don't know what he said.

Ma femme et moi étions très contents de faire[5] votre connaissance[5].

My wife and I were very glad to meet you.

Je suis plus âgé que vous mais plus jeune que lui.

I am older than you but younger than he (is).

Nous lui écrivions toutes les semaines.

We used to write to him every week.

Ne lui dites pas ce que j'ai dit.

Don't tell him what I said.

Dites-lui de se mêler[6] de ses affaires.

Tell him to mind his own business.

Est-ce que c'est la route pour Paris?

Is this the road to Paris?

Est-ce que ces enfants sont les vôtres ou les siens?

Are these children yours or hers?

Laissez-moi tranquille.

Leave me alone (=quiet).

PRON.: 1 boo-sheh; 2 boo-lah*ng*-sheh; 3 eh-peess-e-eh; 4 ko'ăhf-er; 5 fair votr konn-ayss-ah*ng*ss; 6 may-leh

LESSON NINETEEN

90.   1 TO TAKE, **prendre** (prah*ng*dr)

2 taking, **prenant** (pre*r*-nah*ng*)

3 taken, **pris** (pree)

4 take, etc., **je prends** (prah*ng*) tu prends, il prend, nous **prenons** (pre*r*-no*ng*) vous prenez, ils prennent (pre*r*-neh, prenn).

5 I was taking, etc., je prenais, etc. (pre*r*-nay)

6 I took, etc., je **pris** etc. (pree)

7 I will take, etc., je **prendrai** (prah*ng*-dray)

8 I would take, je prendrais

9 take, prenez, let us take, prenons (*Familiar*: take, prends.)

91. The principal DERIVATIVES of **prendre** are the following:

to learn, **apprendre**	to understand, **comprendre**
to surprise, **surprendre**	to undertake, **entreprendre**
	to take back, **reprendre**

EXERCISE 1

1 He doesn't understand your question. 2 Why haven't you learned to (à) swim? 3 Take care. 4 I will not undertake it. 5 Does that surprise you? 6 Does she take sugar? 7 I will take-back my book. 8 Do you understand me? 9 What are you learning, (the) French or (the) English? 10 At what time do you have (take) your bath? 11 Take-back this money.

VOCABULARY: question, **question** *f* (kess-te-o*ng*); to take care, **prendre garde** (prah*ng*dr gä*r*d); bath, **bain m** (ba*ng*).

92. ADVERBS are nearly always formed in French by adding **-ment** to the Adjective, which corresponds to the English *-ly* ending.

If the adjective does not end in a vowel, **-ment** is added to the *feminine* form.

rare, **rare**	rarely, **rarement**
happy, **heureux** (*f* **heureuse**)	happily, **heureusement**

However remember that some of the commonest adverbs (like **mal, bien, souvent, vite**) do not take **-ment**.

90

EXERCISE II

1 It was really interesting. 2 They listened attentively. 3 We were walking slowly. 4 We rarely see them. 5 She replied immediately. 6 Write it carefully. 7 Fortunately he was there. 8 He passed us rapidly.

VOCABULARY: attentive, **attentif**, *f* attentive (ăh-tah*ng*-tiff, ăh-tah*ng*-teev); slow, **lent** (lah*ng*); immediate, **immédiat** (im-meh-d-ah); careful, **soigneux**, *f* soigneuse, (so'ahnh-ye*r*); rapid, **rapide** (răh-pid).

93. The following words, called Adverbs of Quantity, take **de** or **d'** after them if followed by a Noun;

assez, enough	**moins**, less
autant, as much, as many (oh-tah*ng*)	**peu**, little (pe*r*)
beaucoup, much, many, a lot	**plus**, more
combien, how much, how many	**trop**, too much, too many

We have *enough* time	Nous avons **assez de** temps.
How many children has she?	**Combien** d'enfants a-t-elle?
They have *too much* money	Ils ont **trop d'**argent

EXERCISE III

1 Has he spent as much as you? 2 How much sugar did you put in my coffee? 3 Do you speak more languages than he does? 4 I haven't enough money for that. 5 She has put too much salt in the soup. 6 We have less money than they. 7 Have you many friends in France? 8 Give me a little bread. 9 That has given me a great deal of trouble. 10 How many children have they?

VOCABULARY: put, **mis** (mee); a great deal = much; trouble, **peine** *f* (payn).

94.   1 TO SEND, **envoyer** (ah*ng*-vo'ăh-yeh)
     This Verb is quite regular except in the Stem of the FUTURE and CONDITIONAL, thus;

2 sending, envoyant (ah*ng*-vo'ăhyah*ng*)
3 sent, envoyé (ah*ng*-vo'ăh-yeh)
4 I send, etc. j'envoie,* tu envoies, il envoie, nous envoyons, vous envoyez, ils envoient (ah*ng*-vo'ăh, ah*ng*-vo'ăh-yo*ng*, -yeh)

---

* **y** is changed to **i** whenever no sound follows.

5 I was sending, etc., j'envoyais, etc. (ah*ng*-vo'ăh-yay)
6 I sent, etc., j'envoyai, etc. (ah*ng*-vo'ăh-yay)
7 I will send, etc. **j'enverrai,** etc. (**shah***ng*-vair-reh)
8 I would send, etc. j'enverrais, etc.
9 send, envoyez, let us send, envoyons (*Familiar*; send, envoie)

renvoyer (to send back) is of course conjugated in the same way

Exercise IV

1 We are sending a parcel to Paris.   2 Did you send us the tickets?   3 I would send it back at once.   4 Send us the information as soon as possible.   5 Don't send the things back. 6 Will he send it by (the) post?

VOCABULARY: at once, **tout de suite** (too de*r* switt); as soon as possible **aussitôt que possible** (oh-se-toh ke*r* poss-eebl); post, **poste** *f* (posst).

95. Most French Adverbs are placed immediately after the Verb:

she closes the door *gently*   Elle ferme **doucement** la porte

1 Adverbs never come between the Subject and the Verb as in English.

He *rarely* reads the newspaper   Il lit **rarement** le journal

2 Most Adverbs come before the Past Participle in Compound Tenses.

They played *well*   Ils ont **bien** joué

3 **aujourd'hui, hier, demain**; adverbs of place (**ici, là,** etc.) and adverbs consisting of more than one word follow the Past Participle.

We have seen him *today*   Nous l'avons vu **aujourd'hui**
I replied to their letter *at once*   J'ai répondu à leur lettre **tout de suite**

Exercise V

1 She speaks French well.   2 He always wears glasses.   3 I have often been there.   4 We received a letter from him yesterday.   5 She often speaks of you.   6 Have you already eaten?

7 Has the postman been here this morning?   **8** They sent it by return.

96. Sometimes two of the Pronouns in Paragraph 42 occur in one sentence. Both, of course, are placed BEFORE the Verb, **le** or **la** or **l'** or **les** following the other pronoun; as,

I return *it to you*	Je **vous le** rends
He does not show *it (f) to me*	Il ne **me la** montre pas
Don't you give *them to us?*	Ne **nous les** donnez-vous pas?

97. lui and **leur**, however, come after **le, la, les**; as,

We give *it to them*	Nous **le leur** donnons
Didn't you sell *them* to her?	Ne **les lui** avez-vous pas vendus?

In the IMPERATIVE their position is as in English.

Lend *them to me*	**Prêtez-les-moi**

EXERCISE VI

1 He hasn't given it back to me.   **2** I will not show them to him.   **3** We will not give it (f) to them.   **4** Send it to her. **5** Have they sent it to us?   **6** Lend me your knife.   **7** I lent it to your friend, but he didn't give it back to me.   **8** Did you send it to them?   **9** Bring them to me.

CONVERSATIONAL SENTENCES

Avez-vous assez d'argent pour le voyage?	Have you enough money for the journey?
Combien coûte ceci?	How much does this cost?
Il y avait trop de gens là.	There were too many people there.
Pas autant que ça.	Not as much as that.
Je vous l'enverrai aussitôt que possible.	I'll send it to you as soon as possible.
Nous avons pris le train de Paris à Barcelone[1].	We took the train from Paris to Barcelona.
Donnez-le-moi.	Give it to me.
Je ne comprenais pas ce qu'il me disait.	I didn't understand what he was saying to me.
Il parlait trop vite.	He was talking too quickly.

Malheureusement[2] ils ont manqué[3] l'avion.	Unfortunately they missed the plane.
L'équipe[4] a très mal joué.	The team played very badly.
Nous n'avions pas de carte et nous perdions souvent notre chemin.	We had no map and often lost our way.
Les rues étaient mal éclairées[5].	The streets were badly lit.
J'aime un peu de crème[6] dans mon café.	I like a little cream in my coffee.
Ils ont trouvé la gare tout de suite.	They found the station at once.
Merci[7] beaucoup.	Thank you very much.

PRON.: 1 băhr-sser-lonn; 2 măhl-er-rerz-mah*ng*; 3 mah*ng*-keh; 4 eh-keep *f*; 5 eh-klay-reh; 6 kraym; 7 mair-se.

LESSON TWENTY

98. If the IMPERATIVE is used negatively, the Pronouns PRECEDE the Verb in the usual order, thus:

Give *it to me*	Donnez-**le-moi**
Don't give *it to me*	Ne **me le** donnez pas
Lend *them to her*	Prêtez-**les**-**lui**
Don't lend *them to her*	Ne **les lui** prêtez pas

moi if coming before the Verb is changed into **me**.

EXERCISE I

1 Here are the photographs; send them to him. 2 This is my address: don't show it to them. 3 That dress is mine; don't lend it to her. 4 Are these his keys? Give them back to him.

VOCABULARY: photograph, *photographie f* (fo-tograh-fee).

99.   1 TO DO *or* TO MAKE, **faire** (fair)
2 doing *or* making, **faisant** (fer-zah*ng*)
3 done *or* made, **fait*** (fay)

---

* *Fait* does not agree with its preceding direct object when it is followed by an infinitive:

The dresses that I had (to be) cleaned	Les robes que j'ai fait nettoyer

4 I make or I do, etc., je **fais**, tu **fais**, il **fait** (fay), nous
    faisons, vous **faites**, ils **font** (fer-zo*ng*, fayt, fo*ng*)
5 I was making *or* doing, je faisais (fer-zay)
6 I made *or* did, je **fis** (fee)
7 I will make *or* do, je **ferai** (fer-ray)
8 I would make *or* do, je ferais.
9 make, faites, let us make, faisons (*Familiar*: make, fais.)

EXERCISE II

1 What are you doing? 2 I'm doing what you told me.
3 You're always doing the same thing. 4 What has he done
this morning? 5 Let's do something else. 6 What was he
doing? 7 Have you done that? 8 I won't do it. 9 Would
you do that? 10 These children are making too much noise.
11 Do it at once. 12 How many mistakes have you made?

VOCABULARY: same, **même** (maym); something else, **autre chose** *or*
quelque chose d'autre (oh-tr-shohz, kell-ke*r* shohz doh-tr); mistake,
faute *f* (foht).

100. EACH and EVERY followed by a Noun are translated
chaque (shăhck).

EACH ONE, EVERY ONE are translated **chacun,** *f* **chacune**,
(shăhck-u*ng*, shăhck-EEn) according to the Noun they refer
to. (Note that EACH, when meaning EACH ONE, is **chacun.)**

each girl	**chaque** fille
every boy	**chaque** garçon
Each of these girls	**chacune** de ces filles

101.   1 TO RECEIVE, **recevoir** (re*r*-se*r*-vo'ah*r*)
2 receiving, **recevant** (re*r*-se*r*-vah*ng*)
3 received, **reçu** (re*r*-SEE)
4 I receive, etc., je **reçois**, tu reçois, il reçoit (re*r*-so'ăh)
    nous **recevons** vous recevez, ils **reçoivent** (re*r*-se*r*-
    vo*ng*, re*r*-se*r*-veh, re*r*-so'ăhv)
5 I was receiving, je recevais (re*r*-se*r*-vay)
6 I received, je **reçus** (re*r*-SEE)
7 I will receive, je **recevrai** (re*r*-se*r*-vray)
8 I would receive, je recevrais
9 receive, recevez; let us receive, recevons (*Familiar*:
    receive, reçois)

95

1 I receive a letter nearly every day.   2 Each of the candidates received a diploma.   3 You will receive an invitation. 4 Hasn't he received the money (which) we sent him last week? 5 How much did you receive?   6 They won't receive the parcel before the day after tomorrow.

VOCABULARY: candidate, **candidat** *m* (kah*ng*-de-dăh); diploma, **diplome** *m* (de-plohm); invitation, **invitation** *f* (a*ng*-ve-tăh-se-o*ng*); after tomorrow, **après demain** (ăh-pray de*r*-ma*ng*).

102. All Verbs ending in **-evoir** are conjugated like **recevoir.** Frequently called the third regular Conjugation, there are only six others, of which the most important is **devoir**, TO OWE (it also means SHALL, OUGHT TO, MUST). The stem of **devoir** is the letter **d-.**

1 to owe, **devoir**   2 owing, **devant**   3 owed, **dû**   4 I owe etc. je **dois**, ils **doivent**   5 I was owing, je devais   6 I owed, je **dus**   7 I will owe, je **devrai**   8 I would owe, je devrais   9 owe, devez; let us owe, devons (Familiar: owe, dois)

Note that there is no accent in the feminine and plural forms of the past participle (**due, dus, dues**). The other five verbs in this group are: **percevoir, apercevoir** TO PERCEIVE; **concevoir** TO CONCEIVE; **décevoir** TO DISAPPOINT; **redevoir** TO OWE A BALANCE OF A SUM.

1 How much do I owe you?   2 He owes me twenty francs. 3 You must* shut the door.   4 Must I pay this bill?   5 He must* do it.   6 You should* tell the truth.   7 They don't owe him any money.   8 You mustn't write to him.   9 They mustn't* see him.

VOCABULARY: truth, **vérité** *f* (veh-re-teh).

103. SOME and ANY not followed by a Noun, are translated **en,** which is put *before* the Verb, like the Pronouns in Para. 42†

Have you *any* cigarettes?	Avez-vous des cigarettes
Yes, we have *some*	Oui, nous **en** avons

---

* translate MUST, SHALL and SHOULD (meaning 'ought to') by **devoir,** thus: *shall I? must I? am I to?* dois-je (do'ăh**sh**); *he must not,* il ne doit pas; *I should* (= *ought*) *not to,* je ne devrais pas; *you should,* vous devriez.
† Unless the Verb is Imperative Affirmative—see Para. 76.

(a) **en** must be inserted in French, even if not expressed in English:

How many sisters have you?	Combien de soeurs avez-vous?
I have three (*of them*)	J'en ai trois

(b) OF IT, OF THEM, SOME (or ANY) OF IT or OF THEM, are also **en**:

Aren't you speaking *of it*?	N'en parlez-vous pas?
Show us *some of them*	Montrez-nous-**en**

EXERCISE V

1 Will you have some? 2 Here is the money; I spent ten francs of it. 3 He brought his sketches; he has shown me two (of them). 4 How many children does she have? 5 She has three. 6 What is the colour of it? 7 What was the price of them? 8 I've already eaten (the) half of it.

VOCABULARY: will you have, **voulez-vous?** (voo-leh voo); sketch, **croquis** *m* (kro-kee); half, **moitié** *f* (mwăh'te-eh).

104. THERE, TO IT, TO THEM, IN IT, IN THEM, are translated by **y**, which is put before the Verb, like the Pronouns in Para. 42. (THERE, if pointing out a place, is translated **là**)

Is he *there*?	**Y** est-il?
Add this *to it*	Ajoutez-**y** ceci
We shall add this *to them*	Nous **y** ajouterons ceci

1 **y** and **en** follow the other Pronouns which come before the Verb.

2 **en** is placed after **y**, if **y** and **en** occur together.

We shall send *some there*	Nous **y** **en** enverrons.
Add some to it	Ajoutez-**y**-**en**
Give me some	Donnez-m'**en** (instead of 'moi en')

3 **y** must be added, when necessary, to complete the sense.

Was he at home? Yes, he was	Etait-il à la maison? Oui, il **y** était

EXERCISE VI

1 Did you put any water in it? 2 Yes, I put some in (it). 3 Have you been to Paris? 4 Yes, I have (been there). 5 Did you buy some grapes? 6 No, there are none (=it has not

any of them there). 7 Have you put any oil in the salad?
8 No, I will add some to it now.

Vocabulary: oil, **huile** *f* (weel); salad, **salade** *f* (săh-lăhd); to add, **ajouter** (ăh-**shoo**-teh).

LESSON TWENTY-ONE

105.   1 to drink, **boire** (bo'ahr)
   2 drinking, **buvant** (bee-vah*ng*)
   3 drunk, **bu** (bee)
   4 I drink *or* am drinking, je **bois**, tu bois, il boit (bo'ăh),
       nous **buvons**, vous buvez, ils **boivent** (bee-vo*ng*,
       bee-veh, bo'ăhv)
   5 I was drinking, je buvais (bee-vay)
   6 I drank, je **bus**
   7 I will drink, je boirai (bo'ăh-ray)
   8 I would drink, je boirais
   9 drink, buvez; let us drink, buvons (*Familiar*: drink, bois)

Exercise I

1 I don't drink (any) beer.   2 They don't drink (any) wine.
3 She was drinking her coffee.   4 Don't drink this: it isn't very
good.   5 I won't drink any of it.   6 Did you drink any?   7 We
should drink tea and coffee.

106. the whole or the whole of the (my, etc.) is translated:
all the (my, etc.)

Masc. singular: *all* **tout** (too)   Plural: **tous**
Fem. singular: *all* **toute** (toot)   Plural: **toutes**

1 Note that the adjective **tout** must agree in gender and
number with the following noun:

The whole town	Toute la ville
The whole of the book	Tout le livre
All my friends.	Tous mes amis
All the plates	Toutes les assiettes

2 all, referring to a Plural Noun mentioned just previously,
is translated by **tous** or **toutes** (tooss, toot):

Where are our suitcases?	Où sont nos valises?
They are all in the coach	Elles sont toutes dans le car

98

3 EVERYTHING, or ALL meaning 'everything', is translated by **tout**, which is *invariable*:

Everything is lost   Tout est perdu
That is all   C'est tout

EXERCISE II

1 All these cases are mine.   2 The whole house is full of smoke.   3 Where are your friends? Are they all here?   4 Everything is ready.   5 Have you found everything?   6 All his family lives in (= at) Paris.   7 They lost all their money.   8 All these rules are useful.   9 Have you read the whole story?   10 Is this all?

VOCABULARY: smoke, **fumée** *f* (fEE-meh); rule, **règle** *f* (raygl); useful, **utile** (EE-till).

107.   1 TO BE WILLING or WANT TO, **vouloir** (voo-lo'ah*r*)
   2 being willing *or* wanting, **voulant** (voo-lah*ng*)
   3 been willing *or* wanted, **voulu** (voo-lEE)
   4 I am willing *or* want, je **veux**, tu veux, il veut (ve*r*) we want, nous **voulons**, vous voulez, ils **veulent** (voo-long, voo-leh, ve*r*l)
   5 I was willing, je voulais (voo-lay)
   6 I wanted, je **voulus** (voo-lEE)
   7 I will be willing, je **voudrai** (voo-dray)
   8 I would want, je voudrais.
   9 IMPERATIVE: **veuillez** (= will you kindly, be so good as to) (ve*r*'e-yeh).
Veuille (*familiar*) and **veuillons** are very rarely used.

EXERCISE III

1 He doesn't want to* take the plane.   2 Will you fetch it? 3 She didn't want to* learn it.   4 I'd like (want) to* help you. 5 Didn't he want to* listen to you?   6 Will you tell (to) us a story?   7 They don't want to* see us.   8 He will be willing to* pay you.   9 Aren't they willing to* help us?

VOCABULARY: to help, **aider** (ay-deh); to tell, **raconter** (răh-ko*ng*-teh).

---

* TO after any part of **vouloir** *or* **pouvoir** is not translated.

108. Adverbs of Negation always require **ne** before the Verb.

Do you *never* sing?	Ne chantez-vous **jamais**? (shăh-may)
We have *nothing* for you	Nous **n'**avons **rien** pour vous
I see *nobody* here	Je **ne** vois **personne** ici (pair-sonn)

(a) if **personne, rien** or **jamais** comes first, the **ne** still precedes the Verb.

| *Nobody* is here | **Personne** n'est ici |
| *Never* will I do that | **Jamais** je ne ferai cela |

(b) Some more examples of Negations are:

She has *only* two friends = She not has but two friends	Elle **n'**a **que** deux amis
We have *no more* money	Nous **n'**avons **plus** d'argent
He drinks *neither* wine *nor* beer	Il ne boit **ni** vin **ni** bière

'Wine and beer' is '**du** vin et **de la** bière'; but **du, de l', de la** and **des** are omitted after **ni**.

(c) If several of these words occur in the same sentence they go in the following order:

| I shall never give anything to anybody any more. | Je ne donnerai plus jamais rien à personne. |

Exercise IV

1 He drinks nothing. 2 She never listens to me. 3 They had no more of it. 4 We were only three. 5 He is neither old nor young. 6 I shall drink no more. 7 She has never seen me. 8 He eats neither meat nor fish.

Vocabulary: old, **vieux** (ve-e*r*).

109.   1 TO BE ABLE TO (CAN), **pouvoir** (poo-vo'ăh*r*)
2 being able to, **pouvant** (poo-vah*ng*)
3 been able to, **pu** (pee)
4 I am able to *or* I can, je **peux*** (*or* je **puis**), tu peux, il peut (pe*r*, pwe), nous **pouvons**, vous pouvez, ils **peuvent** (poo-vo*ng*, poo-veh, pe*r*v)
5 I was able *or* could, je pouvais (poo-vay)
6 I was able *or* could, je pus (pee)
7 I will be able to, je **pourrai** (poo-reh)

8 I would be able to, je pourrais (poo-**ray**)
There is no IMPERATIVE of pouvoir.

Note that **pu** is invariable. It does not agree with its
preceding direct object:

A thing I couldn't do.   Une chose que je n'ai pas pu faire.

EXERCISE V

1 I can't speak to you today.   2 He was-able-to† do it at
once.   3 I will be able to be there before six o'clock.   4 Would
you be able to go there this afternoon?   5 They can't drink this
tea because it's too strong.   6 We weren't able to understand his
question.   7 I won't be able to return the things (the) next
week.   9 Can't they come?

VOCABULARY: afternoon, **après-midi** *m* or *f* (ah-pray me-de); strong,
fort (for).

Note also that COULD meaning 'would-be-able-to' is translated by the CONDITIONAL of **pouvoir**.

I could speak to him tomorrow.   je pourrais lui parler demain.

110. EVERY, followed by a Noun is generally translated by **tous
les** (*m*) or **toutes les** (*f*) instead of **chaque** (each), as:

every Monday, **tous les** lundis   *every* week, **toutes les** semaines
everybody, everyone (= all the world) **tout le monde**

111. SOME, meaning 'a few', followed by a Noun is **quelques:**

He bought some (a few) handkerchiefs   Il a acheté quelques mouchoirs
                                        (moo-sho'ah**r**)

some one, **quelqu'un**   some (ones), **quelques-uns**

Some of those girls   Quelques-**unes** de ces filles
I have read some (a few, *m*)   J'**en** ai lu quelques-**uns**

---

* For I CAN you may say either **je peux** or **je puis**, but for CAN I? you
may only use **puis-je ?** (or of course **est-ce que je peux ?**).
† In the Past Tense, the IMPERFECT of **vouloir** and **pouvoir** is more
generally used than the Perfect.

1 We meet them every Thursday. 2 They see their friends every six months. 3 Everybody was saying so. 4 Some of his relations were here. 5 We met some of the wives. 6 I have spent a few francs. 7 Some one heard a noise. 8 We have eaten some (a few) apples and (some) pears. 9 Didn't he speak to some of these men?

VOCABULARY: so = it; relations, **parents** *m* (păh-rah*ng*); pear, **poire** *f* (po'ăh**r**).

LESSON TWENTY-TWO

112. 1 TO KNOW, **savoir*** (săh-vo'ahr)
    2 knowing, **sachant** (săh-shah*ng*)
    3 known, **su** (SEE)
    4 I know, je **sais**, tu sais, il sait (say), nous **savons**, vous savez, ils savent (săh-vo*ng*, săh-veh, săhv)
    5 I used to know, je **savais** (săh-vay)
    6 I knew, je **sus**
    7 I will know, je **saurai** (soh-ray)
    8 I would know, je saurais
    9 know, **sachez**, let us know, **sachons** (*Familiar*: know, **sache**)

Notice that the Stem in the Plural Present and in the Imperfect is an exception to Rule 2 in Para. 77, being **sav** ... not **sach** ... In the Imperative the Stem is **sach** ...

1 I know it. 2 We always used to know how to do it. 3 You will know it tomorrow. 4 Don't you know where he lives? 5 If I knew that I'd be rich. 6 Doesn't she know her flight number? 7 He knew it, but he has forgotten it. 8 Can you drive? (= Do you know to drive?)

VOCABULARY: flight number, **numéro de vol** *m* (nEE-meh-ro de*r* vol).

As explained in Paragraph 16 the Feminine of most Adjectives is formed by adding **e** to the Masculine; but those ending in **e** do not change.

---

* **savoir** means to know a fact. To know a person is **connaître**.

113. Some Adjectives undergo a further change, as follows:

		MASC.		FEM.
(a) Final **f** is changed to **ve**	... vif	*lively*	vive
(b) „ **x** „ **se**	jaloux	*jealous*	jalouse
(c) „ **er, et** „ **ère, ète** ...	cher secret	{ *dear* { *secret*	chère secrète
(d) Adjectives ending in **eil, el en** double the final consonant and add **e**	pareil italien	*like* *Italian*	pareille italienne
(e) Monosyllables ending in **s** or **t** also double the final consonant and add **e**	las net	*tired* *clean*	lasse nette

PRON.: (a) veef, veev; (b) shăh-loo, shăh-looz; (c) shair, shair; ser-kray, ser-krayt; (d) păh-ray'e, păh-ray'e; e-tăh-le-ang, e-tăh-le-enn; (e) lăh, lăhss; nett, nett.

The following irregular feminine forms should be learned at once. The less important irregularities are given in the Appendix.

MASC.		FEM.	MASC.		FEM.
blanc	*white*	blanche	franc	*frank*	franche
doux	*soft*	douce	long	*long*	longue
épais	*thick*	épaisse	public	*public*	publique
faux	*false*	fausse	sec	*dry*	sèche
frais	*fresh*	fraîche			

114. 1 TO HOLD, **tenir** (ter-neer)

2 holding, **tenant** (ter-nahng)

3 held, **tenu** (ter-nEE)

4 I hold *or* I am holding, je **tiens**, tu tiens, il tient (te-ang), nous **tenons**, vous tenez, ils **tiennent** (ter-nong, ter-neh, te-enn)

5 I was holding, je **tenais** (ter-nay)

6 I held, je **tins** (tang)

7 I will hold, je **tiendrai** (te-ang-dreh)

8 I would hold, je tiendrais (te-ang-dray)

9 hold, tenez, let us hold, tenons (*Familiar*: hold, tiens)

FOR REFERENCE: 6 tins, tins, tint; tînmes, tîntes, tinrent. All compounds of **tenir** are conjugated in the same way—three examples are: to contain, **contenir**; to belong, **appartenir**; to obtain, **obtenir**.

103

EXERCISE II

1 To whom does this belong? 2 This page contains all the information. 3 His wife was holding the flowers. 4 This house used-to-belong to our ancestors. 5 Hold this. 6 These boxes contain nothing.

VOCABULARY: page, **page** *f* (păh**sh**); ancestors, **ancêtres** *m* or *f* (usually used in the plural) ahng-say-tr.

115. venir (*to come*) is conjugated exactly like **tenir**, thus:

1 to come, **venir** 2 coming, **venant** 3 come, **venu** 4 I come, je **viens**, ils **viennent** 6 I came, je **vins** 7 I shall come, je **viendrai** PERFECT: I have come, je **suis** venu

FOR REFERENCE: 4 viens, viens, vient; venons, venez, viennent. 5 je venais, etc. 6 vins, vins, vint; vînmes, vîntes, vinrent. 8 je viendrais, etc. 9. come, venez, let us come, venons (Familiar: viens, come).

The following are conjugated like **venir**: to become, **devenir**; to come back, **revenir**; to suit, to be convenient, **convenir**.

EXERCISE III

1 He will come back tomorrow. 2 Come here. 3 They used-to-come every day. 4 He comes from Paris. 5 Where do they come from?* 6 I shall not come alone. 7 We would come with you if we had (the) time. 8 He came (past hist.) at the end of (the) last month. 9 Will that be convenient for you?

Venir is used in the following common and very useful construction:

I have just arrived in Paris **Je viens d'arriver** à Paris
They had just eaten **Ils venaient de manger**

116. être is used instead of **avoir** before a number of PAST PARTICIPLES to form the Perfect Tense of some French Verbs, most of which have something to do with motion. The commonest are:

allé, gone (ăh-leh)
devenu, become (de*r*-ve*r*-nEE)
mort, died (moh**r**)
parti, started, gone away (pahr-te)
revenu, come back (re*r*-ve*r*-nEE)
tombé, fallen (to*ng*-beh)

arrivé, arrived (ăh-ree-veh)
entré, entered (ah*ng*-treh)
né, born (neh)
resté, stayed, remained (ress-teh)
ˌ**sorti**, gone out (sor-te)
venu, come (ve*r*-nEE)

---

* Where do they come from = From where do they come?

Generally speaking, if **monter** and **descendre** are used intransitively (without a direct object), they take **être** and not **avoir**:

I went up	Je suis **monté**
They went down	Ils sont **descendus**

But used transitively they take **avoir**:

I went up the stairs	**J'ai monté** l'escalier
He brought the luggage down	**Il a descendu** les bagages

PAST PARTICIPLES following any part of *to be* agree with their Subject (except when reflexive, see Paragraph 125); as,

She has not arrived	Elle n'est pas **arrivée**
Did the men come?	Les hommes sont-ils **venus?**
My sisters will have gone out	Mes soeurs seront **sorties**
My mother was born in France	Ma mère est **née** en France

EXERCISE IV

1 They have gone to the cinema.   2 She didn't come in (enter).   3 Have the girls gone away?   4 Nobody had come. 5 The coaches will have come back.   6 She would have stayed. 7 Did you fall down (sing)?   8 I went alone.

117.   The PLURAL OF ADJECTIVES is formed *from the singular of the same gender*, in the same way as the Plural of Nouns.

	MASC. SING.	FEM. SING.	MASC. PLUR.	FEM. PLUR.
small	**petit**	**petite**	**petits**	**petites**
bad	**mauvais**	**mauvaise**	**mauvais**	**mauvaises**
happy	**heureux**	**heureuse**	**heureux**	**heureuses**
legal	**légal**	**légale**	**légaux**	**légales**
tired	**las**	**lasse**	**las**	**lasses**
beautiful	**beau**	**belle**	**beaux**	**belles**
old	**vieux**	**vieille**	**vieux**	**vieilles**

EXERCISE V

1 They were reading the French newspapers.   2 The church we saw was very old.   3 What beautiful flowers!   4 My friends weren't present.   5 He had (some) big hands and a little head. 6 Buy me some green grapes.   7 These rules are very difficult to (à) understand.

VOCABULARY: present, **présent** (preh-*sahng*); green, **vert** (vair).

LESSON TWENTY-THREE

118.   1 TO GO, **aller** (ăh-leh)

2 going, **allant** (ăh-lah*ng*)

3 gone, **allé** (ăh-leh)

4 I am going, je **vais**, tu **vas**, il **va** (vay, vah), nous allons, vous allez, ils **vont** (ăh-lo*ng*, ăh-leh, vo*ng*)

5 I was going, j'allais (**shă**h-lay)

6 I went, j'allai

7 I will go, **j'irai** (**sh**e-ray)

8 I would go, j'irais

9 go, allez; let us go, allons (*Familiar*: go, va)

I AM ABOUT TO or I AM GOING TO, etc. are translated by **je vais**, etc., TO not being translated; as,

He is *going to write* to him	Il **va** lui écrire
Weren't they *going to* play?	N'**allaient**-ils pas jouer?

EXERCISE I

1 Where are you going?   2 He was going to the theatre.
3 We will go to Paris tomorrow.   4 Why doesn't he go with you?   5 Won't he go alone?   6 Let's go together.   7 Don't go into (= in) the street.   8 Are they going to the boats?   9 I'd go if I had enough money.   10 We are about to begin.   11 I'm not going to buy it.   12 She wasn't going to do it.

119. MYSELF, OURSELVES, etc. following a Verb in English, are translated in French like ME, US, etc.

HIMSELF, HERSELF, THEMSELVES are translated by **se** (or **s'**). These words precede the Verb in the usual way (for exception, see Paragraph 76).

I dress *myself*	Je **m'**habille (măh-be'ye)
We were enjoying *ourselves*	nous **nous** amusions (noo noo zăh-MEE-ze-o*ng*)
Don't flatter *yourself*	ne **vous** flattez pas (flăh-teh)

106

120. SHALL or WILL must always be expressed by the FUTURE TENSE in French when the meaning is future; as,

When I (will) go to Paris next week	Quand j'irai à Paris la semaine prochaine
When I (will) have done it	Quand je l'aurai fait

121. SHOULD or WOULD must be expressed by the CONDITIONAL in French when something would happen conditionally on something else happening; as,

He would pay me if he had the money	Il me payerait s'il avait l'argent
I would write to him if I knew his address	Je lui écrirais si je savais son adresse

122. When SHALL and SHOULD express compulsion or duty— that is, when they are equivalent to *must, am to, have to, ought to,* etc.—**devoir** must be used (see Paragraph 102); as,

Shall I (= am I to) shut the door?	Dois-je fermer la porte?
They *shall* (= must) not do it	Ils ne doivent pas le faire
She *should* (= ought to) pay it	Elle devrait le payer

123. When WILL and WOULD mean *want to, be willing to,* **vouloir** must be used; as,

Will he (= is he willing to) sell it?	Veut-il le vendre?
They *would not* (= did not want to) come	Ils n'ont pas voulu venir
I *will* not give it to you	Je ne veux pas vous le donner

EXERCISE II

(SMALL CAPITALS indicate that **vouloir** or **devoir** is to be used)

1 She WON'T speak to me. 2 You SHOULDN'T say that. 3 We shall wash (ourselves). 4 The children wouldn't enjoy (= amuse) themselves. 5 SHOULDN'T we warn them? 6 They wouldn't come without telling us. 7 They WOULDN'T come with us. 8 I WON'T speak to him. 9 SHALL I go there without you? 10 She SHOULD listen to what I say. 11 They won't find him at home. 12 He WOULDN'T apologize.

VOCABULARY: to wash oneself, **se laver** (lăh-veh); to amuse oneself, **s'amuser** (ăh-mEE-zeh); to warn, **prévenir** (preh-ve*r*-neer); to apologize, **s'excuser** (secks-kEE-zeh).

107

124.   **1** TO RUN, **courir** (koo-reer)
2 running, **courant** (koo-rah*ng*)
3 run, **couru** (koo-rEE)
4 I am running, je **cours**, tu cours, il court (koohr); nous **courons**, vous courez, ils courent (koo-ro*ng*, koo-reh, koohr)
5 I was running, je courais (koo-ray)
6 I ran, je **courus** (koo-rEE)
7 I will run, je **courrai** (koo-ray)
8 I would run, je **courrais**
9 run, courez; let us run, courons (*Familiar*: run, cours)

EXERCISE III

1 The horses are running.   2 Don't run so fast.   3 He was running the whole time.   4 Let's run after them.   5 Why are you running?   6 The boys will run this evening.   7 I wouldn't run if I were (*Imperfect*) you (in your place).

VOCABULARY: so fast, **si vite** (se vitt).

125. When a Verb is followed by MYSELF, HERSELF, YOURSELF, etc., it is called reflexive because the action done reflects back on the doer. The COMPOUND TENSES of all French Verbs used reflexively are formed with **être**. The Past Participle then agrees with preceding Direct Object, thus:

Has she burnt herself?	S'est-elle brulée?
We (*m*) enjoyed ourselves	Nous nous sommes amusés
The girls won't have dressed yet	Les filles ne se seront pas encore habillées

Note carefully that the Verb 'to have' is translated by the corresponding part of 'to be'.

The Participle does not vary in Gender or Number if the Object is INDIRECT:

We said *to* ourselves	Nous nous sommes **dit**
They spoke *to*-each-other (= to themselves)	Ils se sont **parlé**

1 We haven't enjoyed ourselves. 2 They would have dressed (themselves). 3 The boys hadn't washed (themselves). 4 I made a mistake (= deceived myself). 5 They have established themselves. 6 He hadn't been hurrying (himself). 7 Why hasn't she dressed (herself)?

VOCABULARY: to dress oneself, **s'habiller** (săh-bee-yeh); to deceive oneself, **se tromper** (ser tro*ng*-peh); to establish oneself, **s'etablir** (seh-tăh-bleer); to hurry oneself, **se dépêcher** (ser deh-peh-sheh).

LESSON TWENTY-FOUR

126. All the really important irregular Verbs have now been given. To conjugate the remainder, it is only necessary to learn the following.

INFINITIVE	PRES. PART.	PAST. PART.	PRESENT	PAST. HIST.
to follow	**suivre**	**suivant**	**suivi**	**je suis**	**je suivis**
	(swee-vr)	(swe-vah*ng*)	(swe-ve)	(swee)	(swe-ve)
to suffice	**suffire**	**suffisant**	**suffi**	**je suffis**	**je suffis**
to be enough	(SEE-fear)	(SEE-fe-zah*ng*)	(SEE-fee)	(SEE-fee)	(SEE-fee)
to laugh	**rire**	**riant**	**ri**	**je ris**	**je ris**
	(reer)	(re-ah*ng*)	(ree)	(ree)	(ree)

By learning the above parts, and the FUTURE STEM when irregular, the rest of the Verb can always be formed (see Rules in Para. 77 again).

Remember; in the Present Tense, if the First Person Singular ends in **-s**, the Second also ends in **-s**, and the Third in **-t**. The Stem of the Plural is found by taking **-ant** from the Present Participle. Example:

I follow, etc.: je suis, tu suis, il suit, nous suivons, vous suivez, ils suivent.
I was following: je suivais.
I will follow: je suivrai.
I would follow: je suivrais.

EXERCISE I

1 Why are you laughing? 2 He won't follow us. 3 It wasn't enough. 4 Don't laugh so loud. 5 That won't be enough. 6 He'll laugh if he sees that. 7 Has he been following you?

127. Many Verbs are REFLEXIVE in French that are not used reflexively in English, thus:

> to dispute, quarrel, **se disputer** (se*r* diss-PEE-teh)
> to get up, **se lever** (se*r* le*r*-veh)
> to rest, **se reposer** (se*r* re*r*-po-zeh)
> to (go for a) walk, **se promener** (ser pro-me*r*-neh)

They aren't quarrelling.	Ils ne se disputent pas.
When did you get up? (plur.)	Quand vous êtes-vous levés?
She has rested.	Elle s'est reposée.

EXERCISE II

1 They quarrel every day. 2 You rest too often. 3 Did you go for a walk? 4 We quarrelled with the waiter. 5 Have you rested? 6 I'll get up earlier tomorrow. 7 They wouldn't (= did not want to) fight. 8 We must apologize.

VOCABULARY: to fight, **se battre** (se*r*-băhtr).

128. TO between two Verbs is generally translated **de**, unless TO means IN ORDER TO, when it is translated by **pour**; as,

I advise you *to* speak to him	Je vous conseille **de** lui parler
We did it (in order) *to* satisfy them	Nous l'avons fait **pour** les satisfaire

EXERCISE III

1 I forgot to write to him. 2 We waited at the station (in order) to meet them. 3 I regretted having spoken. 4 He said it to reassure you. 5 She tries to help me. 6 They are studying to pass an examination. 7 We work to earn money. 8 He remembers having written this.

VOCABULARY: to regret, **regretter** (re*r*-grett-eh); having spoken = to have spoken (see note Para. 69) to reassure, **rassurer** (răhss-EE-reh); to study, **étudier** (eh-TEE-de-eh); to work, **travailler** (trăh-văh'e-yeh) to earn, **gagner** (găhn-yeh); to remember, **se souvenir** (ser soo-ver-nee*r*, conjugated like **venir**).

110

129. After certain Verbs, TO must be translated **à** instead of **de.** The most important of these Verbs are:

aimer, to like	**avoir,** to have
apprendre, to learn	**inviter,** to invite

I like *to* do that   J'aime **à** faire cela*
He has nothing *to* say   Il n'a rien **à** dire

* Although this is the strict form it is in fact perfectly good colloquial French to leave out **à** and say simply **j'aime faire cela.**

130. TO is not translated after Verbs of an auxiliary nature, such as:

aller, to go	**devoir,** must *or* ought to
laisser, let *or* allow to	**pouvoir,** can *or* be able to
	vouloir, want to *or* be willing to

They wanted *to* see you   Ils voulaient vous voir
Isn't he able *to* come?   Ne peut-il pas venir?

EXERCISE IV

1 He is learning to swim.   2 Aren't you going to book seats? 3 They invited us to come with them.   4 Allow me to pass. 5 We have to go there tomorrow.   6 Weren't they able to help you?   7 We weren't able to find a garage.   8 Do you like dancing?   8 Have you nothing to do?   10 They must try it.

VOCABULARY: to pass, **passer** (pahss-eh); garage, **garage** *m*(gah-rash).

131.

INFINITIVE		PRES. PART.	PAST PART.	PRESENT	PAST HIST.
to feel	**sentir**	**sentant**	**senti**	**je sens**	**je sentis**
to go out	**sortir**	**sortant**	**sorti**	**je sors**	**je sortis**
to go away, leave	**partir**	**partant**	**parti**	**je pars**	**je partis**
to sleep	**dormir**	**dormant**	**dormi**	**je dors**	**je dormis**
to serve	**servir**	**servant**	**servi**	**je sers**	**je servis**
to lie	**mentir**	**mentant**	**menti**	**je mens**	**je mentis**

EXERCISE V

1 Do you feel the draught?   2 She doesn't feel (herself) well.   3 Why did you go out without me?   4 They will leave before six o'clock.   5 Has your wife gone out?   6 At what time will she come back?   7 Let's go out together.   8 He doesn't sleep well.   9 Don't lie.   10 The meal was served upstairs.

VOCABULARY: draught **courant d'air** *m* (koo-rah*ng* dair); together, **ensemble** (ah*ng*-sah*ng*-bl).

132. The Preposition **chez** means literally AT or TO THE PLACE OF:

at my place	**chez moi**	at my brother's	**chez mon frère**
at his house	**chez lui**	to the doctor's	**chez le docteur**
to their place	**chez eux**	at our house	**chez nous**
	from my butcher's	**de chez mon boucher**	

HOME, AT HOME is also frequently translated by **chez moi** (at-the-place-of me), **chez lui**, etc., instead of **à la maison.**

They are going *home*	Ils vont **chez eux** (*or* à la maison)
She isn't *home*	Elle n'est pas **chez elle**
Are they *at home?*	Sont-ils **chez eux?**

133. TO, AT, IN before the name of a town, village or place, are translated by **à**: as,

He lives *in* Paris	Il habite **à** Paris
Are you going *to* London	Allez-vous **à** Londres?

Before names of countries they are generally translated by the following:

1 en in front of (a) feminine singular countries:

> **en** France

> (b) masculine singular countries beginning with a vowel:

> **en** Iran

2 au, aux in front of all others.

> **au** Japon (Japan), **aux** Etats Unis (*m*, United States), **aux** Antilles (*f*, West Indies).

EXERCISE VI

1 He is going home.   2 She was coming out of the hairdresser's.   3 He is sending that letter to Germany.   4 Aren't they in Paris?   5 We met them at my brother's.   6 Isn't he at home?   7 She wasn't at home; she was at her mother's.   8 We met them as they were leaving their house.

VOCABULARY: as, **comme** (komm); 'leaving (their house)' should be translated here by **sortir.**

LESSON TWENTY-FIVE

134. Notice the following peculiarities of Verbs ending in **-er:**

(a) those in **-ger** or **-cer** change the **g** into **ge**, and the **c** into **ç** (cedilla) before a termination beginning with **a, o, u.**

> This is done to soften the **c** and **g** and so keep the sound of the Stem the same as in the Infinitive.

> > juger: we judge, nous jugeons
> > commencer: he began, il commença

(b) **e** and **é** are changed into **è**, if occurring before a SINGLE consonant followed by mute **-e, -es,** or **-ent.**

> > acheter: I buy, j'achète
> > espérer: he hopes, il espère.

(e is always mute except in the termination **-ez**, and in the Infinitive termination **-er**).

(c) Some Verbs in **-ler** and **-ter** double the **l** and **t** before mute **-e, -es, -ent.** The most important of these Verbs are:

épeler to spell; **appeler** to call; **rappeler** to recall; **renouveler** to renew; **jeter** to throw; **feuilleter** to turn over the leaves, browse through.

> > épeler: he spells, il épelle
> > jeter: they throw, ils jettent

(d) Verbs in **-yer** generally change **y** to **i** before mute **-e, -es, -ent.**

> > payer: I pay, je paie *or* paye
> > essuyer: he wipes, il essuie

EXERCISE I

1 They begin, we do not begin; 2 you judge, they were judging; 3 we buy, he doesn't buy; 4 has he led? will you lead? 5 he was repeating, doesn't he repeat? 6 he won't pay you, do not pay him. 7 They will renew their subscription.

VOCABULARY: to lead, **mener** (mer-neh); to repeat, **répéter** (reh-peh-teh); subscription, **abonnement** *m* (ah-bonn-mahng).

135. The following Verbs in **-frir, -vrir** are all conjugated alike:

INFINITIVE		PRES. PART.	PAST PART.	PRESENT	PAST HIST.
to cover	couvrir	couvrant*	couvert	je couvre†	je couvris
to offer	offrir	offrant	offert	j'offre	j'offris
to open	ouvrir	ouvrant	ouvert	j'ouvre	j'ouvris
to suffer	souffrir	souffrant	souffert	je souffre	je souffris

découvrir (to discover) is conjugated like couvrir.

EXERCISE II

1 Do you open the shop at eight o'clock? **2** He is suffering a great deal. (= much). **3** She offered me a glass of wine. **4** What have you discovered? **5** Open the door. **6** Don't cover that plate. **7** Has he offered you anything? (= something) **8** I will open the doors and (the) windows.

136. IMPERSONAL VERBS and expressions are only used in the Third Person Singular (*it* is called impersonal when it doesn't stand for a Noun).

it is raining, **il pleut**   *it* is not necessary, **il ne faut pas**
it is fine, **il fait beau**   *it* was cold, **il faisait froid**

137. THERE IS, there are, etc., are translated by IT THERE HAS, etc.

there is, there are, **il y a**
there will be, **il y aura**
there isn't, **il n'y a pas**
there hasn't been, **il n'y a pas eu**
there hadn't been, **il n'y avait pas eu**

there was, there were, **il y avait**
there would be, **il y aurait**
aren't there? **n'y a-t-il pas?**
has there been? **y a-t-il eu?**
had there been? **y avait-il eu?**

Voilà (= behold) is the translation of THERE IS, THERE ARE, when anything is pointed out; **il y a,** etc., simply expresses existence.

EXERCISE III

1 There are some people who say that. **2** Aren't there any seats for us? **3** There won't be anything to do. **4** Is there a post office in this street? **5** There were no pictures on the wall.

---

* Irregular **-ir** Verbs do not add -iss-. Imperfect: je couvrais, etc.

† If the First Person ends in -e, the Second ends in -es, and the Third in -e, so that the Present of these Verbs takes the same endings as -er Verbs. Note also that in the Imperative the Familiar Form does not take an **s**.

6 Are there any mice in your kitchen? 7 Were there no cigarettes in the packet?

VOCABULARY: people, **personne** *f* even if referring to a male, (pair-sonn); won't be anything = not ... anything, **ne** ... **rien** (See Rule 108); post office, **bureau de poste** *m* (bEE-roh de*r* post); wall, **mur** *m* (mEE*r*); mouse, **souris** *f* (soo-ree); kitchen, **cuisine** *f* (kwee-zeen); packet, **paquet** *m* (păh-kay).

138. PREPOSITIONS never end a French sentence (See Paragraph 39).

Where do you come *from?*	**D'où** venez-vous?
What is he speaking *of?*	**De** quoi parle-t-il?
The man he is writing *to*	L'homme **à** qui il écrit

139. BEFORE (referring to time) = previous to, prior to, **avant.** BEFORE (referring to place) = in front of, in presence of, **devant.**

They left *before* us	Ils sont partis **avant** nous
He was waiting *in front of* the door	Il attendait **devant** la porte

140. même (-self); **mêmes** (-selves); are added to **moi, lui, vous, nous,** etc. (Paragraph 85) when MYSELF, OURSELVES, etc., aren't reflexive. The two words are connected by a hyphen.

The queen herself	**La reine elle-même**

EXERCISE IV

1 What are you speaking about? 2 The cards they were playing with. 3 He leaves before five o'clock. 4 The person we gave it to. 5 We were here before you. 6 The sea was in front of us. 7 The man he is speaking of. 8 Which case did you put it in? 9 He came himself.

141. TO PUT: 1 **mettre,** 2 **mettent,** 3 **mis,** 4 **je mets,** 6 **je mis.** PRESENT TENSE in full: mets, mets, met; mettons, mettez, mettent (may, may, may; mett-o*ng*, mett-eh, mett).

All Verbs ending in **-mettre** are conjugated in the same way: **admettre** to admit, **omettre** to omit, leave out, **permettre,** to permit, allow, **promettre** to promise.

1 Don't you allow it? 2 He promised nothing. 3 We won't allow them to do it. 4 Why have they left this out? 5 They promised us they would come. 6 Wouldn't he allow you to go?

142. WHOSE when Interrogative is translated as TO WHOM? **à qui?**

<blockquote>Whose car is that?   **A qui est cette voiture?**</blockquote>

De qui is used when the following word refers to a person, thus:

<blockquote>Whose doctor is he?   **De qui est-il le docteur?**</blockquote>

143. WHAT, when the SUBJECT, must be translated **qu'est-ce qui?** WHAT, when the OBJECT, is translated **que** or **qu'est-ce que?**

What (is it that) is making that noise?	**Qu'est-ce qui fait ce bruit?**
What have you bought?	**Qu'est-ce que vous avez acheté?** *or* Qu'avez-vous acheté?

144. All Verbs ending in **-indre** are conjugated alike:

<blockquote>

1 TO FEAR, **craindre** (kra*ng*-dr)

2 fearing, **craignant** (krain-yah*ng*)

3 feared, **craint** (kra*ng*)

4 I fear, **je crains,** tu crains, il craint (kra*ng*); nous **craignons,** vous craignez, ils craignent (krain-yo*ng*, krain-yeh, krain-ye*r*)

5 I used to fear, was fearing, **je craignais** (krain-yay)

6 I feared, **je craignis** (krain-yee)

7 I will fear, **je craindrai** (kra*ng*-dray)

8 I would fear, **je craindrais** (kra*ng*-dray)

9 fear, **craignez;** let us fear, **craignons** (*Familiar*: fear, crains)

</blockquote>

1 Whose seat is this? 2 What are you writing? 3 Whose friend is he? 4 What smells so strong? 5 Why is he complaining? 6 What amuses you? 7 Whose clothes are these? 8 He isn't afraid of anything (= he fears nothing). 9 Everybody feared (*imperfect*) him. 10 Why did you complain?

11 Who will paint the picture? 12 Why doesn't he put out the light?

VOCABULARY: to complain, **se plaindre** (se*r* pla*ng*-dr); clothes, **vêtements** *m* (vaytt-mah*ng*); to paint, **peindre** (pa*ng*-dr); to put out the light = to extinguish the light, **éteindre la lumière** (eh-ta*ng*-dr lah ɪɛɛ-me-ai**r**).

145. The INDEFINITE PRONOUN **on** is frequently used in French.

(1) Its literal translation is ONE (used indefinitely).

One doesn't say that	**On** ne dit pas cela

(2) WE, YOU, THEY, PEOPLE, if not referring to a definite person or persons, are translated by **on**, the Verb always being singular.

What are *they* playing (*or* is being played) at the theatre this evening?	Que joue-t-**on** au théâtre ce soir?
Where do *they* sell stamps?	Où vend-**on** des timbres?
People like to enjoy themselves	**On** aime à s'amuser

(3) The English Passive Voice is frequently rendered by **on**,

It is said	**On** dit
It is announced	**On** annonce
French *spoken* here	Ici **on** parle français
That is easily *understood*	**On** comprend cela facilement

On after **et** or **si** is usually changed into **l'on**: if they come, si l'**on** vient. This is optional, and is not done if the next word begins with **l**.

EXERCISE VII

1 There's a knock (= one knocks) at the door. 2 You are wanted = One asks-for you. 3 People are speaking about you. 4 One likes to be at home. 5 People were singing in the street. 6 It is said that she is going to die. 7 If they ask-for your address.

VOCABULARY: to knock, **frapper** (frăh-peh); at (one's own) home, **chez soi** (sheh so'ăh).

146. BETTER is translated by **meilleur** if it is an *adjective* and by **mieux** if it is an *adverb*.

BETTER is an adjective when it describes a person or things, and an Adverb when it describes how something is done.

This apple is *better*	Cette pomme est **meilleure**
She plays *better* than you	Elle joue **mieux** que vous

The same distinction applies to BEST (**le meilleur** and **le mieux**). The Adjectives **pire** (*worse*) and **moindre** (*less*) are sometimes used instead of **plus mauvais** and **plus petit** respectively. The Adverb **pis** (*worse*) is sometimes used instead of **plus mal.**

147. demi (half) is made Feminine if coming AFTER, but not if coming before a Feminine Noun; as,

It was two hours and a half	C'était deux heures et demie
I will come in half an hour	Je viendrai dans une demi-heure

EXERCISE VIII

1 These cigarettes are better than those. **2** She writes better than you. **3** He bought a pound and (a) half of butter. **4** His wine is the best. **5** He is worse than yesterday. **6** She eats less every day. **7** He plays best of all.

LESSON TWENTY-SIX

148. The PRESENT OF THE SUBJUNCTIVE is formed from the PRESENT PARTICIPLE by changing **-ant** into: **-e, -es, -e; -ions, -iez, -ent.** These are the endings of the Present Indicative of **-er** Verbs, with an **i** added in the First and Second Persons Plural.

that I (may) give, etc.	that we (may) give, etc.
que je donne	**que nous donnions**
que tu donnes	**que vous donniez**
qu'il donne	**qu'ils donnent**

Further examples: that (I may) sell, finish, put, etc.

que je	*que tu*	*qu'il*	*que nous*	*que vous*	*qu'ils*
vende	vendes	vende	vendions	vendiez	vendent
finisse	finisses	finisse	finissions	finissiez	finissent
mette	mettes	mette	mettions	mettiez	mettent

EXERCISE I

Form the Present Subjunctive of the following:

1 fermer, attendre, remplir; **2** partir (Paragraph 131), écrire (84), lire (81); **3** savoir (112), voir (77), dire (88). **4** that I may pass; **5** that he may not speak; **6** that we may lose; **7** that you may not give back; **8** that they may succeed; **9** that she may finish; **10** that he may write; **11** that they may not know. **12** that you may sell.

118

149. The only irregular PRESENT SUBJUNCTIVES are given below:

acquérir (acquire) que j'acquière
aller (go) que j'aille
s'asseoir (sit down) que je
           m'asseye
boire (drink) que je boive
falloir (be necessary) qu'il faille
mourir (die) que je meure

mouvoir* (move) que je meuve
prendre (take) que je prenne
recevoir† (receive) que je reçoive
seoir (suit) qu'il siée
tenir (hold) que je tienne
venir (come) que je vienne
valoir (be worth) que je vaille
vouloir (want) que je veuille

Only the First Person Singular need be learned, as all the Persons of the Singular, and the 3rd. Person Plural, have the SAME IRREGULAR STEM.

Examples; **aller** *that I (may)* go, etc. que j'aille, que tu ailles, qu'il aille; que nous allions, que vous alliez, qu'ils aillent.

150. The following four are quite irregular:

	que je	*que tu*	*qu'il*	*que nous*	*que vous*	*qu'ils*
avoir	aie	aies	ait	ayons	ayez	aient
être	sois	sois	soit	soyons	soyez	soient
faire	fasse	fasses	fasse	fassions	fassiez	fassent
pouvoir	puisse	puisses	puisse	puissions	puissiez	puissent

EXERCISE II

Form the Present Subjunctive of the following:

1 aller, faire, boire; 2 pouvoir, venir; 3 avoir, être, vouloir; 4 that I (may) come; 5 that he (may) not be able; 6 that we may be willing; 7 that you may not hold; 8 that they may not go; 9 that we may come back; 10 that you may not receive; 11 that they may do it.

151. The Third Person of the PRESENT SUBJUNCTIVE is used for the Third Person IMPERATIVE (see end of Paragraph 58):

let him have **qu'il ait**
let him speak **qu'il parle**
let them be **qu'ils soient**
let them finish **qu'ils finissent.**

152. The IMPERFECT SUBJUNCTIVE of all Verbs (without exception) is formed from the PAST HISTORIC by changing the final letter of the 1st Person Singular into: **-sse, -sses, -^t, -ssions, -ssiez, -ssent.**

---

* Very rarely used. The usual verbs for *to move* are **bouger** and **remuer.**

† All Verbs ending in **-evoir** are conjugated like **recevoir.**

In the 3rd. Person Sing., the vowel preceding the **t** takes a circumflex accent.

EXAMPLES:

that I had or *that I might have*		*that I was* or *that I might be*	
que j'eusse	que nous eussions	que je fusse	que nous fussions
que tu eusses	que vous eussiez	que tu fusses	que vous fussiez
qu'il eût	qu'ils eussent	qu'il fût	qu'il fussent

that I gave, finished, received or *that I might give, finish, receive*

que je	que tu	qu'il	que nous	que vous	qu'ils
donnasse	donnasses	donnât	donnassions	donnassiez	donnassent
finisse	finisses	finît	finissions	finissiez	finissent
reçusse	reçusses	reçût	reçussions	reçussiez	reçussent

NOTE: We have placed **que** before the Subjunctive and given an English translation. Both practices, however, are misleading. **Que** is not always followed by the Subjunctive, and **may** and **might** are frequently an incorrect translation.

EXERCISE III

Form the Imperfect Subjunctive of the following:

1 avoir, être, fermer;   2 attendre, remplir, lire (81);   3 pouvoir (109), tenir (114), prendre (90).   4 that I replied *or* might reply;   5 that she might not succeed;   6 that they might not have;   7 that she might come (115);   8 that we might speak;   9 that you might be;   10 that he might write (84).

153.   1 to be necessary, **falloir**
3 been necessary, **fallu** (invariable)
4 it is necessary, **il faut**
5 it was necessary, **il fallait**
6 it was necessary, **il fallut**
7 it will be necessary, **il faudra**
8 it would ne necessary, **il faudrait**

The Verb following **falloir**, unless an Infinitive, *must* be in the Subjunctive.

154, The Subjunctive is used in RELATIVE SENTENCES: (1) if following a Superlative; (2) if following: *seul, premier, dernier.*

The biggest dog (that) I saw	Le plus grand chien que j'**aie** vu
The only man who knows it	Le seul homme qui le **sache**

120

155. The Subjunctive must be used after certain CONJUNCTIONS, the most important of which are:

afin que, so that   **avant que,** before   **jusqu'à ce que,** until
pour que, in order that   **quoique, bien que,** (al)though

We will do it, though it is late   Nous le ferons, bien qu'il soit tard
I will wait until he comes   J'attendrai jusqu'à ce qu'il vienne

EXERCISE IV

1 It is the only thing he sells.   2 The best book I have ever read.   3 The finest picture he has painted.   4 Give it to the first man who comes.   5 Wait until I'm ready.   6 Although he is rich he isn't happy.   7 We will speak to them before they have finished it.   8 He has come so that we may-be-able-to speak of-it.

156. The Subjunctive is used after most Verbs used NEGATIVELY or INTERROGATIVELY.

Is it likely that she will* come?   Est-il probable qu'elle vienne?
He doesn't believe they will* leave   Il ne croit pas qu'ils partent

After **dire, savoir** and **informer, penser, croire** and **voir** the Subjunctive is not used (unless some doubt is implied in the statement), as, I don't know what he said, Je ne sais pas ce qu'il a dit.

157. The Subjunctive is used after IMPERSONAL VERBS and expressions, except those denoting certainty or probability; as,

It is necessary for me to leave   Il faut que je **parte**
It is right that he should* be punished   Il est juste qu'il **soit** puni
It is better that he should* come   Il vaut mieux qu'il **vienne**

EXERCISE V

1 Do you think he'll* be at home?   2 I don't believe she wants to dance.   3 I didn't think (Imperf.) he would* come.   4 Is it necessary that we should* leave.   5 Isn't it (= probable) that he will see* it?   6 Don't you know that he will be there?   7 He didn't say that he could (Imperf.) do it.   8 Is it possible that the money is his?   9 I don't expect (= think) that he will take any of it.

VOCABULARY: I believe, **je crois** (from **croire**).

---

* See Paragraph 158.

158. For all practical purposes the Subjunctive has only two living Tenses, the Present and the Perfect. The Pluperfect is never used in conversation and the Imperfect only rarely. However, the Imperfect is still part of the grammatical structure of spoken French and so some practice in it is included here. The Present Subjunctive is always used unless the first Verb is Imperfect or Conditional. After these two, the Imperfect Subjunctive is used.

From this Rule it follows that: he is, was, will be, should be, would be, may be, might be, etc. can only be translated in a Subjunctive clause by **soit** or **fût**.

159. The Subjunctive is used after certain Verbs followed by **que**, the most important of which are:

vouloir, to want, wish   **falloir,** to be necessary   **désirer,** to desire
   craindre, to fear   **regretter,** to regret   **douter,** to doubt
         souhaiter, to wish, hope

I'm sorry she is here	Je regrette qu'elle **soit** ici
We want them to be there	Nous désirons qu'ils **soient** là
He doesn't want me to see it	Il ne veut pas que je le **voie**

160. A few of the Verbs and Conjunctions which govern the Subjunctive may take **ne** before the following verb, unless the first verb is Interrogative or Negative. This insertion of **ne** is now optional. The most important are:

> **avoir peur, craindre,** to be afraid, to fear
> **prendre garde,** to take cover, watch out
> **empêcher,** to prevent
> **à moins que,** unless

He's afraid that you know it	Il craint que vous (**ne**) le sachiez
BUT: Is he afraid that you know it?	**Craint-il que vous le sachiez?**

Exercise VI

1 We're sorry that he didn't find us.   2 She's afraid that he will come.   3 Is it necessary for us to wait (= that we wait)? 4 I doubted whether (= that) they would come.   5 I'm afraid he won't wait for you.   6 We were afraid we wouldn't see you. 7 We wish (Conditional) they hadn't begun.   8 I wish (Conditional) she wasn't here.

161. falloir (See Paragraph 153) is frequently used for MUST, HAVE TO, and other words denoting compulsion. The English must be changed like this:

I *shall have to* do it = it will be necessary that I do it
Il faudra que je le fasse
Ought you not to wait? = is it not necessary that you wait?
Ne faut-il pas que vous attendiez?
He *must* leave = it is necessary that he leaves
Il faut qu'il parte

Exercise VII

1 Must you do it?   2 You'll have to write to him.   3 He wouldn't have to finish it.   4 We must know it.   5 It isn't necessary for us to (= that we) pay that duty.   6 It wasn't necessary (Imperf.) for them to speak (= that they spoke).

VOCABULARY: duty, **droits** (*m pl*).

162. When WANT, WISH, etc. are followed in English by an Object and an Infinitive, the construction must be changed like this:

I want *you to go* there with him = I want *that you* go there with him
Je veux que vous y alliez avec lui
They wanted *him to come* = They wanted *that he* came
Ils voulaient qu'il vînt

163. SHALL I? SHALL WE? are frequently translated like this:

Shall we shut it?   **Voulez-vous que nous le fermions?**
Shall I not finish that?   **Ne voulez-vous pas que je finisse cela?**

Exercise VIII

1 Does he want her to (= that she) read it?   2 They want me to speak to him.   3 Will he want you to write to them?   4 She wants you to accept this.   5 They won't want us to keep it.   6 Doesn't he want us to stay there?   7 We don't want them to hear us.   8 Did you want (Imperf.) me to do (= that I did) it for you?   9 Shall I do it for him?   10 Shall we not go there?   11 Shall I not send it to him?   12 Shall we fetch it?   13 Shall I shut the window?

APPENDIX

IRREGULAR PLURALS AND FEMININES

1. The following NOUNS ending in **-al** take **-s** in the Plural:

bal, *dancing ball*; carnaval, *carnival*; chacal, *jackal*; festival, *festival*; récital, *recital*; régal, *treat*

2. The following NOUNS ending in **-au, -eu** take **-s** in the plural:

landau, pram; bleu, *blue, bruise;* pneu, *tyre.*

3. The following NOUNS ending in **-ou** add **x**:

bijou, *jewel*; caillou, *stone, pebble*; chou, *cabbage*; genou, *knee*; hibou, *owl*; joujou, *toy (baby talk)*; pou, *louse.*

4. The following NOUNS ending in **-ail** change **-ail** into **-aux**:

travail, *work*; bail, *lease*; corail, *coral*; émail, *enamel*; soupirail, *vent, air-hole*; vantail, *leaf (of door or shutter)*; vitrail, *stained glass* or *leaded glass window.*

The Plural of **ail,** *garlic,* is **ails;** the Plural of **bétail,** *cattle,* is **bestiaux.**

5. Other irregular Plurals are:

aïeul, *grandfather*	aïeux, *ancestors*	or aïeuls, *grandfathers*	
ciel, *sky or heaven*	cieux, *heavens*	or ciels, *skies*	
oeil, *eye*	yeux, *eyes*	or oeils-de-boeuf, *oval windows.*	

6. The following ADJECTIVES have irregular Feminine forms:

m		f	m		f
absous	*absolved*	absoute	exprès	*express*	expresse
bas	*low*	basse	faux	*false*	fausse
beau*	*fine*	belle	favori	*favourite*	favorite
bénin	*benign*	bénigne	fou*	*foolish, mad*	folle
blanc	*white*	blanche	frais	*fresh*	fraîche
bon	*good*	bonne	franc	*honest*	franche
caduc	*decrepit*	caduque	gentil	*kind, nice*	gentille
coi	*quiet*	coite	gras	*fat*	grasse
dissous	*dissolved*	dissoute	grec	*Greek*	grecque
doux	*soft, gentle*	douce	gros	*big*	grosse
épais	*thick*	épaisse	hébreu	*Hebrew*	hébraïque

* Before a Masculine Noun beginning with a VOWEL or an H mute, **bel, fol,** are used instead of **beau, fou.**

jumeau	*twin*	jumelle	public	*public*	publique
long	*long*	longue	roux	*red*	rousse
malin	*cunning*	maligne	sec	*dry*	sèche
mou*	*soft*	molle	sot	*stupid*	sotte
muet	*dumb*	muette	sujet	*subject*	sujette
muscat	*muscatel*	muscade	tiers	*third*	tierce
nouveau*	*new*	nouvelle	traître	*treacherous*	traîtresse
nul	*no (not one)*	nulle	turc	*Turkish*	turque
oblong	*oblong*	oblongue	vieux*	*old*	vieille
préfix	*prefixed*	préfixe	violet	*violet*	violette

* Before a Masculine Noun beginning with a VOWEL or an H mute, **mol, nouvel, vieil**, are used instead of **mou, nouveau, vieux.**

7. Colours have no separate feminine or plural form if they are formed from nouns. (Exceptions: écarlate, pourpre and rose.)

An olive dress   Une robe olive
Olive dresses   Des robes olive

8. The following ADJECTIVES in **-al** take **s** in the Plural:

bancal, *bandy-legged, wobbly*; fatal, *fatal*; final, *final*; glacial, *icy*; natal, *native*; naval, *naval*.

9. NOUNS AND ADJECTIVES ending in **-eur** (derived from a Present Participle) change into **-euse**; as,

danseur, *dancer*, danseuse;   menteur, *liar*, menteuse;
(EXCEPT: vengeur, *revenger*, vengeresse; enchanteur, *enchanter*, enchanteresse and a few other seldom-used words)

10. Those in **-teur** change into **-trice**; as,

acteur, *actor*, actrice;   inventeur, *inventor*, inventrice;
(EXCEPT: chanteur, *singer*, chanteuse; serviteur, *servant*, servante)

11. **majeur, meilleur, mineur** and those ending in **-érieur** add **e**.

supérieur, *superior*, supérieure;   extérieur, *exterior*, extérieure

Adjectives ending in **-gu** take a diaresis over the **e**, to show that the **u** is pronounced: aigu, *acute*, aiguë; (aigue would be pronounced: aig)

12. In COMPOUND NOUNS, both parts are made Plural except in the following cases:

(a) No change is made if the Compound is formed from a Verb and Adverb, as: passe-partout, *latch-key* and *latch-keys*.

(b) Only the Noun changes if formed with Noun and Verb, or Noun and Preposition: sous-officier, *sub-officer*, sous-officiers. porte-monnaie, *purse*, does not change in the Plural.

(c) Only the first Noun changes if the parts are joined by a Preposition: chemin de fer, *railway*, chemins de fer; hotel de ville, *town hall*, hôtels de ville.

EXCEPTIONS: Monsieur, Messieurs; Madame, Mesdames; Mademoiselle, Mesdemoiselles; Monseigneur, Messeigneurs; gentilhomme, gentilshommes.

13. ADVERBS are formed from Adjectives ending in -ant or -ent by changing the termination -nt to -mment; as,

constant, *constantly*, constamment; prudent, *prudently*, prudemment. EXCEPTIONS: lent, *slowly*, lentement; présent, *presently*, présentement; véhément, *vehement*, véhémentement.

14. The following ADVERBS take an acute accent over the e preceding -ment:

aveugle	*blindly*	aveuglément
commode	*conveniently*	commodément
commun	*commonly*	communément
conforme	*conformably*	conformément
confus	*confusedly*	confusément
diffus	*diffusely*	diffusément
énorme	*enormously*	enormément
exprès	*expressly*	expressément
immense	*immensely*	immensément
impuni	*with impunity*	impunément
obscur	*darkly*	obscurément
opinâtre	*obstinately*	opiniâtrément
précis	*precisely*	précisément
profond	*deeply*	profondément
uniforme	*uniformly*	uniformément

15. beau, fou, mou, nouveau form the ADVERB from heir Feminine:

bellement, follement, mollement, nouvellement

16. gentil, nicely, gentiment, is quite irregular.

126

INDEX

Included are most words introduced in the earlier exercises, as well as cross-references to points of grammar (**questions, pronouns, future tense** etc.). The numbers indicate Paragraphs dealing with that particular item; we make it clear if a page number is thus referred to.

FRENCH
IN THREE MONTHS
II

IDIOMS, READING, VOCABULARIES

INTRODUCTION

Having worked through the grammar lessons in Part I and mastered the basic constructions of the language, the reader will be looking for help with the everyday colloquial expressions that are so necessary for a working grasp of conversational French, Obviously it is impossible to include an exhaustive collection of French idioms: there is only space here to give some of the most common and most useful. Our point of reference has therefore been the verb. We have chosen the most often-used verbs and listed examples of the expressions and idioms derived from them. The reader should try to foresee what he might want to say in a given situation and build up a vocabulary of phrase and sentence using these examples as a basis.

Following the idioms there is a handful of extracts from some well-known French writers. One of the great satisfactions of learning a foreign language is that a new literature becomes available. You should get into the habit of reading French as soon as possible: and there is no reason for not starting with the best. The two fables of La Fontaine, Baudelaire's poem, Maupassant's short story and the extract from Albert Camus's novel *La Peste* will show the reader something—a very small something—of what French literature has to offer. The word-for-word English equivalents given underneath the text are of course not meant to be a translation, but to show the characteristic structures and style of written French. Try as far as possible to read the pieces without referring to the crib; and try reading them aloud.

The selection of French proverbs that follows gives further examples of traditional idiom. Lastly we have included a number of specialized vocabularies covering those situations in which the visitor to France is most likely to find himself.

IDIOMS

AVOIR—*to have*

J'ai besoin de ...	*I need ...*
J'ai chaud, froid, faim, soif	*I'm hot, cold, hungry, thirsty*
J'ai envie de me coucher	*I want to go to bed*
J'avais raison et il avait tort	*I was right and he was wrong*
J'aurai vingt ans le mois prochain	*I shall be twenty next month*
Le match a eu lieu hier	*The match took place yesterday*
Qu'avez-vous?	*What's the matter with you?*
Il a quelque chose	*There's something the matter with him*
J'en ai assez	*I've had enough*
En avoir à quelqu'un	*To have a grudge against someone*
Vous n'avez pas à vous inquiéter	*You have no need to worry*
Il y a	*There is, there are*
Il y a un an, un mois	*A year, month ago*
Il y a du vent, brouillard	*It's windy, foggy*
Combien y a-t-il d'ici à ...?	*How far is it from here to . . .?*
On m'a eu	*I've been had (cheated)*
J'ai eu beau essayer de ...	*Try as I might I couldn't ...*
Vous n'avez qu'à attendre	*You'll just have to wait*
Vous avez eu de la chance	*You were lucky*
Avoir affaire à quelqu'un	*To have dealings with someone*
J'en ai marre	*I'm fed up with it*

ÊTRE—*to be*

Soit	*So be it*
Ainsi soit-il	*Amen*
Etre bien, mal avec quelqu'un	*To be on good, bad terms with someone*
Il est docteur, ingénieur	*He's a doctor, engineer*
Nous sommes le quinze	*Today is the fifteenth*

133

Il est de leurs amis	*He is a friend of theirs*
Comme si de rien n'était	*As if nothing had happened*
S'il en fut jamais	*If ever there was one*
Je n'en suis pas encore là!	*I haven't come to that yet!*
Je ne sais plus où j'en suis	*I don't know where I am any more, I'm in a complete muddle*
Il en est qui disent que ...	*There are some who say that ...*
Je suis à vous dans un moment	*I'll be with you in a moment*
C'est à vous de commencer	*It's your turn to start*
C'est à vous de faire cela	*It's your job to do that*
Soyez le bienvenu!	*Welcome!*
Il viendra soit cette semaine soit la semaine prochaine	*He'll come either this week or next*

FAIRE—*to do, make*

Il fait beau, mauvais temps	*It's fine, bad weather*
Je ne sais que faire	*I don't know what to do*
J'ai fort à faire	*I've got my hands full, a lot to do*
Toute réfléxion faite	*All things considered*
Nous avons fait une promenade	*We went for a walk*
C'est bien fait	*It serves you right*
Il faisait du cinquante à l'heure	*He was doing fifty miles an hour*
Faites comme chez vous	*Make yourself at home*
Que faire?	*What shall I, we, you (or any pronoun, any tense) do?*
Cela fera mon affaire	*That will suit me very well*
Qu'est-ce que ça fait?	*What does it matter?*
Qu'est-ce que cela peut me faire?	*What's that to me, what do I care?*
Cela ne fait rien	*It doesn't matter*
Si cela ne te fait rien	*If you don't mind*
Faire une valise	*To pack a case*
Faire les cartes	*To shuffle cards*
Je veux faire du théâtre	*I want to be an actor, actress*

134

Il fait sa médecine	*He's studying to be a doctor*
Cette robe fait très jeune	*That dress makes you look very young*
Ne fais pas l'idiot	*Don't play the fool*
Elle n'en fait qu'à sa tête	*She goes her own way*
Ne vous en faites pas	*Don't worry*
Faites venir le médecin	*Call the doctor*
Ils nous ont fait venir	*They sent for us*
Il a fait construire une maison	*He had a house built*
Je ne suis pas arrivé à me faire comprendre	*I couldn't make myself understood*
Je me suis fait couper les cheveux, photographier	*I had my hair cut, photo taken*
Il se fait vieux	*He's looking old*
Je me suis fait à la vie de campagne	*I got used to, adapted myself to, country life*
Cela fait que je suis toujours ici	*Consequently I'm still here*
On m'a fait ouvrir ma valise	*They made me open my case*
Faire manger les enfants	*To feed the children*
Je veux faire réparer ma voiture	*I want to have my car repaired*
Un bruit s'est fait entendre	*A noise was heard*
Il se fait tard	*It's getting late*
Un fromage fait	*A ripe cheese*
Un steak bien fait	*A well-done steak*
Vêtements tout faits	*Off-the-peg clothes*
Faire suivre une lettre	*To forward a letter*
A faire suivre	*Please forward*
Faire-part de mariage	*Notification of a marriage*
Faire quelque chose au petit bonheur la chance	*To do something in a random, happy-go-lucky way*
Il s'est fait prendre en train de chiper des pommes	*He was caught pinching apples*
Cela ne se fait pas	*That isn't done*
Il n'y a rien à faire	*There's nothing we can do about it*
Il ne faisait que se plaindre	*All he did was to complain*

ALLER—*to go*

Aller en voiture, en autobus, en avion, en bateau, en train
To go by car, bus, plane, boat, train

Aller à pied, à cheval
To go on foot, on horseback

Aller à la pêche, à la chasse, en ville, en vacances
To go fishing, hunting, into town, on holiday

Aller chez quelqu'un
To visit someone

Il ira loin
He will go far, will do well

Les affaires vont bien, mal
Business is good, bad

Tout va bien
Everything's going well

Comment allez-vous?
How are you?

Ça va
I'm fine

Cela va sans dire
That goes without saying, that's obvious

Cela vous va
That fits, suits you

Le bleu ne lui va pas
Blue doesn't suit her

Allons-y!
Let's go, let's get on with it!

Je vais m'en occuper
I'm going to take care of it

Il va de soi que ...
It stands to reason that ...

S'en aller
To go away

Va-t-en! Allez-vous-en!
Go away!

Allons-nous-en!
Let's go!

Y aller carrément
To go ahead and do something

Les taches ne veulent pas s'en aller
The marks won't come off

Il faut que je m'en aille
I must be going

Mes forces s'en allaient
My strength was failing

Billet d'aller et retour
Return ticket

Aller de mieux en mieux, de mal en pis
To get better and better, go from bad to worse

Aller bon train, grand train
To go at a good pace, like the wind

Aller son petit bonhomme de chemin
To go your own sweet way

Tout va comme sur des roulettes
Everything's going smoothly, like clockwork

Tu te laisses aller
You're letting yourself go, becoming careless

Laisse-toi aller	*Let yourself go, relax*
Allez voir ce qu'il fait	*Go and see what he's doing*

VENIR—*to come*

Viens ici, venez ici!	*Come here!*
Venez donc!	*Come on now, come along!*
D'où venez-vous?	*Where have you, do you, come from?*
Il vient de Londres	*He's a Londoner*
Dans les mois à venir	*In the months to come*
Faire venir quelque chose	*To have something sent*
Vin venu de France	*Wine from France*
Venir de faire quelque chose	*To have just done something*
Je viens de manger	*I have just eaten*
Elle venait de se lever	*She had just got up*
D'où vient-il que . . .?	*How does it happen that . . .?*
Je viendrai si je peux	*I'll come if I can*

PRENDRE—*to take*

Prendre une chambre, un appartement	*To take a room, a flat*
Prendre un bain, le déjeuner	*To have a bath, lunch*
J'ai pris un billet	*I bought a ticket*
J'ai pris des renseignements	*I found out the information*
Prenez garde!	*Be careful!*
Où a-t-il pris cela?	*Where did he get that idea?*
Il prend les choses trop au sérieux	*He takes things too seriously*
Il a très mal pris la mort de son père	*He took his father's death very badly*
C'est à prendre ou à laisser	*Take it or leave it*
A tout prendre	*Everything considered, on the whole*
En prendre à son aise	*To take things easily*
Il ne voulait pas se faire prendre	*He didn't want to be caught*

Qu'est-ce qui vous prend?	*What has got into you?*
Je passerai vous prendre à trois heures	*I'll pick you up at three o'clock*
On m'a pris pour ma soeur	*I was taken for my sister*
Bottes qui prennent l'eau	*Boots that let in water*
Elle prend de mauvaises habitudes	*She's getting bad habits*
Prenez à gauche	*Take the left turning, bear to the left*
Une mode qui a vite pris	*A fashion that quickly caught on*
Je me suis pris la main dans la porte	*I caught my hand in the door*
Je ne sais pas comment m'y prendre	*I don't know how to set about it*
Il s'y prend mal	*He's going the wrong way about it*
Prendre la mouche	*To take offence, get angry*
Prendre les choses comme elles sont	*To take things as they are*
Cela prendra longtemps	*That will take a long time*
Elle prend des heures à s'habiller	*She takes hours dressing*

DIRE—*to say, tell*

Envoyer dire à quelqu'un que . . .	*Send word to someone that . . .*
Qu'en dira-t-on?	*What will people say?*
Je dis ce que je pense	*I speak my mind*
Je vous l'avais bien dit!	*Didn't I tell you!*
Comme on dit	*As the saying goes*
Comment est-ce que cela se dit en français?	*How do you say that in French?*
Cela ne se dit pas	*That's not how you say it*
Dire que oui, non	*To say yes, no*
Je ne sais comment dire	*I don't know how to put it*
A vrai dire . . .	*To tell the truth . . .*
C'est tout dit	*I need say no more*
Tout est dit	*That's the end of the matter*

138

Tout n'est pas dit	*We haven't heard the last of it*
A ce qu'il dit	*According to him*
Cela va sans dire	*That goes without saying, stands to reason*
On dit que ...	*They say that ...*
On aurait dit que ...	*It was as if ...*
On dirait un vagabond	*You'd think he was a tramp*
On se dirait en Angleterre	*You'd think you were in England*
Il n'y a pas à dire	*There's no doubt about it*
Je lui ai fait dire que ...	*I sent word to him that ...*
Je ne me le suis pas fait dire deux fois	*I didn't have to be told twice*
Faites ce qu'on vous dit	*Do as you're told*
Dites-lui d'entrer	*Tell him to come in*
Cela ne me dit rien	*That doesn't appeal to me*
Qu'est-ce que cela veut dire?	*What does that mean?*
Que veut dire ce mot?	*What does this word mean?*
Ce n'est pas à dire que ...	*That's not to say that ...*
Dites-moi ce que vous avez fait	*Tell me what you've done*
A l'heure dite	*At the appointed time*
Un livre qui est soi-disant bon	*A supposedly good book*
Si vous venez à trois heures, disons	*If you come at, say, three o'clock*
Vous n'avez qu'à le dire	*You only have to mention it*
Il m'a donné le prix juste du billet, c'est-à-dire, dix livres	*He gave me the exact price of the ticket, that's to say, ten pounds*

VOIR—*to see*

Cela vaut la peine d'être vu	*That's well worth seeing*
Il faut le voir pour le croire	*It has to be seen to be believed*
Voir c'est croire	*Seeing is believing*
A le voir on dirait ...	*By the look of him you'd say ...*
Quelque chose qui se voit de loin	*Something that can be seen from far away*

On n'y voit rien, on n'y voit goutte	*You can't see a thing here*
Je l'ai vu de mes propres yeux	*I saw it with my own eyes*
Faire voir quelque chose à quelqu'un	*To show someone something*
Faites voir	*Let me see it*
Allons voir	*Let's go and see*
Je l'ai vu tomber	*I saw him fall*
Quelles pièces avez-vous vues ?	*What plays did you see?*
Cela se voit	*That's obvious, apparent*
Nous nous voyons souvent	*We see a lot of each other*
A ce que je vois …	*As far as I can see …*
Cela n'a rien à voir à l'affaire	*That has nothing to do with it*
Je ne peux pas le voir	*I can't bear the sight of him*
Vu les circonstances …	*Considering circumstances …*
A perte de vue	*As far as the eye can see*
Voyons !	*Come, come!*
Tu ne feras pas ça, voyons !	*Surely you won't do that!*
On verra	*We shall see*

VOULOIR—*to wish, want*

Vous l'avez voulu	*You've only yourself to blame, you asked for it*
Faites comme vous voudrez	*Do as you please*
Il ne sait pas ce qu'il veut	*He doesn't know what to do, his own mind*
Que voulez-vous ?	*What do you want?*
Qu'il le veuille ou non	*Whether he likes it or not*
Que voulez-vous que j'y fasse ?	*How can I help it, what do you expect me to do about it?*
Tant que vous voudrez	*As much as you like*
C'est tout ce que vous voulez ?	*Is that all you want?*
Combien en voulez-vous ?	*How much do you want, are you asking for it?*
Je ne veux pas de cela	*I want none of it*

Je ne lui veux pas de mal	*I don't wish him any harm*
En vouloir à quelqu'un	*To have a grudge against, be annoyed with, someone*
Je ne sais pas pourquoi il m'en voulait	*I don't know why he had it in for me*
Je veux qu'il vienne	*I want him to come*
La voiture ne veut pas démarrer	*The car won't start*
Il ne voulait pas s'en aller	*He didn't want to go*
J'aurais bien voulu les voir	*I'd quite like to have seen them*
Je veux que tu sois heureux	*I want you to be happy*
Je voudrais une bouteille de vin	*I'd like a bottle of wine*
Si vous voulez	*If you like*
Je veux bien	*I'm quite willing, I don't mind*
Si vous le voulez bien	*If you don't mind*
Il voulait absolument me voir	*He insisted on seeing me*
Dieu veuille que ...	*God grant that ...*

FALLOIR—*to be necessary*

Il me faut de l'argent	*I need some money*
Avez-vous tout ce qu'il vous faut?	*Have you everything you need?*
C'est juste ce qu'il me faut	*It's just what I need*
Que vous faut-il?	*What do you need?*
Voilà ce qu'il vous faut	*This is just the thing for you*
Il lui faut trois jours pour faire cela	*He needs three days to do that*
Nous ferons tout ce qu'il faudra	*We'll do everything necessary*
Se conduire comme il faut	*To behave properly*
Elle est très comme il faut	*She's very prim and proper*
Il faut partir	*I, you, we must go*
Il me faut partir	*I must go*
Il nous faut partir	*We must go*
Il faut nous dépêcher	*We must hurry*
Il fallait le dire!	*You should have said so, mentioned it*

METTRE—*to put*

Mettre le couvert	*To lay the table*
On l'a mis à la porte	*They turned him out*
Mettre le feu à quelque chose	*To set fire to something*
Qu'est-ce que je dois mettre?	*What should I wear?*
Mettre à chauffer de l'eau	*To put some water on to boil*
Mettre en vente une maison, un appartement	*To put a house, flat, up for sale*
Se mettre à table	*To sit down to table*
Mettez-vous là	*Sit there*
Je ne savais où me mettre	*I didn't know where to put myself*
Se mettre à faire quelque chose	*To begin to do something*
Il s'est mis à rire	*He began to laugh*
Se mettre en colère	*To get angry*
Nous nous sommes mis en route	*We started out (on the the journey)*
Si elle arrive, mettons, demain matin	*If she arrives, let's say, for example, tomorrow morning*

VALOIR—*to be worth*

Ces pommes valent trois francs le kilo	*These apples are three francs a kilo*
Combien vaut ceci?	*How much is this?*
J'ai payé deux livres à valoir	*I paid two pounds on account*
Il ne vaut pas le pain qu'il mange	*He's not worth his salt*
Ce film ne vaut pas grand chose	*This film isn't up to much*
Moins nous parlerons mieux cela vaudra	*The less said the better*
Un vaurien, une vaurienne	*A good-for-nothing*
Un franc vaut cent centimes	*One franc is equal to a hundred centimes*

L'un vaut l'autre	*One is as good as, as bad as, the other*
Il vaudrait mieux partir maintenant	*It would be better to leave now*
Il vaut mieux être laborieux que d'être paresseux	*It's better to work hard than be lazy*
Mieux vaut tard que jamais	*Better late than never*
Une gentillesse en vaut une autre	*One good turn deserves another*
Cela vaut la peine d'être visité	*That is worth visiting*
Ça vaut le coup	*It's worth it*
Ça ne vaut pas le coup	*It's not worth it*
Vaille que vaille	*For better or worse*

MOURIR—*to die*

Il est mort la semaine dernière	*He died last week*
Il y a dix ans qu'elle est morte	*It's ten years since she died*
Je meurs de soif	*I'm dying of thirst*
Je meurs de faim	*I'm dying of hunger*
Je mourais de peur	*I was frightened to death*
Je m'ennuie à mourir	*I'm bored to death*
Il m'ennuie à mourir	*He bores me to death*
Nous mourrons d'envie de partir en vacances	*We're dying to get away on holiday*
Elle mourait d'envie de me le dire	*She was dying to tell me about it*
C'est à mourir de rire	*It's killing (very funny)*
Mort et enterré	*Dead and buried*
Bel et bien mort	*Well and truly dead, dead as a doornail*
Faire le mort	*To lie low, to sham death*

143

POUVOIR—*to be able*

Je ne peux pas le faire	*I can't do it*
Ça ne peut pas se faire	*It can't de done*
On n'y peut rien	*It can't be helped*
Je n'y peux rien	*I can't do anything about it*
Elle a été on ne peut plus gentille	*She was as nice as anyone could be*
Je n'en peux plus	*I can't go on, I'm exhausted*
Sauve qui peut	*Every man for himself*
Advienne que pourra	*Come what may*

SAVOIR—*to know*

Je ne sais pas	*I don't know*
Je le sais par coeur	*I know it by heart*
Savez-vous le chemin?	*Do you know the way?*
Il en sait plus d'une	*He knows a thing or two*
Savoir c'est pouvoir	*Knowledge is power*
Je ne savais pas qu'il était là	*I didn't know he was there*
Je sais bien!	*I know!*
Nous ne savons rien de rien	*We don't know a thing*
Tu ne sais pas ce qu'on va faire?	*I'll tell you what we'll do*
Je n'en sais rien	*I know nothing about it*
Sans le savoir	*Without knowing, unconsciously*
Elle le fait sans le savoir	*She does it without realizing it*
Pas je sache	*Not that I know of*
Autant qu'il sache	*As far as he knows*
On ne sait jamais	*You never know*
Je sais ce que je veux	*I know what I want*
Il ne savait que dire	*He was at a loss to know what to say*
Sachez bien que . . .	*Bear in mind that . . .*
Il aurait dû me le faire savoir	*He ought to have let me know*
Savez-vous nager?	*Can you swim?*
Savez-vous comment y aller?	*Do you know how to get there?*
Il a écrit je ne sais quoi	*He has written something or other*

Dieu seul le sait! — *God only knows!*
Dieu sait quand on mangera! — *God knows when we're going to eat!*

TENIR—*to hold*

Tiens, tenez ma main — *Hold my hand*

Cette voiture tient bien la route — *This car holds the road well*

Tiens! — *Well, well!*

Tenez, je vais vous montrer — *Here, I'll show you*

Ce compartiment ne tient que six personnes — *This compartment only holds six people*

Il tient de sa mère — *He takes after his mother*

Une pièce bien tenue — *A tidy, well-kept room*

Il tient un petit hôtel — *He runs a small hotel*

Tenir sa promesse — *To keep one's promise*

Tenez votre gauche — *Keep to the left*

Cette armoire tient trop de place — *This cupboard takes up too much room*

La corde tient bien — *The rope is holding*

C'est une histoire qui ne tient pas debout — *It's a story that doesn't stand up, ring true*

Il ne tient pas en place — *He's restless, can't keep still*

Je ne tenais plus en place — *I couldn't keep still*

Tenez bon! — *Hold tight!*

Une couleur qui tient bien — *A fast colour*

Je tiens beaucoup à mon chien — *I'm very fond of my dog*

Nous tenons à y aller — *We're keen on going*

Nous irons puisqu'il y tient tellement — *We'll go since he's so set on it*

Il ne tient qu'à vous — *It rests with you*

Elle ne se tenait pas de joie — *She was beside herself with joy*

Je ne sais pas à quoi m'en tenir — *I don't know what to believe*

CROIRE—*to believe, think*

Je ne vous crois pas	*I don't believe you*
Est-ce qu'il vient? Oui, je crois	*Is he coming? Yes, I think so*
Je crois qu'il viendra	*I think he'll come*
Je ne crois pas qu'il vienne	*I don't think he'll come*
Je le crois bien!	*I should think so!*
Je crois bien qu'il est parti	*I do believe, I'm afraid that, he has gone*
N'en croyez rien	*Don't believe a word of it*
Je te croyais perdu	*I thought you were lost*
Je croyais bien faire	*I thought I was doing the right thing*
Il ne pouvait pas en croire ses yeux	*He couldn't believe his eyes*
A l'en croire ...	*According to him ...*
Qu'est-ce qu'elle se croit	*How she fancies herself!*
C'est à ne pas y croire	*It's unbelievable, beyond belief*

DEVOIR—*to owe, have to do*

Tu dois obéir à tes parents	*You must obey your parents*
Il ne sait pas ce qu'il doit faire	*He doesn't know what to do*
Vous devriez voir ce film	*You ought to see this film*
Il croyait devoir le faire	*He thought it his duty to do it*
Vous devez être fatigué	*You must be tired*
Il doit y en avoir beaucoup	*There must be a lot of them*
Vous me devez trois francs	*You owe me three francs*
C'est à lui que je dois tout	*I owe it all to him*
Faire son devoir	*To do one's duty*
Faire ses devoirs	*To do one's homework*

146

SERVIR—*to serve*

Cela m'a beaucoup servi	*That was very useful to me*
Ça ne sert à rien de pleurer	*It's no use crying*
À quoi cela sert-il?	*What's the use of that?*
Servez-vous	*Help yourself*
Je me sers de ceci pour ...	*I use this for ...*
Je m'en sers comme salon	*I use it as a sitting room*
Il a servi pendant la dernière guerre	*He served during the last war*
Le dîner est servi	*Dinner is served*
Est-ce que je peux vous servir?	*Can I serve you?*
Vous servez-vous de cette chaise?	*Are you using, do you use, this chair?*

SENTIR—*to feel, smell*

Je sens que je vais m'ennuyer	*I feel I'm going to be bored*
Je ne me sens pas très bien	*I don't feel very well*
Elle se fait sentir	*She makes her presence felt*
Je me sens beaucoup plus jeune	*I feel much younger*
Il sent le danger	*He smells danger*
Ce parfum sent bon	*This perfume smells nice*
Je ne sens rien	*I can't smell anything*
Ça sent le gaz	*There's a smell of gas*
Je ne peux pas la sentir	*I can't stand her*
Je le sentais venir de loin	*I could feel it coming*
Ces vêtements sentent le moisi	*These clothes smell musty, mouldy*
Elle ne se sent pas de joie	*She's beside herself with joy*
Je me sens tout chose	*I feel all funny*
Je me suis senti idiot	*I felt stupid*

READING TEXTS

LE CORBEAU ET LE RENARD
THE CROW AND THE FOX

Maître Corbeau, sur un arbre perché,
Master Crow, on a tree perched,

Tenait en son bec un fromage.
Was-holding in his beak a cheese.

Maître Renard, par l'odeur alléché,
Master Fox, by the smell attracted,

Lui tint à peu près ce langage;
To-him held [spoke] more or less this speech:

Hé! bonjour, Monsieur du Corbeau,
Hey! good day, Mr. (of the) Crow,

Que vous êtes joli! que vous me semblez beau!
How you are pretty! how you to-me seem handsome!

Sans mentir, si votre ramage
Without to-lie, if your singing

Se rapporte à votre plumage,
Is equal to your plumage,

Vous êtes le phénix des hôtes de ces bois.
You are the phoenix of the inhabitants of these woods.

A ces mots le Corbeau ne se sent pas de joie;
At these words the crow himself feels not of joy [was beside himself with joy]

Et, pour montrer sa belle voix,
And, for to-show his beautiful voice,

Il ouvre un large bec, laisse tomber sa proie,
He opens a large beak, lets to-fall [drops] his prey.

Le Renard s'en saisit, et dit: Mon bon Monsieur,
The Fox (himself) of-it seizes, and says: My good Sir,

Apprenez que tout flatteur
Learn that every flatterer

Vit aux dépens de celui qui l'écoute.
Lives at-the expenses of he who him listens-to.

Cette leçon vaut bien un fromage, sans doute.
This lesson is-worth well a cheese, without doubt.

Le Corbeau, honteux et confus,
The Crow, ashamed and confused,

Jura, mais un peu tard, qu'on ne l'y prendrait plus.
Swore, but a little late, that one him there would-take no more.

LA FONTAINE (1621-95)

148

L'ALOUETTE ET SES PETITS AVEC LE MAITRE D'UN CHAMP
THE SKYLARK AND HER LITTLE-ONES WITH THE MASTER [OWNER] OF A FIELD

Les alouettes font leur nid
The skylarks   make their nest

Dans les blés, quand ils sont en   herbe,
In   the corn, when   they are   in [the] blade,

C'est-à-dire environ le temps
That is-to-say   about   the time

Que tout   aime et que tout   pullule dans le monde,
That everything loves and that everything multiplies in   the world,

Monstres marins au   fond de l'onde,
Monsters   marine   at-the bottom of the wave [ocean],

Tigres dans les forêts, alouettes aux champs.
Tigers in   the forests, skylarks in-the fields.

Une pourtant de ces dernières
One   however   of these last

Avait laissé passer la moitié d'un printemps
Had   let   to-pass the half   of a   spring

Sans goûter le plaisir des amours printanières.
Without to-taste the pleasure of the loves   of-spring.

A toute force enfin elle se   résolut
Nevertheless   at-last she (herself) resolved

D'imiter la   nature et d'être mère encore.
To imitate (the) nature   and to-be   mother again.

Elle bâtit un nid, pond, couve et fait éclore
She   builds a nest, lays,   incubates and makes to-hatch

A la hâte: le tout   alla du mieux qu'il put.
In (the) haste: (the) everything went of the best   that it could.

Les blés d'alentour mûrs avant que la nitée
The corn of round-about ripe before   (that) the brood

Se trouvât assez forte encore
(It at) found   enough strong yet

Pour voler et prendre l'essor,
(For) to-fly and to-take   the flight [to take wing],

De mille   soins divers l'Alouette agitée
By a-thousand cares various the skylark   agitated

S'en va chercher pâture, avertit ses enfants
Goes-away to-look-for food,   warns her children

D'être toujours au guet   et faire   sentinelle.
To-be   always   on-the-watch and to make [mount] guard.

Si le possesseur de ces champs
If the owner   of these fields

Vient avec son fils, comme il viendra, dit-elle,
Comes with his son, when   he will-come, said-she

Ecoutez bien: selon ce qu'il dira
Listen well: according-to that which he will-say

Chacun de nous décampera.
Each-one of us will-decamp.

Sitôt que l'Alouette eut quitté sa famille,
As soon as the skylark had left her family,

Le possesseur du champ vient avec son fils.
The owner of-the field comes with his son.

Ces blés sont mûrs, dit-il: allez chez nos amis
This corn is ripe, said-he: go to-the-house-of our friends

Les prier que chacun, apportant sa faucille,
Them to-ask that each-one, bringing his sickle,

Nous vienne aider demain dès la pointe du jour.
To-us comes to-help tomorrow from the point [break] of-the day.

Notre Alouette de retour
Our skylark of return [returning]

Trouve en alarme sa couvée.
Finds in alarm her brood.

L'un commence: Il a dit que, l'aurore levée,
(The) one begins: He said that, the dawn risen,

L'on fît venir demain ses amis pour l'aider.
(The) one makes to-come tomorrow his friends for him to-help.

—S'il n'a dit que cela, repartit l'Alouette,
—If he said only that, answered the skylark.

Rien ne nous presse encore de changer de retraite;
Nothing us presses yet (of) to-change (of) retreat;

Mais c'est demain qu'il faut tout de bon écouter.
But it is tomorrow that it is-necessary everything in real earnest to listen.

Cependant soyez gais; voilà de quoi manger.
Meanwhile be gay; there-is of what [something] to eat.

Eux repus, tout s'endort, les petits et la mère.
Them repasted, everyone goes to sleep, the little-ones and the mother.

L'aube du jour arrive, et d'amis point du tout.
The dawn of-the day arrives, and of friends none of the [at] all.

L'Alouette à l'essor, le maître s'en vient faire
The Skylark on the wing, the owner then comes to-do

Sa ronde ainsi qu'à l'ordinaire.
His round as at the ordinary [as usual].

Ces blés ne devraient pas, dit-il, être debout.
This corn ought not, said-he, to-be standing.

Nos amis ont grand tort, et tort qui se repose
Our friends have great wrong [are very wrong], and wrong whoever (himself) relies

Sur de tels paresseux, à servir ainsi lents.
On any such lazy-people, (to) to-serve thus slow.

Mon fils, allez chez   nos parents
My   son, go to-the-houses-of our   relations

Les prier de la même chose.
Them to-ask (of) the same   thing.

L'épouvante est au   nid plus forte que jamais.
The terror   is in-the nest more strong than ever.

—Il a dit ses parents, mère! c'est à cette heure ...
—He said his relations, mother! it is at this time ...

—Non, mes enfants; dormez en paix:
—No,   my children; sleep in peace:

Ne bougeons de notre demeure.
Not let-us-move from our   dwelling.

L'Alouette eut raison;   car personne ne vint.
The Skylark has reason [was right]; because nobody   came.

Pour la troisième fois, le maître se   souvint
For   the third   time, the owner (himself) remembered

De visiter ses blés. Notre erreur est extrême,
To-visit his corn. Our error is extreme,

Dit-il, de nous attendre à   d'autres gens que nous.
Said-he, ourselves to-wait-for [rely on] other people than ourselves.

Il n'est meilleur ami ni parent que soi-même.
There isn't better   friend or relation than oneself.

Retenez bien cela, mon fils. Et savez-vous
Remember well that, my son. And do you know

Ce qu'il faut   faire? Il faut   qu'avec notre famille
That which it is-necessary to-do? It is-necessary that with our   household

Nous prenions dès demain chacun une faucille:
We   take   from tomorrow each-one a   sickle:

C'est là notre plus court;   et nous achèverons
It is then our most short [easiest way]; and we   will-finish

Notre moisson quand nous pourrons.
Our harvest when we   will-be-able.

Dès lors que ce dessein fut su   de l'Alouette:
From when this plan   was known of the Skylark:

—C'est ce coup qu'il est bon de partir, mes enfants!
—It is this time that it is good to-leave, my children!

Et les petits, en   même temps,
And the little-ones, in [at the] same time,

Voletants, se   culebutants,
Fluttering, (themselves) tumbling,

Délogèrent tous   sans trompette.
Left-the-home all-of-them without trumpet [making a noise].

LA FONTAINE (1621-95)

151

LE GOÛT DU NÉANT
THE TASTE OF-(THE) NOTHINGNESS

Morne esprit, autrefois amoureux de la lutte,
Dejected spirit, once enamoured of the struggle,

L'Espoir, dont l'éperon attisait ton ardeur,
(The) Hope, of-which the spur was-stirring your ardour,

Ne veut plus t'enfourcher! Couche-toi sans pudeur,
Wishes no longer you to-mount! Lie-down-yourself without shame,

Vieux cheval dont le pied à chaque obstacle butte.
Old horse of-whom the foot at each obstacle stumbles.

Résigne-toi, mon coeur; dors ton sommeil de brute.
Resign-yourself, my heart; sleep your sleep of brute.

Esprit vaincu, fourbu! Pour toi, vieux maraudeur,
Spirit conquered, worn-out! For you, old plunderer,

L'amour n'a plus de goût, non plus que la dispute;
(The) love has no longer any taste, no more than (the) argument;

Adieu donc, chants du cuivre et soupirs de la flûte!
Goodbye then, songs of-(the) brass and sighs of the flute!

Plaisirs, ne tentez plus un coeur sombre et boudeur!
Pleasures, tempt no longer a heart gloomy and sulky!

Le Printemps adorable a perdu son odeur!
The Spring adorable has lost its odour!

Et le Temps m'engloutit minute par minute,
And (the) Time me engulfs minute by minute,

Comme la neige immense un corps pris de roideur;
Like the snow immense a body taken with stiffening;

Je contemple d'en haut le globe en sa rondeur
I contemplate from in [on] high the globe in its roundness

Et je n'y cherche plus l'abri d'une cahute.
And I there look-for no longer the shelter of a hut.

Avalanche, veux-tu m'emporter dans ta chute?
Avalanche, will-you me carry-off in your fall?

CHARLES BAUDELAIRE (1821-67)

UN DUEL
A DUEL

La guerre était finie; les Allemands occupaient la France;
The war was finished; the Germans were-occupying (the) France;
de Paris les premiers trains sortaient, allant aux frontières
from Paris the first trains were-leaving, going to-the frontiers
nouvelles, traversant avec lenteur les campagnes et les villages.
new, crossing with slowness the countryside and the villages.
Les premiers voyageurs regardaient par les portières les plaines
The first travellers were-looking-at through the doors the plains
ruinées. Devant les portes des maisons restées debout, des
ruined. Before the doors of-the houses remained [still] standing, some
soldats prussiens fumaient leur pipe, à cheval sur des chaises.
soldiers Prussian were-smoking their pipes, at horse on [straddling] chairs.
Quand on passait par les villes, on voyait des régiments entiers
When one was-passing by the towns, one was-seeing regiments entire
manoeuvrant sur les places.
manoeuvring on the squares.

M. Dubois, gros marchand riche et pacifique, allait
M. Dubois, fat merchant rich and peaceable, was-going
rejoindre en Suisse sa femme et sa fille, envoyées par
to-rejoin in Switzerland his wife and his daughter sent by
prudence à l'étranger, avant l'invasion, et maintenant
prudence [for safety] abroad, before the invasion, and now
qu'il gagnait la frontière, il voyait pour la première fois
that he was-reaching the frontier, he was-seeing for the first time
des Prussiens. Il regardait avec une terreur irritée ces
(some) Prussians. He was-looking-at with a terror annoyed these
hommes barbus et armés installés comme chez eux sur la terre
men bearded and armed installed as-if at-home on the soil
de France.
of France.

Dans son compartiment, deux Anglais, venus pour voir,
In his compartment, two Englishmen, come (for) to-see,
regardaient de leurs yeux tranquilles et curieux. Ils étaient
were-looking with their eyes quiet and curious. They were
gros aussi tous deux et causaient en leur langue.
fat too all two [both of them] and were-speaking in their language.

Tout à coup, le train s'étant arrêté à la gare d'une
Suddenly, the train (itself) being [having] stopped at the station of a
petite ville, un officier prussien monta dans le compartiment.
small town, an officer Prussian climbed into the compartment.

153

Il était grand et barbu jusqu'aux yeux. Les Anglais aussitôt
He was   tall   and bearded as-far-as to-the eyes.   The Englishmen at-once

se   mirent   à le contempler avec des sourires de
themselves put [began] him to contemplate with   smiles   of

curiosité satisfaite, tandis que M. Dubois faisait   semblant
curiosity   satisfied,   while   (that) M. Dubois was-making semblance [pretended]

de lire un journal, blotti dans son coin, comme un voleur
to read a   newspaper, huddled in his   corner like   a   thief

en face d'un gendarme.
opposite   a   policeman.

Le train se remit en marche. Soudain l'officier prussien,
The train   started up again.   Suddenly the officer Prussian,

indiquant un village, prononça en français:
indicating a   village, pronounced in French:

—J'ai tué douze Français dans ce village.
—I (have) killed twelve Frenchmen in   that village.

Les Anglais, tout à fait intéressés, demandèrent aussitôt:
The Englishmen, completely   interested,   asked   at-once:

—Aoh! Quel est le nom de ce village?
—Oh!   What is the name of that village?

Le Prussien répondit: "Phalsbourg".
The Prussian   replied: "Phalsbourg".

Et il regardait M. Dubois en riant   orgueilleusement.
And he looked-at M. Dubois (in) laughing haughtily.

Le train roulait, traversant toujours des villages occupés.
The train   was-rolling, crossing   always [still]   villages occupied.

On voyait   les soldats allemands le long des routes, au bord
One was-seeing (the) soldiers German   along   the roads,   at-the side

des champs. On les voyait   partout.
of-the fields.   One them was-seeing everywhere.

L'officier tendit la main:
The officer   held-out the hand:

—Si j'avais le commandement, j'aurais tué tout le monde.
—If I had   the command,   I would-have killed everybody.

Plus de France!
No more   France!

Les Anglais, par   politesse, répondirent simplement:
The Englishmen, through politeness, answered   simply:

—Aoh! yes.
—Oh! yes.

Il continua:
He continued:

—Dans vingt ans toute l'Europe, toute, appartiendra à nous.
—In   twenty years all   (the) Europe. all,   will-belong   to us.

La Prusse plus forte que tous!
(The) Prussia more strong than everyone!

154

Les Anglais, inquiets, ne répondaient plus. Alors l'officier
The Englishmen, uneasy, answered no more. Then the officer

se mit à rire. Il insultait la France écrasée, insultait les
began to to-laugh. He insulted (the) France crushed, insulted the

ennemis à terre. Et soudain il mit ses bottes contre les cuisses
enemies on-the ground. And suddenly he put his boots against the thighs

de M. Dubois, qui détournait les yeux, rouge jusqu'aux
of M. Dubois, who turned-away the eyes, red as-far-as to-the

oreilles.
ears.

L'officier tira sa pipe, et regardant fixement le Français:
The officer drew [out] his pipe and looking-at fixedly the Frenchman:

—Vous n'auriez pas de tabac?
—You wouldn't have any tobacco?

M. Dubois répondit:
M. Dubois replied:

—Non, monsieur!
—No, sir!

L'Allemand reprit:
The German retook [went on]:

—Je vous prie d'aller en acheter quand le train s'arrêtera.
—I you beg to-go some to-buy when the train (itself) will-stop.

Et il se mit à rire de nouveau.
And he began to to-laugh anew.

—Je vous donnerai un pourboire!
—I you will-give a tip!

Le train siffla, ralentissant sa marche. Puis il s'arrêta
The train whistled, slowing-down its speed. Then it stopped

tout à fait.
completely.

L'Allemand ouvrit la portière et, prenant par le bras M.
The German opened the door and, taking by the arm M.

Dubois:
Dubois:

—Allez faire ma commission, vite, vite!
—Go to-do my errand, quickly, quickly!

La machine déjà sifflait pour repartir. Alors brusquement
The engine already was-whistling for to-restart. Then quickly

M. Dubois s'élança sur le quai et malgré les gestes
M. Dubois (himself) sprang on-to the platform and in-spite-of the gestures

du chef de gare, il se précipita dans le compartiment voisin.
of-the station master, he (himself) dashed into the compartment neighbouring.

Il était seul! Le train s'arrêta de nouveau dans une station.
He was alone! The train stopped again in a station.

155

Et tout à coup l'officier parut à la portière et monta, suivi
And all at once the officer appeared at the door and climbed-in, followed

bientôt des deux Anglais que la curiosité poussait. L'Allemand
soon by-the two Englishmen whom (the) curiosity was-pushing. The German

s'assit en face du Français et, riant toujours:
sat down opposite the Frenchman and, laughing still:

—Vous n'avez pas voulu faire ma commission.
—You have not wished to-do my errand.

M. Dubois répondit:
M. Dubois replied:

—Non, monsieur!
—No, sir!

Le train venait de repartir.
The train was-coming of to-restart [had just restarted].

L'officier dit:
The officer said:

—Je vais couper votre moustache pour bourrer ma pipe.
—I am-going to cut your moustache for to-fill my pipe.

Et il avança la main vers la figure de son voisin. Les
And he advanced the hand towards the face of his neighbour. The

Anglais regardaient de leurs yeux fixes.
Englishmen were-looking with their eyes fixed.

Déjà l'Allemand avait pris la moustache et tirait dessus,
Already the German had taken the moustache and was-pulling on-it,

quand M. Dubois, le saisissant au collet, le rejeta sur la
when M. Dubois, him seizing at-the collar, him threw-back on the

banquette. Puis fou de colère il se mit à lui taper furieusement
seat. Then mad with anger, he began to (to-him) to-hit furiously

des coups de poing par la figure. Le Prussien essaya de tirer
with blows of fist on the face. The Prussian tried to-draw

son sabre, mais M. Dubois tapait, tapait sans repos, sans
his sabre, but M. Dubois was-hitting, was-hitting without rest, without

savoir où tombaient les coups. Le sang coulait: l'Allemand,
to-know where were-falling the blows. The blood was-flowing: the German,

étranglé, crachait ses dents, essayait, mais en vain, de rejeter
throttled, spat [out] his teeth, tried, but in vain, to-throw-back

ce gros homme exaspéré. Les Anglais, pleins de joie et de
this fat man exasperated. The Englishmen, full of joy and of

curiosité, s'étaient levés et rapprochés pour mieux voir.
curiosity, had risen and come-nearer for better to-see.

Et soudain M. Dubois, épuisé par un pareil effort,
And suddenly M. Dubois, exhausted by a like [such an] effort,

se rassit sans dire un mot.
sat-down-again without to-say a word.

Le Prussien ne se   jeta pas sur lui, tant   il demeurait
The Prussian   himself threw not on   him, so-much he was-remaining

stupide d'étonnement et de douleur. Enfin il prononça:
stupid   with astonishment and with pain.   At-last he pronounced:

—Si vous ne voulez pas me   rendre raison   avec le
If   you   will   not to-me render reason [satisfaction] with the

pistolet je vous tuerai.
pistol   I you will-kill.

M. Dubois répondit:
M. Dubois replied:

—Quand vous voudrez. Je veux bien.
—When   you   will-wish. I wish well [I am quite willing].

L'Allemand reprit.
The German   went-on.

—Voici Strasbourg, je prendrai deux officiers pour témoins.
—Here-is Strasbourg, I shall-take two   officers   for   witnesses.

J'ai le temps avant que le train reparte.
I have the time   before (that) the train   restarts.

M. Dubois dit aux Anglais:
M. Dubois said to-the Englishmen:

—Voulez-vous être mes témoins?
—Will-you   (to)-be my witnesses?

Tous deux répondirent ensemble:
Both   replied   together:

—Aoh, Yes!

Et le train s'arrêta.
And the train   stopped.

En une minute, le Prussien avait trouvé deux camarades qui
In one minute, the Prussian had   found   two   comrades   who

apportèrent des pistolets, et on gagna   les remparts.
brought   (some) pistols, and one gained [they reached] the ramparts.

M. Dubois n'avait jamais tenu un pistolet. On le plaça à
M. Dubois had   never   held a pistol. They him placed at

vingt pas de son ennemi. On lui   demanda:
twenty paces from his enemy. They to-him asked:

—Etes-vous prêt?
—Are-you   ready?

En répondant "oui, monsieur!" il s'aperçut qu'un des
In answering "yes, sir!"   he noticed   that one of-the

Anglais avait ouvert son parapluie pour se garantir du soleil.
Englishmen had   opened his umbrella   for himself to-protect from-the sun.

Une voix commanda:
A voice commanded:

—Feu!
—Fire!

157

M. Dubois tira,　　au hasard, sans　attendre, et il aperçut
M.　Dubois　　drew [fired], at　random,　without to-wait,　　and he noticed

avec stupeur le Prussien, debout en face de lui, qui chancelait,
with stupor　the Prussian,　standing opposite　　him, who staggered,

levait les bras et tombait raide sur le nez.
lifted　the arms and fell　　stiff　　on　the nose [flat on his face].

Il l'avait tué!
He him had killed!

Le train partait. Ils sautèrent dans leur voiture. Alors
The train　was-leaving. They jumped　into　their carriage.　Then

les Anglais, ôtant leurs toques de voyage, les levèrent en les
the Englishmen, doffing their　travelling-caps,　　　them raised　while them

agitant, puis trois fois de suite　ils crièrent:
waving,　then　three times in succession they cried:

—Hip, hip, hip, hurrah!

Puis ils tendirent gravement, l'un après l'autre, la main
Then they held-out　gravely,　(the) one after　the other,　the hand

droite à M. Dubois, et ils retournèrent s'asseoir côte à côte dans
right　to M. Dubois,　and they returned　　to-sit-down side by side　in

leur coin.
their corner.

GUY DE MAUPASSANT (1850-1893)

LA PESTE
THE PLAGUE

Après dîner, Rieux et sa mère vinrent s'installer près du
After　dinner,　Rieux and his mother came themselves to-install near　the

malade. La nuit commençait pour lui dans la lutte et Rieux
sick-man. The night was-beginning　for　him in　the struggle and Rieux

savait que ce dur combat avec l'ange de la peste devait durer
knew　that this hard fight　with　the angel of the plague must　last

jusqu'à l'aube. Tarrou luttait　immobile. Pas une seule fois,
until　the dawn. Tarrou　was-fighting motionless.　Not one　single time,

non plus, il ne parla. Rieux suivait seulement les phases du
either,　he (not) spoke. Rieux　followed only　the stages of-the

combat aux yeux de son ami, tour à tour ouverts ou fermés,
combat in-the eyes of his　friend, turn by turn open　or closed,

le regard fixé sur un objet ou ramené sur le docteur et sa
the gaze fixed on an object or brought-back on the doctor and his

mère. Chaque fois que le docteur rencontrait ce regard, Tarrou
mother. Each time that the doctor met this look, Tarrou

souriait, dans un grand effort.
smiled, in a great effort.

Il pleuvait. Dans l'ombre de la pièce, Rieux, un instant
It was-raining. In the darkness of the room, Rieux, a moment

distrait par la pluie, contemplait de nouveau Tarrou. Sa mère
distracted by the rain, contemplated once more Tarrou. His mother

tricotait, levant de temps en temps la tête pour regarder atten-
was-knitting, lifting from time to time the head for to-look-at atten-

tivement le malade. Le docteur avait fait maintenant tout ce
tively the sick-man. The doctor had done now all that

qu'il y avait à faire. Après la pluie, le silence s'épaissit dans la
there was to do. After the rain, the silence (itself) thickened in the

chambre, pleine seulement du tumulte d'une guerre invisible.
bedroom, full only of-the tumult of a war invisible.

Rieux se leva pour faire boire le malade et revint s'asseoir.
Rieux himself raised for to-make to-drink the sick-man and came-again to sit down.

Des passants marchaient rapidement sur le trottoir. Le
(Some) passers-by were-walking quickly on the pavement. The

docteur pour la première fois reconnut que cette nuit, pleine de
doctor for the first time realized that this night, full of

promeneurs tardifs et sans les timbres d'ambulances, était
walkers late and without the sirens of ambulances, was

semblable à celles d'autrefois. C'était une nuit délivrée de la
similar to those of before. It was a night delivered from the

peste.
plague.

Le froid du matin commençait à se faire sentir dans la
The cold of-the morning began to itself to-make to-feel in the

chambre. Le docteur frissona et, regardant Tarrou, il comprit
bedroom. The doctor shivered and, looking-at Tarrou, he understood

qu'une pause avait eu lieu et que le malade dormait. A la
that a pause had had [taken] place and that the sick-man was-sleeping. At the

fenêtre le jour était encore noir. Quand le docteur avança vers
window the day was still dark. When the doctor advanced towards

le lit, Tarrou le regardait de ses yeux sans expression.
the bed, Tarrou him looked-at with his eyes without expression.

—Vous avez dormi, n'est-ce pas? demanda Rieux.
—You have slept, haven't you? asked Rieux.

—Oui.
—Yes.

159

—Respirez-vous mieux?
—Are you breathing   better?

—Un peu. Cela veut-il dire quelque chose?
—A little.   That wishes-it to-say [Does that mean] some thing?

Rieux ne répondit pas tout de suite, mais au bout d'un
Rieux   answered   not   at   once,   but at-the end   of a

moment il dit:
moment   he said:

—Non, Tarrou, cela ne veut rien dire.
—No,   Tarrou,   that means nothing.

—Merci, dit Tarrou. Répondez-moi toujours exactement.
—Thanks, said Tarrou.   Answer-me   always   truthfully.

Rieux s'était assis au pied du lit. Il sentait près de lui les
Rieux was [had] sat down at the foot of the bed. He felt   near   him the

jambes du   malade, longues et dures. Tarrou respirait plus
legs   of-the sick-man, long   and hard. Tarrou was-breathing more

fortement.
strongly.

—La fièvre va   reprendre, n'est-ca pas, Rieux? dit-il
—The fever is-going to-retake, isn't it,   Rieux? said-he

d'une voix essoufflée.
in a voice breathless.

—Oui, dit Rieux. Buvez.
—Yes,   said Rieux. Drink.

L'autre but et laissa retomber sa tête.
The other drank and let   to-fall back his head.

—C'est long, dit-il.
—It's   long,   said-he.

Rieux lui   prit le bras, et soudain la fièvre reflua visiblement
Rieux to-him took the arm. and suddenly the fever re-flowed visibly

jusqu'à son font. Mais ses yeux brillèrent encore de tout
as-far-as his forehead. But his eyes shone   still   with all

l'éclat   du courage.
the brightness of the courage.

A midi, la fièvre était à son sommet. Dans les intervalles de
At noon, the fever, was at its height.   in   the ntervals   oı

la fièvre, Tarrou de loin en loin   regardait encore ses amis. Mais
the fever, Tarrou from further and further looked-a stil· his friend·. But

bientôt ses yeux s'ouvrirent de moins en moins souvent. Rieux
soon   his eyes (themselves) opened less and less often.   Rieux

n'avait plus devant lui qu'un masque inerte où   le sourire
had no more in-front-of him than a mask   lifeless where the smile

avait disparu. Cette forme humaine qui lui avait été si proche,
had disappeared. This form human   which to-him had been so close,

160

brûlée par un mal surhumain, s'immergeait à ses yeux
burned by a suffering superhuman, (itself) was-sinking before his eyes

dans les eaux de la peste et il ne pouvait rien contre ce
into the waters of the plague and he could [do] nothing against this

naufrage. Et à la fin, ce furent bien les larmes de l'impuissance
shipwreck. And at the end, it was really the tears of (the) impotence

qui empêchèrent Rieux de voir Tarrou se tourner brusquement
that prevented Rieux from seeing Tarrou (himself) turn suddenly

contre le mur, et expirer dans une plainte creuse, comme si,
against the wall, and die in [with] a groan hollow, as if,

quelque part en lui, une corde essentielle s'était rompue.
some where in him, a cord essential (itself) had broken.

from *La Peste* (The Plague) by ALBERT CAMUS (1913-1960)
© Editions Gallimard

PROVERBS

A méchant ouvrier, point de bon outil
To the bad workman no tool is good

L'appétit vient en mangeant
The appetite comes with eating

L'argent est un bon serviteur et un mauvais maître
Money is a good servant and a bad master

Autres temps, autres moeurs
Other times, other customs

Aux grands maux les grands remèdes
To great evils great remedies

Beaucoup de bruit pour rien
Much (noise) ado about nothing

Les beaux esprits se rencontrent
Great minds think alike

Bien mal acquis ne profite jamais
There is never profit from ill-gotten gains

Bonne renommée vaut mieux que ceinture dorée
A good reputation is worth more than wealth

Les bons comptes font les bons amis
Good accounts make good friends

Ce que femme veut, Dieu le veut
What woman wants, God wants (i.e. they always manage to get it)

C'est en forgeant qu'on devient forgeron
It is by working at the forge that you become a blacksmith

Chacun pour soi et Dieu pour tous
Every man for himself and God for everybody

Chat échaudé craint l'eau froide
A scalded cat fears cold water (i.e. even the appearance of what has harmed it)

Le chat parti, les souris dansent
When the cat's away the mice (dance) will play

Comme on fait son lit, on se couche
As you make your bed, you lie on it

Comparaison n'est pas raison
Comparisons prove nothing

Contentement passe richesse
Happiness is worth more than wealth

Déshabiller saint Pierre pour habiller saint Paul
(Undress) Rob Peter to (dress) pay Paul

Deux avis valent mieux qu'un
Two (opinions) heads are better than one

De deux maux il faut choisir le moindre
Choose the lesser of two evils

Dis-moi qui tu hantes, je te dirai qui tu es
Tell me who your friends are, I will tell you what you are

Donner un oeuf pour avoir un boeuf
(To give an) To set a (egg) sprat to catch a (an ox) mackerel

L'enfer est pavé de bonnes intentions
Hell is paved with good intentions

L'exception confirme la règle
The exception proves the rule

Fais ce que dois, advienne que pourra
Do what you must, come what may

La fin justifie les moyens
The end justifies the means

Les grands diseurs ne sont pas les grands faiseurs
The great talkers are not the great doers

L'habitude est une seconde nature
Habit is a second nature

Heureux au jeu, malheureux en amour
Lucky at cards, unlucky in love

Il faut battre le fer pendant qu'il est chaud
You must strike while the iron is hot

Il n'y a pas de fumée sans feu
There's no smoke without a fire

Il n'y a que la vérité qui blesse
It is only the truth that hurts

Il n'y a que le premier pas qui coûte
It is only the first step that is difficult

Il y a loin de la coupe aux lèvres
There's many a slip 'twixt cup and lip

Loin des yeux, loin du coeur
Out of sight, out of mind

Les loups ne se mangent pas entre eux
(Wolves) Dog doesn't eat dog

Mains froides, coeur chaud
Cold hands, warm heart

Mettre la charrue avant les boeufs
To put the (plough) cart before the (oxen) horse

Mieux vaut tard que jamais
Better late than never

Ne fais pas à autrui ce que tu ne voudrais pas qu'on te fît
Don't do to others what you wouldn't have done to you

Nécessité fait loi
Necessity knows no law

N'éveillez pas le chat qui dort
Let sleeping (cat) dogs lie

Nul n'est prophète en son pays
No man is a prophet in his own country

Oeil pour oeil, dent pour dent
An eye for an eye, a tooth for a tooth

L'oisiveté est mère de tous les vices
Idleness is the mother of all vice

On ne fait pas d'omelette sans casser d'oeufs
You can't make an omelette without breaking eggs

163

On reconnaît l'arbre à ses fruits
You recognize the tree by its fruits

Pierre qui roule n'amasse pas mousse
A rolling stone gathers no moss

Plus ça change, plus c'est la même chose
The more things change, the more they stay the same

Point de nouvelles, bonnes nouvelles
No news is good news

Qui aime bien châtie bien
Who loves well punishes well

Quiconque se sert de l'épée périra par l'épée
Who lives by the sword shall die by the sword

Qui ne risque rien n'a rien
Who risks nothing has nothing

Qui sème le vent récolte la tempête
Who sows the wind reaps the storm

Qui se ressemble s'assemble
Birds of a feather flock together

Qui veut la fin veut les moyens
Who wishes the end wishes the means

Rira bien qui rira le dernier
He who laughs last laughs longest

Si jeunesse savait, si vieillesse pouvait
If only youth knew, if only old-age could

Tel père, tel fils
Like father, like son

Tout est bien qui finit bien
All's well that ends well

Tout vient à point à qui sait attendre
Everything comes to him who waits

Une hirondelle ne fait pas le printemps
One swallow doesn't make a (spring) summer

Un tiens vaut mieux que deux tu l'auras
A bird in hand is worth two in the bush

Vouloir, c'est pouvoir
Where there's a will there's a way

164

TRAVELLING

By car ...

accelerator, accélérateur *m*, *back axle*, pont arrière *m*; *battery*, batterie *f*; *bend*, virage *m*; *big end*, tête de bielle *f*; *body*, châssis *m*; *bolt*, boulon *m*; *bonnet*, capot *m*; boot, coffre *m*; *brake*, frein *m*; *brake* (v), freiner; *brake lining*, garniture de frein *f*; *breakdown*, panne *f*; *break down* (v), tomber en panne; *breakdown van*, voiture de dépannage *f*; *bulb*, lampe *f*; *bumper*, pare-chocs *m*; *camshaft*, arbre à cames *m*; *can*, bidon *m*; *car*, voiture *f*; *caravan*, caravane *f*; *carburettor*, carburateur *m*; *clutch*, embrayage *m*; *choke*, starter *m*; *distributor*, distributeur *m*; *diversion*, route deviée *f*; *door*, portière *f*; *drive* (v), conduire; *driver*, chauffeur *m*; *driving licence*, permit de conduire *m*; *dynamo*, dynamo *f*; *engine*. moteur *m*; *exhaust*, échappement *m*; *fan*, ventilateur *m*; *fan belt*, courroie de ventilateur *f*; *funnel*, entonnoir *m*; *garage*, garage *m*; *gear*, vitesse *f*; *gear-box*, boîte de vitesses *f*; *gear lever*, levier de vitesses; *grease*, graisse *f*; *handle*, manivelle *f*; *hood*, capote *f*; *horn*, klaxon *m*; *highway code*, code le de route *m*; *hub*, moyeu *m*; *ignition*, allumage *m*; *ignition key*, clef de contact *f*; *indicator*, clignotant *m*; *inner tube*, chambre à air *f*; *insurance certificate*, certificat d'assurance *m*; *jack*, cric *m*; *lights (head)*, phares *m*; *lights (side)*, feux de position *m*; *lights (rear)*, feux arrière; *lorry*, camion *m*; *lubrication*, graissage *m*; *luggage rack*, porte-baggages *m*; *mechanic*, garagiste *m*; *or* mécanicien *m*; *mirror*, rétroviseur *m*; *motorist*, automobiliste *mf*; *motorway*, autoroute *f*; *number plate*, plaque d'immatriculation *f*; *nut*, écrou *m*; *oil*, huile *f*; *one way*, sens unique; *overheat* (v), chauffer; *park* (v), stationner, se garer; *No parking*, stationnement interdit; *pedestrian*, piéton *m*; *petrol*, essence *f*; *petrol pump*, pompe à essence *f*; *piston ring*, segment de piston *m*; *plug*, bougie *f*; *propeller shaft*, arbre de transmission *m*; *puncture*, crevaison *f*; *radiator*, radiateur *m*; *repair* (v), réparer; *right of way*, priorité *f*; *rim*, jante *f*; *road*, route *f*; *road (major)*, route de priorité *f*; *road (minor)*, route secondaire *f*; *road closed*, route barrée *f*; *run out of petrol*, avoir une panne d'essence; *screw*, vis *f*; *screwdriver*, tournevis *m*; *shock absorber*, amortisseur *m*; *skid*, déraper; *spanner*, clé *f*; *spares*, pièces de remplacement *f*; *speed*, vitesse *f*; *speed limit*, limite de vitesse *f*; *speedometer*, indicateur de vitesse *m*; *spring*, ressort *m*; *starter*, démarreur *m*; *steering wheel*, volant *m*; *street*, rue *f*; *tank*, réservoir à essence *m*; *toll*, péage *m*; *traffic lights*, feux de circulation *m*; *trailer*, remorque *f*; *transmission*, transmission *f*; *two-stroke mixture*, mélange deux temps *m*; *tyre*, pneu *m*; *tyre* (*spare*), roue de secours *f*; *tyre* (*tubeless*), pneu à chambre incorporée *m*; *tyre* (*pressure*), pression des pneus *f*; *underpass*, souterrain *m*; *uneven road*, chaussée deformée *f*; *valve*, valve *f*; *van*, camionnette *f*; *vehicle*, véhicule *f*; *washer*, rondelle *f*; *wheel*, roue *f*; *wheel* (*rear*), roue arrière *f*; *wheel* (*front*), roue avant *f*; *window*, glace *f*; *window* (*rear*), glace arrière *f*; *windscreen*, pare-brise *m*; *windscreen wiper*, essuie-glace *m*; *wing*, aile *f*.

By Train, Boat and Plane . . .

aeroplane, avion *m*; *air conditioner*, climatiseur *m*; *air hostess*, hôtesse de l'air *f*; *airline*, ligne aérienne *f*; *airport*, aéroport *m*; *air terminal*, aérogare *f*; *altitude*, altitude *f*; *anchor*, ancre *f*; *arrival*, arrivée *f*; *ashtray*, cendrier *m*; *boat*, bateau *m*; *booking office*, guichet *m*; *bunk*, couchette *f*; *bus*, autobus *m*; *cabin*, cabine *f*; *captain*, capitaine *m*; *case*, valise *f*; *change trains*, changer de train; *Channel*, Manche *f*; *cloudy*, nuageux; *coach*, car *m*; *compartment*, compartiment *m*; *connection*, correspondance *f*; *control tower*, tour *f* de contrôle; *corridor*, couloir *m*; *crew*, équipage *m*; *crossing*, traversée *f*; *Customs*, Douane *f*; *Customs duty*, droits *m* de Douane; *Customs officer*, Douanier *m*; *deck*, pont *m*; *declare*, déclarer; *delayed*, retardé; *departure*, départ *m*; *destination*, destination *f*; *dining car*, wagon-restaurant *m*; *disembark*, débarquer; *door*, portière *f*; *embark*, embarquer; *emergency exit*, sortie *f* de secours; *engine*, moteur *m*; *enquiry office*, bureau *m* de renseignements; *entrance*, entrée *f*; *escalator*, escalier roulant *m*; *exit*, sortie *f*; *fare*, prix *m*; *ferry*, ferry *m*; *flight*, vol *m*; *fog*, brouillard *m*; *foghorn*, sirène *f*; *funnel*, cheminée *f*; *get on* (*a train etc.*), monter dans; *get off*, descendre de; *goods train*, train *m* de marchandise; *guard*, chef de train *m*; *hand luggage*, bagages *m* à main; *heating*, chauffage *m*; *jet aircraft*, avion *m* à réaction; *jet engine*, réacteur *m*; *label*, étiquette *f*; *land* (v), atterrir; *late*, en retard; *lavatory*, toilette *f*; *left-luggage office*, consigne *m*; *lifeboat*, canot *m* de sauvetage; *life-jacket*, gilet *m* de sauvetage; *lift*, ascenseur *m*; *luggage*, bagages *m*; *luggage rack*, porte-bagages *m*; *luggage van*, fourgon *m*; *ocean*, océan *m*; *passport*, passeport *m*; *pilot*, pilote *m*; *platform*, quai *m*; *port*, port *m*; *porter*, porteur *m*; *propeller*, hélice *f*; *queue*, queue *f*; *queue* (v), faire la queue; *route*, route *f*; *runway*, piste *f*; *sea*, mer *f*; *seat*, place *f*; *seat belt*, ceinture de sécurité *f*; *seat reservation*, réservation *f*; *sleeper*, place *f* de wagon-lit; *sleeping berth*, couchette *f*; *speed*, vitesse *f*; *station*, gare *f*; *stationmaster*, chef de gare *m*; *steward*, steward *m*; *stop*, arrêt *m*; *stop* (v), s'arrêter; *storm*, orage *m*; *take-off*, décollage *m*; *taxi*, taxi *m*; *terminus*, terminus *m*; *ticket (single)*, billet simple *m*; *ticket (return)*, billet aller et retour; *ticket inspector*, contrôleur *m*; *timetable*, horaire *m*; *tip*, pourboire *m*; *track*, voie *f*; *train*, train *m*; *train (express)*, rapide *m*; *travel* (v), voyager; *tray*, plateau *m*; *trunk*, malle *f*; *underground*, métro *m*; *waiting room*, salle d'attente *f*; *weather report*, prévisions *f* météorologiques; *window*, fenêtre *f*.

EATING AND DRINKING

almond, amande *f*; *anchovy*, anchois *m*; *aperitif*, apéritif *m*; *apple*, pomme *f*; *apricot*, abricot *m*; *artichoke (globe)* artichaut *m*, *(Jerusalem)* topinambour *m*; *asparagus*, asperge *f*; *aubergine*, aubergine *f*; *avocado*, avocat *m*; *bacon*, bacon *m*; *banana*, banane *f*; *basil*, basilic *m*; *batter*, pâte à frire *f*; *bay leaf*, laurier *m*; *bean*, haricot *m*; *beef*, boeuf *m*; *beer*, bière *f*; *beetroot*, betterave *f*; *biscuit*, biscuit *m or* gâteau sec *m*; *blackberry*, mûre *f*; *blackcurrant*, cassis *m*; *boar*, sanglier *m*; *boiled*, bouilli *or* à l'eau *(for vegetables)*; *bone*, os *m*; *brains*, cervelle *f*: *brandy*, cognac *m*; *brazil nut*, noix *f* du Brésil; *bread*, pain *m*; *breadcrumbs (uncooked)* chapelure *f (cooked)* gratin *m*; *broth*, bouillon *m*; *brussels sprouts*, choux de Bruxelles *m*; *butter*, beurre *m*; *cabbage*, chou *m*; *cake*, gâteau *m*; *caper*, câpre *f*; *caraway*, cumin *m*; *cheese*, fromage *m*; *chervil*, cerfeuil *m*; *cherry*, cerise *f*; *chicken*, poulet *m*; *chicory*, endive *f*; *chive*, ciboulette *f*; *chocolate*, chocolat *m*; *chop*, côtelette *f*; *cider*, cidre *m*; *cinnamon*. cannelle *f*; *clam*, peigne *m*; *clove*, clou de girofle *m*; *cockle*, coque *f*; *cocoa*, cacao, *m*; *coconut* noix *f* de coco *m*; *cod*, morue *f*; *coffee*, café *m*; *coriander*, coriandre *f*; *cornflour*, farine de maïs *f*; *crab*, crabe *m*; *cream*, crème *f*; *cucumber*, concombre *m*; *damson*, prune *f* de Damas; *date*, datte *f*; *dessert*, dessert *m*; *diet*, régime *m*; *dough*, pâte *f* à pain; *duck*, canard *m*; *duckling*, caneton *m*; *eel*, anguille *f*; *egg*, oeuf *m*; *eggplant*, aubergine *f*; *escallop (of meat)* escalope *f*; *fat*, graisse *f*; *fennel*, fenouil *m*; *fig*, figue *f*; *fish*, poisson *m*; *fizzy*, gazeux; *non-fizzy*, non-gazeux; *flan*, flan *m*; *flour*, farine *f*; *fruit*, fruit *m*; *game*, gibier *m*; *garlic*, ail *m*; *giblets*, abatis *m*; *gherkin*, cornichon *m*; *gin*, gin *m*; *goose*, oie *f*; *gooseberry*, groseille *f* à maquereau; *grape*, raisin *m*; *grapefruit*, pamplemousse *m*; *gravy*, jus (de viande) *m*; *greengage*, reine-Claude *f*; *green pepper*, poivron *m*; *grilled*, grillé; *haddock*, haddock *m*; *hake*, merluche *f*; *ham*, jambon *m*; *hare*, lièvre *m*; *heart*, coeur *m*; *herbs*, herbes *f*; *herring*, hareng *m*; *ice cream*, glace *f*; *ice cube*, glaçon *m*; *icing sugar*, sucre glace *m*; *jam*, confitures *f pl*; *jelly*, gelée *f*; *kidney*, rognon *m*; *lamb*, agneau *m*; *lard*, saindoux *m*; *leek*, poireau *m*; *lemon*, citron *m*; *lemonade* (*fizzy*) limonade ; (*still*), citronade *f*; *lemon juice*, citron pressé *m*; *lentil*, lentille *f*; *lettuce*, laitue *f*; *liver*, foie *m*; *lobster*, langouste *f*, homard *n*; *lollipop*, sucette *f*; *macaroon*, macaron *m*; *mackerel*, maquereau *m*; *marmalade*, confitures d'oranges *f*; *marrow*, courge *f*; *marrow* (*baby*), courgette *f*; *marzipan*, pâte d'amandes *f*; *meat*, viande *f*; *melon*, melon *m*; *meringue*, meringue *f*; *milk*, lait *m*; *minced meat*, viande hachée *f*; *mineral water*, eau minérale *f*; *mint*, menthe *f*; *mushroom*, champignon *m*; *mussel*, moule *f*; *mustard*, moutarde *f*; *mutton*, mouton *m*; *mutton* (*leg of*), gigot *m*; *nougat*, nougat *m*; *nut*, noix *f*; *nutmeg*, noix de muscade *f*; *oil*, huile *f*; *olive*, olive *f*; *omelette*, omelette *f*, *onion*, oignon *m*; *orange*, orange *f*; *orangeade*, orangeade *f*; *orange juice*, jus d'orange *m*; *oyster*, huître *f*; *pancake*, crêpe *f*; *paprika*, paprika *m*; *parsley*, persil *m*; *partridge*, perdrix *f*, *pasta*, pâtes *f*; *pastry*, pâte *f*; *pastries*, pâtisseries *f*; *pâté*, pâté *m*; *pea*, pois *m*; *peach*, pêche *f*; *peanut*, cacahuète *f*; *pear*, poire *f*; *pepper*, poivre *m*; *pheasant*, faisan *m*; *picnic*, pique-nique *m*; *pigeon*, pigeon *m*; *pineapple*, ananas *m*; *plaice*, carrelet *m*; *plum*, prune *f*; *poached*, poché; *pork*, porc *m*; *port*, porto *m*; *potato*, pomme de terre *f*; *poultry*, volaille *f*; *prawn*, bouquet *m*; *prune*, pruneau *m*; *quail*, caille *f*; *rabbit*, lapin *m*; *radish*, radis *m*; *raisin*, raisin sec *m*; *raspberry*, framboise *f*; *redcurrant*, groseille rouge *f*; *rhubarb*, rhubarbe *f*; *rice*, riz *m*; *roast*, rôti *m*; *roe* (*hard*) oeufs de poisson (*m*); *roe* (*soft*) laitance *f*; *roll*, petit pain *m*; *rosemary*, romarin *m*; *rum*, rhum *m*; *saffron*, safran *m*; *sage*, sauge *m*; *salad*, salade *f*; *salmon*, saumon *m*; *salt*, sel *m*; *sandwich*, sandwich *m*; *sardine*, sardine *f*; *sauce*, sauce *f*; *sausage* (*cooked*), saucisson *m*; *sausage* (*raw*), saucisse *f*; *scallop*, coquille St. Jacques *f*; *seasoning*, assaisonnement *m*; *semolina*, semoule *f*; *shallot*, échalote *f*; *sherry*, sherry *m*; *shrimp*, crevette *f*; *skate*, raie *f*; *smoked*, fumé; *soda water*, soda *m*; *sole*,

sole *f*; *soup*, soupe *f* or potage *m*; *spaghetti*, spaghetti *m pl*; *spice*, épice *f*; *spinach*, épinard *m*; *starter*, hors d'oeuvre *m*; *steak*, steak *m*; *stew*, ragoût *m*; *stock*, bouillon *m*; *strawberry*, fraise *f*; *stuffed*, farci; *stuffing*, farce *f*; *suet*, graisse de rognon *m*; *sugar*, sucre *m* ; *sultana*, raisin sec de Smyrne *m* ; *sweets*, bonbons *m*; *sweetbreads*, ris *m*; *syrup*, sirop *m*; *tangerine*, mandarine *f*; *tarragon*, estragon *m*; *tart*, tarte *f*; *tea*, thé *m*; *thyme*, thym *m*; *toast*, toast *m*, or pain grillé *m*; *toffee*, caramel *m*; *tomato*, tomate *f*; *tongue*, langue *f*; *tonic water*, tonic *m*; *tripe*, tripes *f pl*; *trout*, truite *f*; *tuna*, thon *m*; *turbot*, turbot *m*; *turkey*, dinde *f*; *turnip*, navet *m*; *vanilla*, vanille *f*; *veal*, veau *m*; *vegetable*, légume *m*; *vinegar*, vinaigre *m*; *vitamin*, vitamine *f*; *walnut*, noix *f*; *water*, eau *f*; *watercress*, cresson *m*; *whiting*, merlan *m*; *wine*, vin *m*; *winkle*, bigorneau *m*; *woodcock*, bécasse *f*; *yeast*, levure *f*; *yoghurt*, yahourt *m*.

HOUSE AND HOUSEHOLD

address book, carnet d'adresses *m*; *ant*, fourmi *f*; *armchair*, fauteuil *m*; *ashtray*, cendrier *m*; *axe*, hache *f*; *balcony*, balcon *m*; *basket*, panier *m*; *bath*, baignoire *f*; *bathroom*, salle *f* de bain; *beam*, poutre *f*; *bed*, lit *m*; *bed (double)*, lit à deux personnes *m*; *bedroom*, chambre *f*; *bedbug*, punaise *f* (des lits); *bee*, abeille *f*; *binoculars*, jumelles *f*; *blanket*, couverture *f*; *bleach*, blanc de lessive *m*; *block of flats*, immeuble *m*; *blotting paper*, buvard *m*; *bluebottle*, mouche à viande *f*; *biro*, stylo à bille *m*; *boiler*, chaudière *f*; *bolt*, boulon *m*; *bolt (door)* verrou *m*; *book*, livre *m*; *bookcase*, bibliothèque *f*; *bottle*, bouteille *f*; *bowl (eating)* bol *m*; *bowl (washing)*, cuvette *f*; *box*, boîte *f*; *brick*, brique *f*; *briefcase*, serviette *f*; *broom*, balai *m*; *brush*, brosse *f*; *bucket*, seau *m*; *button*, bouton *m*; *camp-bed*, lit de camp *m*; *candle*, bougie *f*; *candle-stick*, porte-bougie *m*; *carpet (fitted)* moquette *f*; *carpet (loose)* tapis *m*; *ceiling*, plafond *m*; *cellar*, cave *f*; *cellotape*, cellotape *m*; *central heating*, chauffage central *m*; *chair*, chaise *f*; *chest*, coffre *m*; *chimney*, cheminée *f*; *clock*, pendule *f*; *clothespeg*, pince à linge *f*; *cloakroom*, vestiaire *m*; *coal*, charbon *m*; *coat hanger*, cintre *m*; *comb*, peigne *m*; *cooker*, cuisinière *f*; *corkscrew*, tire-bouchon *m*; *cot*, lit d'enfant *m*; *cotton*, fil à coudre *m*; *cottonwool*, coton hydrophile *m*; *cupboard*, placard *m*; *cushion*, coussin *m*; *curtain*, rideau *m*; *decanter*, carafe *f*; *deck chair*, chaise longue *f*; *desk*, bureau *m*; *detergent*, détergent *m*; *diction-*

ary, dictionnaire *m*; *dining-room*, salle à manger *f*; *dishcloth*, torchon, *m* serpillière *f*; *doll*, poupée *f*; *doll's house*, maison de poupée *f*; *door*, porte *f*; *door (front)*, porte de devant *f*; *door (back)*, porte de derrière *f*; *doorbell*, sonnette *f*; *doorknob*, poignée *f*; *drain*, égout *m*; *drainpipe*, tuyau d'écoulement *m*; *draught*, courant d'air *m*; *drawer*, tiroir *m*; *drawing-pin*, punaise *f*; *dry rot*, pourriture sèche *f*; *dust*, poussière *f*; *dustbin*, poubelle *f*; *duster*, chiffon *m* (à épousseter); *eggcup*, coquetier *m*; *eiderdown*, édredon *m*; *elastic*, élastique *m*; *electricity*, électricité *f*; *envelope*, enveloppe *f*; *file (for documents)* dossier *m*; *file (tool)* lime *f*; *filter*, filtre *m*; *fire*, feu, *m*; *fireplace*, cheminée *f*; *flannel*, gant de toilette *m*; *flat*, appartement *m*; *flea*, puce *f*; *floor*, plancher *m*; *flower pot*, pot à fleurs *m*; *fly*, mouche *f*; *fork*, fourchette *f*; *fountain pen*, stylo *m*; *fridge*, réfrigérateur *m*; *frying pan*, poêle *f*; *funnel*, entonnoir *m*; *furnished*, meublé; *fuse*, plomb *m*; *garden*, jardin *m*; *gas*, gaz *m*; *gas cylinder*, bombonne à gaz *f*; *gas meter*, compteur à gaz *m*; *glass*, verre *m*; *greenhouse*, serre *f*; *ground sheet*, tapis de sol *m*; *gutter*, gouttière *f*; *glue*, colle *f*; *hairbrush*, brosse à cheveux *f*; *hall*, entrée *f*; *hammer*, marteau *m*; *handbag*, sac à main *m*; *high chair*, chaise haute *f*; *hinge*, charnière *f*; *hoe*, sarcloir *m*; *hook*, crochet *m*; *hook and eye*, agrafe et oeillet *m*; *hot water bottle*, bouillotte *f*; *ink*, encre *f*; *insulation*, isolation *f*; *iron*, fer à repasser *m*; *iron* (v), repasser; *ironing board*, planche à repasser *f*; *jamb*, chambranle *m* (de porte); *jug*, cruche *f*; *kettle*, bouilloire *f*; *key*, clef *or* clé *f*; *keyhole*, trou de serrure *m*; *kitchen*, cuisine *f*; *knife*, couteau *m*; *knit*, tricoter; *knitting needle*, aiguille à tricoter *f*; *ladder*, échelle *f*; *ladle*, louche *f*; *lamp (bedside)*, lampe de chevet *f*; *lampshade*, abat-jour *m*; *laundry*, lessive *f*; *lavatory*, toilette *f*; *lavatory paper*, papier hygiénique *m*; *lawn*, pelouse *f*; *lawnmower*, tondeuse *f*; *letterbox*, boîte aux lettres *f*; *light*, lumière *f*; *light switch*, interrupteur *m*; *lighter*, briquet *m*; *lighter flint*, pierre à briquet *f*; *lighter fuel*, essence à briquet *f*; *lightning conductor*, paratonnerre *m*; *lock*, serrure *f*; *magazine*, périodique *m*; *map*, carte *f*; *mat*, paillasson *m*; *matches*, allumettes *f pl*; *mattress*, matelas *m*; *methylated spirit*, alcool à bruler *m*; *mirror*, glace *f*; *mosquito*, moustique *m*; *mouse*, souris *f*; *nail*, clou *m*; *nailbrush*, brosse à ongles *f*; *nailfile*, lime à ongles *f*; *napkin*, serviette de table *f*; *nappy*, couche *f*; *needle*, aiguille *f*; *nib*, plume *f*; *nut*, écrou *m*; *oil can*, bidon *m*; *oven*, four *m*; *paint*, peinture *f*; *paper*, papier *m*; *paper clip*, agrafe *f*; *paper tissues*, mouchoirs en papier *m*; *paraffin*, pétrole *m*; *pencil*, crayon *m*; *penknife*, canif *m*; *photograph*, photographie *f*; *piano*, piano *m*; *picture*, tableau *m*; *pillow*, oreiller *m*; *pillowcase*, taie d'oreiller *f*; *pin*, épingle *f*; *plate*, assiette *f*; *pliers*, pinces *f pl*; *plug*, prise (électrique) *f*; *polish*, cirage *m*; *popper*, pression *f*; *pram*, landeau *m*; *primus stove*, réchaud portatif *m or* primus *m*; *pushchair*, poussette *f*; *radiator*, radiateur *m*; *rake*, rateau *m*; *rat*, rat *m*; *razor*, rasoir *m*; *razor blade*, lame de rasoir *f*; *razor (electric)*, rasoir électrique *m*; *record*, disque *m*; *record player*, électrophone *m*; *rent*, loyer *m*; *roof*, toit *m*; *room*, pièce *f*; *rope*, corde *f*; *rubber*, gomme *f*; *rubbish*, ordures *f pl*; *rucksack*, sac à dos *m*; *safety pin*, épingle de sûreté *f*; *satchel*, cartable *m*; *saucepan*, casserole *f*; *saucer*, soucoupe *f*; *saw*, scie *f*; *scales (bathroom)*, pèse-personnes *m*; *scissors*, ciseaux *m pl*; *screw*, vis *f*; *screwdriver*, tourne-vis *m*; *scrubbing brush*, brosse dure *f*; *sewing machine*, machine à coudre *f*; *shampoo*, shampooing *m*; *shaving brush*, blaireau *m*; *shaving soap*, savon à barbe *m*; *shears*, cisailles *f pl*; *shoe brush*, brosse à chaussures *f*; *shower*, douche *f*; *shutter*, volet *m*; *sink*, évier *m*; *sitting room*, salon *m*; *soap*, savon *m*; *sofa*, canapé *m*; *spanner*, clé *f*; *spoon*, cuillère *f*; *stairs*, escalier *m*; *stamp (postage)*, timbre *m*; *stool*, tabouret *m*; *strap*, courroie *f*; *string*, ficelle *f*; *suitcase*, valise *f*; *sun tan cream*, crème pour bronzer *f*; *table*, table *f*; *tablecloth*, nappe *f*; *talc*, talc *m*; *tap*, robinet *m*; *tape measure*, mètre *m*; *tape recorder*, magnétophone *m*; *teapot*, théière *f*; *telephone*, téléphone *m*; *telephone directory*, bottin *m*; *telephone number*, numéro de téléphone *m*; *telephone operator*, téléphoniste *mf*; *television*, télévision *f*; *thermos*, thermos *m*; *thermostat*, thermostat *m*; *thimble*, dé à coudre *m*; *tile*, tuile *f*; *tin opener*, ouvre-boîtes *m*; *toothbrush*, brosse à dents *f*; *toothpaste*, pâte dentifrice *f*; *torch*, lampe de poche *f*; *towel*, serviette de toilette *f*; *tray*, plateau *m*; *trunk*, malle *f*; *tweezers*, pinces à épiler *f pl*; *typewriter*, machine à écrire *f*; *umbrella*, parapluie *m*; *unfurnished*, non meublé; *vacuum cleaner*, aspirateur *m*; *vase*, vase *m*; *voltage*, voltage *m*; *walking stick*, canne *f*; *wall*, mur *m*; *wallet*, portefeuille *m*; *wardrobe*, armoire *f*; *washbasin*, lavabo *m*; *washer*, rondelle *f*; *washing line*, corde à linge *f*; *washing machine*, machine à laver *f*; *wasp*, guêpe *f*; *waste paper basket*, corbeille à papier *f*; *water-colour*, aquarelle *f*; *water heater*, chauffe-eau *m*;

waterproof, imperméable; *wheelbarrow*, brouette *f*; *wire*, fil de fer *m*; *wireless*, radio *f*; *wool*, laine *f*; *writing paper*, papier à lettres *m*.

SHOPS AND SERVICES

antique dealer, antiquaire *m*; *art gallery*, galerie *f*; *baker*, boulangerie *f*; *book shop*, librairie *f*; *builder*, constructeur *m*; *butcher*, boucherie *f*; *café*, café *m*; *cake shop*, pâtisserie *f*; *carpenter*, menuisier *m*; *chemist*, pharmacie *f*; *cinema*, cinéma *m*; *cleaners*, teinturerie *f*; *comedy*, comédie *f*; *confectioner*, confiserie *f*; *dairy*, laiterie *f*; *decorator/painter*, peintre décorateur *m*; *department store*, grand magasin *m*; *do the shopping*, faire les courses; *draper*, mercerie *f*; *dustmen*, boueux *m pl*; *electrician*, électricien *m*; *estate agent*, agent immobilier *m*; *film*, film *m*; *fireman*, pompier *m*; *fishmonger*, marchand de poisson *m*; *fruiterer*, marchand de fruits *m*; *gas company*, compagnie de gaz *f*; *garage*, garage *m*; *grocer*, épicerie *f*; *hairdresser*, coiffeur *m*; *hire a car*, louer une voiture; *ironmonger*, quincaillerie *f*; *jeweller*, bijoutier *m*; *library*, bibliothèque *f*; *market*, marché *m*; *museum*, musée *m*; *newsagent*, marchand de journaux *m*; *office*, bureau *m*; *perfumery*, parfumerie *f*; *play*, pièce *f*; *plumber*, plombier *m*; *police station*, commissariat de police *m*; *policeman*, agent de police *m*; *postman*, facteur *m*; *post office*, bureau de poste *m*; *restaurant*, restaurant *m*; *retailer*, marchand au détail *m*; *shoe repairer*, cordonnier *m*; *shoe shop*, magasin de chaussures *m*; *snackbar*, snackbar *m*; *stationer*, papeterie *f*; *supermarket*, supermarché *m*; *swimming pool*, piscine *f*; *tailor*, tailleur *m*; *theatre*, théâtre *m*; *tobacconist*, marchand de tabac *m*; *travel agency*, agence de voyages *f*; *wholesaler*, commerçant en gros *m*; *window cleaner*, laveur de carreaux *m*; *wine merchant*, marchand de vin *m*; *zoo*, jardin zoologique *m*.

CLOTHES, ETC.

anorak, anorak *m*; *apron*, tablier *m*; *bathing costume*, maillot de bain *m*; *belt*, ceinture *f*; *beret*, béret, *m*; *bikini*, bikini *m*; *blouse*, chemisier *m*; *boots*, bottes *f*; *bow tie*, noeud papillon *m*; *bracelet*, bracelet *m*; *braces*, bretelles *f*; *brassiere*, soutien-gorge *m*; *brooch*, broche *f*; *buckle*, boucle *f*; *buttonhole*, boutonnière *f*; *cap*, casquette *f*; *cape*, cape *f*; *clothing*, vêtements *m pl*; *coat*, manteau *m*; *collar*, col *m*; *collar stud*, bouton de col *m*; *corset*, corset *m*; *cotton*, coton *m*; *cuff*, manchette *f*; *cufflinks*, boutons de manchettes *m*; *curlers*, bigoudis *m*; *darn* (v) repriser; *dress*, robe *f*; *dress* (v) s'habiller; *dress-suit*, smoking *m*; *dressing-gown*, robe de chambre *f*; *dry-clean* (v) nettoyer à sec; *earring*, boucle d'oreille *f*; *embroider* (v) broder; *embroidery*, broderie *f*; *engagement ring*, bague de fiançailles *f*; *eye pencil*, crayon pour les sourcils *m*; *face-powder*, poudre *f*; *fringe*, frange *f*; *glove*, gant *m*; *hair-clip*, épingle à cheveux *f*; *hair-net*, filet à cheveux *m*; *hairpin*, épingle neige *f*; *hat*, chapeau *m*; *handkerchief*, mouchoir *m*; *jacket*, veste *f*; *jeans*, jeans *m*; *knickers*, culotte *f*; *lace*, dentelle *f*; *lapel*, revers *m*; *lawn*, batiste *f*; *leather*, cuir *m*; *lipstick*, rouge à levres *m*; *make-up*, maquillage *m*; *nail-varnish*, vernis à ongles *m*; *necklace*, collier *m*; *nightdress*, chemise de nuit *f*; *nylon*, nylon *m*; *overall*, blouse *f*; *overcoat*, pardessus *m*; *pants*, caleçon, slip *m*; *petticoat*, jupon *m*; *pocket*, poche *f*; *pony-tail*, queue de cheval *f*; *powder-compact*, poudrier *m*; *pyjamas*, pyjama *m*; *raincoat*, imperméable *m*; *ribbon*, ruban *m*; *ring*, bague *f*; *rollers (hair)*, rouleaux *m*; *sandals*, sandales *f*; *satin*, satin *m*; *scarf*, écharpe *f*, foulard *m*; *sew* (v), coudre; *shawl*, châle *m*; *shirt*, chemise *f*; *shoes*, chaussures *f*; *shoe-laces*, lacets de chaussures *m*; *silk*, soie *f*; *size*, taille *f*; *skirt*, jupe *f*; *sleeve*, manche *f*; *slippers*, chaussons *m*, pantoufles *f*; *socks*, chaussettes *f*; *starch*, amidon *m*; *stockings*, bas *m*; *suit (man's)*, costume *m*; *suit (woman's)*, tailleur *m*; *sun glasses*, lunettes *f* de soleil; *T-shirt*, T-shirt *m*; *tennis shoes*, chaussures *m* de tennis; *tie*, cravate *f*; *tights*, collant *m*; *trousers*, pantalon *m*; *undress* (v), déshabiller; *uniform*, uniforme *f*; *veil*, voile *m*; *velvet*, velours *m*; *waistcoat*, gilet *m*; *wedding ring*, alliance *f*; *wellington boots*, bottes *f* en caoutchouc; *wig*, perruque *f*; *zip fastener*, fermeture éclair *f*.

BODY

adam's apple, pomme d'adam *f*; *ankle*, cheville *f*; *arm*, bras *m*; *artery*, artère *f*; *back*, dos *m*; *beard*, barbe *f*; *bladder*, vessie *f*; *blood*, sang *m*; *body*, corps *m*; *bone*, os *m*; *brain*, cerveau *m*; *breast*, sein *m*; *buttock*, fesse *f*; *cheek*, joue *f*; *chest*, poitrine *f*; *chin*, menton *m*; *ear*, oreille *f*; *eardrum*, tympan *m*; *ear lobe*, lobe *m*; *elbow*, coude *m*; *eye*, oeil *m*; *eyeball*, globe oculaire *m*; *eyebrow*, sourcil *m*; *eyelash*, cil *m*; *face*, visage *m*; *fist*, poing *m*; *forehead*, front *m*; *gall bladder*, vessicule biliaire *f*; *gland*, glande *f*; *gums*, gencives *f pl*; *hair*, cheveux *m pl*; *hand*, main *f*;

head, tête *f*; *heart*, coeur *m*; *hip*, hanche *f*; *intestine*, intestin *m*; *joint*, articulation *f*; *knee*, genou *m*; *kneecap*, rotule *f*; *kidney*, rein *m*; *leg*, jambe *f*; *lip*, lèvre *f*; *liver*, foie *m*; *lung*, poumon *m*; *mouth*, bouche *f*; *muscle*, muscle *m*; *nail*, ongle *m*; *navel*, nombril *m*; *neck*, cou *m*; *nipple*, mamelon *m*; *nose*, nez *m*; *nostril*, narine *f*; *organ*, organe *m*; *palate*, palais *m*; *palm*, paume *f*; *pancreas*, pancréas *m*; *parting (hair)*, raie *f*; *shoulder*, épaule *f*; *skin*, peau *f*; *skull*, crâne *m*; *spleen*, rate *f*; *stomach*, estomac *m*; *teeth*, dents *f*; *thigh*, cuisse *f*; *throat*, gorge *f*; *thumb*, pouce *m*; *toes*, orteils *m* or doigts de pied *m*; *tongue*, langue *f*; *tonsil*, amygdale *f*; *vein*, veine *f*; *wrist*, poignée *f*.

MEDICAL

abortion, avortement *m*; *abscess*, abcès *m*; *accident*, accident *m*; *acne*, acné *f*; *allergic*, allergique; *allergy*, allergie *f*; *anaesthetic*, anesthésie *f*; *antibiotic*, antibiotique *m*; *antibody*, anticorps *m*; *antidote*, antidote *m*; *antiseptic*, antiseptique *m*; *appendicitis*, appendicite *f*; *arthritis*, arthrite *f*; *aspirin*, aspirine *f*; *athlete's foot*, pied de l'athlète *m*; *backache*, mal au dos *m*; *bacteria*, bactérie *f*; *bandage* (v) mettre un pansement; *bandage*, pansement *m*; *bandage (crepe)*, bande Velpeau *f*; *birth*, naissance *f*; *blackhead*, point noir *m*; *bleed* (v) saigner; *blister*, ampoule *f*; *blood*, sang *m*; *blood group*, groupe sanguin *m*; *boil*, furoncle *m*; *broken*, cassé; *bronchitis*, bronchite *f*; *bruise*, bleu *m*; *bump*, bosse *f*; *burn*, brûlure *f*; *cancer*, cancer *m*; *casualty ward*, salle *f* des accidentés; *catarrh*, catarrhe *m*; *cerebral haemorrhage*, hemorragie cérébrale *f*; *chicken pox*, varicelle *f*; *choke* (v), s'étouffer or s'étrangler; *clot*, caillot *m*; *cold*, rhume *m*; *concussion*, commotion cérébrale *f*; *constipation*, constipation *f*; *consultant*, médecin consultant *m*; *convalescence*, convalescence *f*; *corn*, cor *m*; *cough* (v) tousser; *cough*, toux *f*; *cough mixture*, sirop *m* contre la toux; *cramp*, crampe *f*; *cut*, coupure *f*; *cyst*, kyste *m*; *dandruff*, pellicules *f pl*; *dentist*, dentiste *m*; *diabetes*, diabète *m*; *diarrhoea*, diarrhée *f*; *disinfectant*, désinfectant *m*; *doctor*, docteur or médecin *m*; *dose*, dose *f*; *drug*, drogue *f*; *earache*, mal *m* aux oreilles; *emetic*, émétique *m*; *enema*, lavement *m*; *epidemic*, épidemie *f*; *epilepsy*, épilepsie *f*; *faint* (v), s'évanouir; *false teeth*, fausses dents *f pl*; *fever*, fièvre *f*; *filling (dental)*, plombage *m*; *flat feet*, pieds plats *m pl*; *flu*, grippe *f*; *fracture*, fracture *f*; *gallstone*, calcul biliaire *m*; *gargle* (v) se gargariser; *germ*, microbe *m*; *german measles*, rubéole *f*; *graft*, greffe *f*; *graze*, écorchure *f*; *haemorrhage*, hémorragie *f*; *hay fever*, rhume des foins *m*; *headache*, mal à la tête *f*; *heart attack*, crise cardiaque *f*; *hernia*, hernie *f*; *hospital*, hôpital *m*; *ill*, malade; *illness*, maladie *f*; *injection*, piqûre *f*; *injured*, blessé; *inoculation*, inoculation *f*; *insect bite*, piqûre d'insecte *f*; *insomnia*, insomnie *f*; *iodine*, iode *m*; *laxative*, laxatif *m*; *laryngitis*, laryngite *f*; *measles*, rougeole *f*; *medicine*, médicament *m*; *menstrual period*, règles *f pl*; *miscarriage*, fausse couche *f*; *mole*, grain *m* de beauté; *mumps*, oreillons *m pl*; *nervous breakdown*, depression nerveuse *f*; *nose bleed*, saignement du nez *m*; *nurse*, infirmière *f*; *ointment*, pommade *f*; *operating theatre*, salle d'opération *f*; *operation*, opération *f*; *pain*, douleur *f*; *patient*, malade *m f*; *piles*, hémorroïdes *f*; *pill*, pilule *f*; *pleurisy*, pleurésie *f*; *pneumonia*, pneumonie *f*; *poison*, poison *m*; *poultice*, cataplasme *m*; *pregnancy*, grossesse *f*; *pregnant*, enceinte; *prescription*, ordonnance *f*; *rash*, éruption *f*; *Red Cross*, La Croix Rouge; *rheumatism*, rhumatisme *m*; *sanitary towels*, serviettes hygiéniques *f*; *scratch*, égratignure *f*; *sea sickness*, mal *m* de mer; *sedative*, calmant *m*; *shivering*, frissonnement *m*; *sighted (short)*, myope, *(long)* presbyte; *sinus*, sinusite *f*; *sleeping pill*, somnifère *m*; *sling*, écharpe *f*; *slipped disc*, hernie discale *f*; *small pox*, variole *f*; *sore throat*, mal *m* à la gorge; *spectacles*, lunettes *f pl*; *splint*, éclisse *f*; *splinter*, écharde *f*; *spot*, bouton *m*; *sprain*, foulure *f*; *stiff neck*, torticolis *m*; *sting*, piqûre *f*; *stitch* (surgical) point *m* de suture; *stomach ache*, mal à l'estomac *m*; *stomach upset*, estomac dérangé *m*; *stretcher*, civière *f*; *stroke*, attaque *f*; *stye*, compère-loriot *m or* orgelet *m*; *sunburn*, coup de soleil *m*; *sunstroke*, insolation *f*; *surgeon*, chirurgien *m*; *surgery*, chirurgie *f*; *swelling*, enflure *f*; *tablet*, cachet *m or* comprimé *m*; *tapeworm*, ver solitaire *m or* ténia *m*; *temperature*, température *f*; *thermometer*, thermomètre *m*; *therapy*, thérapie *f*; *tonsilitis*, angine *f or* inflammation *f* des amygdales; *toothache*, mal *m* aux dents; *truss*, bandage herniaire *m*; *tuberculosis*, tuberculose *f*; *tumor*, tumeur *f*; *ulcer*, ulcère *m*; *unconscious*, sans connaissance; *varicose vein*, varice *f*; *verruca*, verrue plantaire *f*; *virus*, virus *m*; *visiting hours*, heures de visite *f*; *vomit* (v), vomir; *water on the knee*, épanchement *m* de synovie; *ward*, salle *f*; *wart*, verrue *f*; *whooping cough*, coqueluche *f*; *X-ray*, radio (graphie) *f*; *yellow jaundice*, jaunisse *f*.

FRENCH
IN THREE MONTHS

III

KEY TO GRAMMAR EXERCISES

Key to Lesson 1

EXERCISE I. 1 un frère; 2 une soeur; 3 un billet; 4 une mère; 5 un jour; 6 une porte; 7 un hôtel; 8 une gare; 9 un ami; 10 le livre; 11 la porte; 12 le père; 13 l'église; 14 la table; 15 la valise; 16 l'adresse; 17 le jour; 18 l'heure; 19 l'hôtel; 20 la mère; 21 l'ami.

EXERCISE II. 1 Les livres; 2 les pères; 3 les tables; 4 les valises; 5 les hôtels; 6 les adresses; 7 les billets; 8 les heures.

EXERCISE III. 1 il a acheté une voiture; 2 nous avons trouvé deux valises; 3 elles ont reçu une lettre. 4 le frère et la soeur ont acheté un chien; 5 J'ai reçu deux paquets; 6 vous avez trouvé les passeports; 7 elle a une télévision.

EXERCISE IV. 1 de notre porte; 2 à vos hôtels; 3 les portes de notre église; 4 à leur table; 5 de votre hôtel à notre porte; 6 à leur église; 7 de nos billets; 8 de leurs amis.

Key to Lesson 2

EXERCISE I. 1 un couteau, les couteaux; 2 un bras, deux bras; 3 le journal, les journaux; 4 la voix, les voix; 5 le feu, les feux; 6 un fils, trois fils.

EXERCISE II. 1 Ai-je rencontré vos neveux? 2 Ont-ils envoyé une carte postale? 3 Avez-vous écrit l'adresse? 4 Avons-nous reçu les journaux? 5 A-t-il vu les animaux? 6 Ont-elles écrit à leurs amis? 7 Ils ont deux fils; 8 Avez-vous vu vos amis? 9 Ont-ils acheté votre maison? 10 A-t-elle reçu le paquet?

EXERCISE III. 1 mon livre; 2 son père; 3 mon chapeau; 4 sa mère; 5 mes bras; 6 ses chemises; 7 ma chambre; 8 sa mère; 9 son sac à main; 10 sa famille; 11 sa famille; 12 ses chapeaux.

EXERCISE IV. 1 son écriture; 2 son école; 3 sa chambre; 4 son oncle; 5 sa rue; 6 son épaule; 7 son épaule.

EXERCISE V. 1 N'avez-vous pas mon livre? 2 Il n'a pas vu son écriture; 3 Nous n'avons pas trouvé les gants; 4 N'ont-ils pas écrit à vos amis? 5 Je n'ai pas lu sa lettre.

Key to Lesson 3

EXERCISE I. 1 quelle école? 2 quels mois? 3 quelles chambres? 4 quel homme! 5 quelles voix? 6 quelle famille? 7 quelle gare?

EXERCISE II. 1 cette voiture; 2 cette fleur; 3 ces couteaux; 4 ces fourchettes; 5 cet enfant; 6 ce restaurant; 7 cette heure; 8 ces jours; 9 cet hôtel; 10 ces jardins; 11 ce magasin.

EXERCISE III. 1 le mari de ma soeur; 2 la voiture de votre père; 3 la couleur de cette fleur; 4 l'adresse de ma soeur; 5 la robe de quelle fille? 6 les valises de ces voyageurs; 7 la mère de votre ami; 8 Avez-vous trouvé les gants de cette dame? 9 Son mari a écrit à l'ami de son frère; 10 Leurs nièces n'ont pas lu la lettre de cette dame; 11 Les fenêtres de nos voisins.

EXERCISE IV. 1 Qui est là? 2 Où sont nos amis? 3 Je suis très fatigué; 4 Il est très riche; 5 Elle est à l'église; 6 Nous sommes à son hôtel; 7 Vous êtes en retard; 8 Le livre est sur la table; 9 Qui sont ces hommes? 10 Où sont nos journaux? 11 Vos amis sont à la gare.

EXERCISE V. 1 Nos amis sont absents; 2 Ces hommes sont riches; 3 Sa maison est trop petite; 4 Nous sommes fatigués; 5 Cette eau est chaude; 6 Cette pomme est mauvaise; 7 Vous êtes très aimable; 8 Je suis malade; 9 Cette chambre est très froide; 10 Ma voiture est très petite.

Key to Lesson 4

EXERCISE I. 1 Elle n'est pas jeune. 2 Cette lampe n'est pas très jolie. 3 N'es-tu pas satisfait? 4 N'est-il pas trop vieux? 5 Ne suis-je pas en retard? 6 Nous ne sommes pas fatiguées. 7 Ces gants sont trop petits. 8 Mon manteau n'est pas sale. 9 Vos voisins sont très riches.

EXERCISE II. 1 Le facteur a-t-il apporté une lettre? 2 Cette dame a-t-elle acheté votre manteau? 3 Ces fleurs sont-elles très jolies? 4 Votre fille est-elle à l'école? 5 Cet homme a-t-il deux fils ou trois? 6 Le docteur a-t-il vu votre pied? 7 Les journaux ne sont-ils pas sur la table? 8 Le garçon n'est-il pas ici? 9 Sa maison est-elle grande?

EXERCISE III. 1 J'ai reçu; 2 Mon ami a brisé le verre; 3 Avez-vous entendu le bruit? 4 Elle a perdu son briquet; 5 Le docteur a-t-il lu ma lettre? 6 Il n'a pas ouvert le paquet. 7 N'ont-ils pas vu l'incendie? 8 Nous n'avons pas ouvert la porte.

EXERCISE IV. 1 du jardin; 2 au docteur; 3 du couteau; 4 au bateau; 5 de la maison; 6 à l'hôtel; 7 Avez-vous reçu le message du directeur? 8 Le premier jour de la semaine; 9 Le dernier jour du mois. 10 Avez-vous vu la voiture du docteur?

Key to Lesson 5

EXERCISE I. 1 Avez-vous entendu sa voix? Oui, elle est très forte. 2 J'ai lu sa lettre; elle est très courte. 3 Nous avons acheté ce roman; il est très intéressant. 4 Avez-vous acheté la maison? Non, elle est vendue. 5 Où sont les pommes? Elles ne sont pas bonnes.

EXERCISE II. 1 Les pages des livres; 2 les plumes des oiseaux; 3 les pantalons des garçons; 4 les chaussures des filles; 5 Nous avons donné l'argent aux enfants. 6 Ils ont parlé aux femmes des ouvriers. 7 J'ai écrit au dentiste de notre ami. 8 Nous avons envoyé le paquet aux amis de votre père. 9 Ils ont vu les phares des fenêtres de notre maison.

EXERCISE III. 1 de la bière; 2 du lait; 3 du poisson; 4 des verres; 5 du beurre; 6 du sel; 7 de la salade; 8 de l'eau; 9 des fleurs; 10 Il a acheté du fromage et du vin. 11 Avez-vous trouvé de l'argent sur la table? 12 Ils ont eu de la soupe. 13 Avez-vous entendu du bruit? 14 J'ai de la monnaie.

EXERCISE IV. 1 Nous n'avons pas d'argent. 2 N'a-t-il pas d'allumettes? 3 N'avez-vous pas de monnaie? 4 Je n'ai pas de temps. 5 Elle n'a pas de billet. 6 N'avons-nous pas de sucre? 7 Cette pièce n'a pas de fenêtres. 8 N'ont-ils pas de bière? 9 Ils n'ont pas reçu de lettres. 10 Les hommes ont eu du pain, du fromage et du vin. 11 Avez-vous des amis à Paris?

Key to Lesson 6

EXERCISE I. 1 il parle; 2 nous remercions; 3 vous passez; 4 ils acceptent; 5 je visite; 6 il ferme; 7 elles ferment; 8 nous parlons; 9 elle remercie; 10 ils passent; 11 j'accepte; 12 elle visite.

EXERCISE II. 1 Elle donne du pain et du beurre aux enfants. 2 Les hommes parlent à leurs femmes. 3 Son mari remercie le directeur. 4 Nous parlons aux hommes. 5 Vous acceptez son argent. 6 Ils visitent la maison. 7 Elle ferme la porte. 8 Les hommes passent devant la maison. 9 Nous donnons du pain aux oiseaux. 10 Ils ferment les fenêtres. 11 Il visite cette école. 12 Ils remercient leurs amis.

EXERCISE III. 1 Il fume sa pipe. 2 Nous coupons l'herbe. 3 Elle cherche l'adresse. 4 Ils allument le feu. 5 Je porte les bagages. 6 Vous mangez trop. 7 Il porte un manteau. 8 J'arrive demain matin. 9 Elle donne de l'argent à mon frère.

EXERCISE IV. Fument-ils des cigares ou des cigarettes? 2 Cherche-t-elle un appartement? 3 Arrive-t-il le matin ou le soir? 4 Allumez-vous votre pipe? 5 Ces hommes mangent-ils du fromage? 6 Ferment-elles leurs portes? 7 Acceptent-ils ces cadeaux? 8 Cherchez-vous votre briquet? 9 Votre ami parle-t-il à son voisin?

Key to Lesson 7

EXERCISE I. 1 Il ne trouve pas le chemin. 2 Ils ne payent pas leurs dettes. 3 N'habitez-vous pas dans cette maison? 4 Ne travaille-t-elle pas souvent? 5 Ne cherchent-elles pas leurs chaussures? 6 Pourquoi ne coupez-vous pas cette ficelle? 7 Il n'habite pas là. 8 Ne chanté-je pas bien? 9 Il ne voyage pas par avion. 10 Pourquoi ne regardez-vous pas le menu?

EXERCISE II. 1 Qui ferme la porte? 2 Qui a mis les allumettes sur la table? 3 Que regardez-vous? 4 Qu'a-t-elle accepté? 5 Qui cherchent-ils? 6 Qui a ouvert la fenêtre? 7 Qu'avez-vous dit? 8 Que porte-il? 9 Qui a voyagé par bateau? 10 Qu'avons-nous payé? 11 Que donne-t-il à l'agent? 13 A qui avez-vous écrit?

EXERCISE III. 1 pour son fils; 2 dans le feu; 3 sur le bateau; 4 sous la table; 5 avec votre couteau; 6 sans cet argent.

EXERCISE IV.ˈ 1 J'ai payé; 2 nous avons visité; 3 elle a donné; 4 il n'a pas trouvé; 5 ont-ils passé? 6 N'avez-vous pas accepté? 7 Il a cherché son manteau; 8 Ils ont fermé la porte. 9 Nous n'avons pas parlé au docteur. 10 N'ai-je pas donné d'argent au garçon?

EXERCISE V. 1 Il n'allume pas le feu. 2 N'ont-ils pas allumé le feu? 3 Nous n'aimons pas cette chambre. 4 N'ont-ils pas cherché votre montre? 5 Ne regardez-vous pas le journal? 6 J'ai payé votre addition.

Key to Lesson 8

EXERCISE I. 1 J'ai votre adresse et vous avez la mienne. 2 A-t-elle pris mon billet ou le sien? 3 Nous avons leurs clefs et ils ont les nôtres. 4 Il n'a pas apporté mon addition mais la leur. 5 Avez-vous rencontré mes fils ou les siens? 6 J'ai perdu sa montre et la mienne. 7 Ils n'ont pas acheté mes tableaux mais les siens. 8 N'a-t-il pas dépensé son argent et le vôtre?

EXERCISE II. 1 Sur quoi avez-vous écrit l'adresse? 2 Qu'avez-vous dit? 3 Quel tableau ont-ils acheté? 4 Qui a-t-il rencontré à l'aéroport? 5 Dans quoi a-t-elle envoyé les choses? 6 Pourquoi chantez-vous? 7 Qu'a-t-il trouvé dans le livre?

EXERCISE III. 1 une ville anglaise; 2 des voitures allemandes; 3 des vaisseaux français; 4 cette table ronde; 5 ces hommes riches; 6 ma main droite; 7 son rasoir électrique; 8 Ont-ils apporté ces fleurs jaunes? 9 Avez-vous bu du vin rouge?

EXERCISE IV. 1 une porte fermée; 2 deux enfants perdus; 3 La ficelle est coupée. 4 Ses dettes sont payées. 5 Les fenêtres sont-elles ouvertes? 6 Les enfants ne sont pas encore trouvés. 7 A-t-il vendu ses chevaux? 8 Ses chevaux ne sont pas encore vendus. 9 Ont-ils bu l'eau?

Key to Lesson 9

EXERCISE I. 1 Ils le portent. 2 Nous leur donnons les fleurs. 3 Je la fume. 4 Elle nous cherche. 5 Vous les trouvez. 6 Il vous rencontre. 7 Les dames nous parlent. 8 Le docteur lui parle. 9 La fille lui chante une chanson.

EXERCISE II. 1 Nous l'invitons. 2 Je l'invite. 3 Elle nous oublie. 4 Ils m'oublient. 5 Nous l'acceptons. 6 Ils les acceptent. 7 Le garçon l'apporte. 8 Les enfants leur parlent. 9 Ils la trouvent. 10 Votre soeur le regarde. 11 Il l'aime. 12 Nous les aimons. 13 Il nous apporte du pain et du beurre. 14 Vos amis vous cherchent. 15 Nous les rencontrons. 16 Ma mère lui parle. 17 Vous les oubliez. 18 Où est la lettre? 19 Il l'écrit. 20 Vos fils les portent-ils?

EXERCISE III. 1 Vous parle-t-il? 2 Nous ne l'aimons pas. 3 Les remerciez-vous? 4 Nous regarde-t-il? 5 Les apportent-ils? 6 Me regardez-vous? 7 Nous vous remercions. 8 Votre ami nous cherche-t-

il? 9 Ils la cassent. 10 Pourquoi les cachez-vous? 11 L'avez-vous?
12 Nous les avons.

EXERCISE IV. 1 Il ne le trouve pas. 2 Ne nous remerciez-vous pas?
3 Ne lui parlez-vous pas? 4 Nous ne leur donnons pas les livres.
5 Pourquoi ne me regardez-vous pas? 6 Il ne la cache pas. 7 Pourquoi
ne nous apporte-elle pas le menu? 8 Mon ami ne les aime pas. 9 Pourquoi ne me montrez-vous pas sa lettre? 10 Ne les rencontrez-vous pas
tous les jours? 11 Pourquoi ne fume-t-il pas des cigarettes françaises?
12 Il ne les aime pas. 13 Pourquoi cette fenêtre n'est-elle pas fermée?
14 Je la ferme.

Key to Lesson 10

EXERCISE I. 1 il perd; 2 nous rendons; 3 vous vendez; 4 ils
répondent; 5 j'attends; 6 elle vend; 7 ils perdent; 8 nous répondons;
9 vous attendez; 10 votre ami rend; 11 elle répond; 12 ces hommes
perdent; 13 Ils nous répondent toujours par retour du courrier. 14
Avez-vous vu sa maison? Oui, il la vend. 15 Il nous attend à cinq heures.

EXERCISE II. 1 Vend-elle? 2 perdez-vous? 3 répondent-ils? 4 Je
ne rends pas; 5 elle n'attend pas; 6 ne vendons-nous pas? 7 ne rend-
elle pas? 8 Pourqoui ne répondez-vous pas? 9 J'attends le train. 10 Ne
vendent-ils pas de timbres? 11 Je lui prête souvent mes livres mais il ne
les rend pas. 12 J'ai rencontré votre frère aujourd'hui; ne l'attendez-
vous pas ce soir?

EXERCISE III. 1 Elle a entendu sa voix. 2 Ils ont vendu leur voiture.
3 Le rend-il? 4 A-t-il rendu l'argent? 5 Ne m'attendez-vous pas?
6 N'avez-vous pas attendu votre femme hier? 7 Le pharmacien ne le
vend-il pas? 8 Nous avons descendu les escaliers.

Key to Lesson 11

EXERCISE I. 1 Ils ne vous ont pas écrit. 2 Lui avez-vous parlé?
3 Nous ne leur avons pas répondu. 4 Ne l'ont-ils pas trouvé? 5 Je lui
ai apporté les lettres. 6 Nous l'avons vu aujourd'hui. 7 Elle ne m'a pas
donné son numéro de téléphone. 8 Ils ne l'ont pas perdu.

EXERCISE II. 1 Ils ne finissent pas leur repas. 2 Le remplissent-ils?
3 Nous ne choisissons pas ces couleurs. 4 Ne punissez-vous pas votre
chien? 5 Pourquoi ne remplit-elle pas le verre? 6 Pourquoi choisissez-
vous les tâches difficiles? 7 Il finit votre costume aujourd'hui. 8 Elle
réussit d'habitude.

EXERCISE III. 1 Pourquoi n'avez-vous pas rempli la bouteille? 2 Ils
n'ont pas encore fini leur travail. 3 Nous n'avons pas choisi ce vin.
4 A-t-elle choisi une bague? 5 Obéissez-vous à ses ordres? 6 Ne l'ont-
ils pas trop puni? 7 Nous avons essayé et nous avons réussi. 8 Ont-ils
choisi?

EXERCISE IV. 1 Pourquoi l'homme vous a-t-il parlé? 2 Où habite
votre frère (*better than* Votre frère où habite-t-il?). 3 Comment l'agent

vous a-t-il trouvé? 4 Qu'est-ce que votre ami vous a envoyé *or* Que vous a envoyé votre ami? 5 Où sont mes valises? 6 Qu'est-ce que votre femme a entendu *better than* Qu' a entendu votre femme? 7 Que vend ce magasin?

Key to Lesson 12

EXERCISE I. 1 une bonne chose; 2 ces belles pommes; 3 ce petit chat; 4 une jolie fleur; 5 quel petit pied! 6 un vieil ami; 7 ces grands fleuves; 8 sa belle bague; 9 une mauvaise opinion; 10 ces méchants hommes; 11 ce gros oiseau; 12 une nouvelle voiture.

EXERCISE II. 1 Voici du (*or* de) vieux vin. 2 Voici de belles fleurs. 3 Voilà un gros avion. 4 Voilà de grosses montagnes. 5 Voici un bon endroit. 6 Voilà de petits lacs. 7 Voici de jeunes animaux. 8 Voilà du (*or* de) bon beurre et du (*or* de) bon fromage. 9 Ils nous ont donné de la (*or* de) bonne viande mais du (*or* de) mauvais vin.

EXERCISE III. 1 Avez-vous du (*or* de) bon beurre? 2 Nous avons bu du (*or* de) vieux vin. 3 Ils ont acheté de belles bagues. 4 Nous avons une mauvaise opinion de vous. 5 Elle porte un nouveau chapeau tous les jours.

EXERCISE IV. 1 Notre chambre est plus grande que la vôtre. 2 Votre jardin est plus petit que le nôtre. 3 Cet arbre est-il le plus haut du jardin? *or* Est-ce que cet arbre est le plus haut du jardin? 4 Les jumeaux sont les plus jeunes de la famille. 5 Son pied est plus petit que le sien. 6 N'est-elle pas plus jolie que sa soeur? 7 La femme la plus pauvre de la ville habite là.

EXERCISE V. 1 Ma voiture est aussi rapide que la sienne. 2 Il est moins intelligent que son frère. 3 Cette plage est la meilleure de la région. 4 Mes mains ne sont pas si sales que les vôtres. 5 Sa bague est la moins belle. 6 La montagne la plus haute du monde. 7 N'est-il pas le meilleur pianiste en Europe? 8 Ma cuisine est aussi bonne que la sienne. 9 Il a gagné moins de dix francs aujourd'hui. 10 Je lui ai donné plus de huit mille francs.

Key to Lesson 13

EXERCISE I. 1 Il sera ici demain. 2 Nous serons là. 3 Je parlerai à son père. 4 Il vendra sa maison. 5 Aurez-vous le temps demain? 6 Le programme finira à huit heures. 7 Ils répondront à notre lettre par retour de courrier. 8 Aurez-vous de l'argent la semaine prochaine? 9 Je ne lui donnerai pas l'argent. 10 Où habiteront-ils? 11 Ne seront-ils pas en retard?

EXERCISE II. 1 Je lui parlerai demain. 2 Nous leur rendrons le livre. 3 Il ne le finira pas avant ce soir. 4 Ne nous chercheront-ils pas si nous sommes en retard? 5 Ils ne lui répondront pas. 6 Ne vous attendra-t-elle pas? 7 Vous l'aurez. 8 Nous ne le trouverons pas à la maison. 9 Ne l'accepteront-ils pas?

EXERCISE III. 1 Ne soyez pas en retard. 2 Répondez à sa lettre par retour de courrier. 3 Demandons le menu. 4 Remplissez les verres.

183

5 Ne fumez pas ici. 6 Regardez ces tableaux. 7 Ne mangez pas cette nourriture. 8 Ne vendez pas vos livres. 9 Fermez la fenêtre. 10 Ne dépensons pas cet argent. 11 Coupez du pain. 12 Soyez raisonnable.

EXERCISE IV. 1 Quel sera son salaire? 2 Quel est son nom? 3 Quelle est votre maison? 4 Quels sont vos amis? 5 Quelle est son adresse? 6 Quelle est sa soeur? 7 Quelle est votre taille? 8 Lequel de ces enfants est le plus jeune? 9 Laquelle de ces chambres est la plus chère? 10 Quel journal avez-vous acheté?

Key to Lesson 14

EXERCISE I. 1 Vous ne seriez pas heureux là. 2 Il ne serait pas là à temps. 3 J'aimerais un verre de vin. 4 Ils ne perdraient pas le chemin. 5 Ils n'auraient pas le temps. 6 Elle serait seule. 7 Nous dépenserions trop d'argent. 8 Ils ne seraient pas à la maison. 9 Auriez-vous payé l'addition?

EXERCISE II. 1 L'homme qui nous a parlé. 2 Le café que nous avons bu ce matin. 3 Une maison qui donne sur la mer. 4 La lettre qui est sur la table est pour votre ami. 5 Les journaux qui sont ici sont français. 6 Nous n'aimons pas la nourriture qu'ils mangent. 7 Le film que nous avons vu hier.

EXERCISE III. 1 L'hôtel que nous avons choisi est plein. 2 Le bruit que j'ai entendu. 3 Où est l'argent que je vous ai donné? 4 Voilà l'homme que j'ai rencontré hier.

EXERCISE IV. 1 Quelle page avez-vous lue? 2 J'ai trouvé les timbres que vous avez perdus. 3 Le facteur a apporté trois lettres pour vous; les avez-vous reçues? 4 Quels animaux avez-vous vus? 5 Est-ce que l'eau qu'il vous a apportée est chaude? 6 Leur maison est très grande; l'avez vous vue?

Key to Lesson 15

EXERCISE I. 1 Je lui donnais une leçon. 2 Elle avait deux soeurs. 3 Ils étaient seuls. 4 Elle jouait du piano. 5 Ils écoutaient la musique. 6 Nous attendions son avion. 7 Elle nous parlait. 8 Je fumais une cigarette. 9 Il avait mal à la tête. 10 Nous étions à la maison. 11 Vous aviez tort; J'avais raison.

EXERCISE II. 1 Ils jouaient tous les jours. 2 Il gagnait beaucoup d'argent. 4 Nous étudions ensemble le français. 4 Ils allaient au marché avec leurs paniers. 5 Ne jouaient-ils pas aux cartes hier soir? 6 Elle gagnait toujours et je perdais toujours. 7 Il finissait son repas. 8 Ils n'étaient pas ici. 9 Nous avions une petite maison. 10 Ils n'avaient pas le temps. 11 N'était-elle pas française?

EXERCISE III. 1 Le train dans lequel il voyageait était en retard. 2 Les moyens par lesquels il gagnait sa vie. 3 L'homme avec lequel (or avec qui) j'ai discuté l'affaire hier n'est pas là. 4 La fille pour laquelle (or pour qui) vous avez acheté les chaussures. 5 L'enveloppe sur laquelle il a écrit l'adresse. 6 L'homme par lequel (or par qui) il a envoyé l'argent.

EXERCISE IV. 1 Avez-vous loué les chambres dont nous parlions? 2 Où est la liste de laquelle il copiait les noms? 3 Voilà l'homme à qui (or auquel) je l'ai donné. 4 Le feu dont nous avons entendu parler était très grave. 5 Nous parlions de notre fils et non (pas) du vôtre. 6 Nous l'avons prêté à nos amis et non (pas) aux leurs. 7 Auquel de ces hommes l'avez-vous envoyé? 8 Desquelles de ces filles parliez-vous? 9 L'ont-ils appris de ma fille ou de la sienne?

Key to Lesson 16

EXERCISE I. 1 En parlant à son ami; 2 en tournant le coin; 3 en visitant Athènes; 4 sans répondre à la lettre; 5 après avoir écrit; 6 j'ai le plaisir de vous informer; 7 pour avoir perdu l'argent; 8 en cherchant la rue; 9 sans attendre une réponse; 10 ayant perdu le chemin; 11 pour avoir vendu; 12 en entendant le bruit.

EXERCISE II. 1 Donnez ceci à votre frère. 2 Ceci coûte plus que cela. 3 Pourquoi n'avez-vous pas choisi cela? 4 C'est la meilleure couleur. 5 Est-ce que ce n'était pas stupide? or Ce n'était pas stupide? 6 C'est trop cher. 7 Ce sera intéressant. 8 Ne lui montrez pas ceci. 9 C'est trop petit. 10 Ceci ne semble pas très lourd.. 11 Est-te que ce ne sera pas difficile? or Ce ne sera pas difficile? 12 Ce n'était pas facile.

EXERCISE III. 1 il parla; 2 je ne la cherchai pas; 3 nous acceptâmes; 4 vous oubliâtes; 5 ils coupèrent; 6 nous trouvâmes; 7 ils ne donnèrent pas; 8 nous quittâmes la ville; 9 nous fermâmes la porte; 10 ils ne payèrent pas l'addition; 11 il me regarda.

EXERCISE IV. 1 nous finîmes; 2 il ne vendit pas; 3 vous choisîtes; 4 nous perdîmes; 5 ils repondirent; 6 elle rendit; 7 je remplis; 8 ils ne réussirent pas.

EXERCISE V. 1 je fus; 2 elle eut; 3 nous fûmes; 4 ils eurent; 5 elles furent; 6 nous eûmes; 7 je n'eus pas; 8 il ne fut pas. 9 ils ne furent pas.

EXERCISE VI. 1 C'est mon appartement. 2 Est-ce que c'est votre place? or C'est votre place? 3 Ce sont (or c'est) mes clefs. 4 Ce ne sont pas (or ce n'est pas) ses enfants. 5 Est-ce que ce n'est pas votre billet? or Ce n'est pas votre billet? 6 Est-ce que c'était notre autobus? or C'était notre autobus? 7 Est-ce que ce sera votre adresse? 8 C'était notre train. 9 Est-ce que ce n'est pas son magasin? or Ce n'est pas son magasin? 10 C'étaient quels oiseaux?

EXERCISE VII. 1 C'était son mari. 2 Est-ce que ce sont vos chaussures? 3 Ce n'était pas mon opinion. 4 C'est bon. 5 Ce sont (or c'est) des Allemands. 6 Est-ce que c'est un Espagnol? or C'est un Espagnol? 7 Est-ce que c'était cher? 8 Ce ne sont pas (or ce n'est pas) des Français.

EXERCISE VIII. 1 Donnez-lui mon adresse. 2 Montrez-nous le chemin. 3 Prêtez-leur l'argent. 4 Envoyez-nous les lettres. 5 Téléphonez-moi ce soir. 6 Ne l'acceptez pas. 7 Finissons-le. 8 Ne lui donnez pas de vin. 9 Ne les vendez pas. 10 Embrassez-moi. 11 Ne les dérangez pas. 12 Ne nous oubliez pas.

EXERCISE I. 1 Voyez-vous cet homme? 2 Je vous verrai demain. 3 Je l'ai vu la semaine dernière. 4 Les avez-vous vus? 5 Ils virent le bateau. 6 Ils ne nous voient pas. 7 En voyant cela. 8 Après l'avoir vu. 9 Nous les voyions tous les jours. 10 Je les verrais, s'ils étaient là.

EXERCISE II. 1 Avez-vous vu ce film-ci ou celui-là? 2 Quel est le prix de ces pommes? 3 Celles-ci coûtent deux francs, et celles-là deux francs cinquante. 4 Cette bouteille-ci est pleine et celle-là est vide. 5 Voici plusieurs pièces de monnaie; celles-ci sont anglaises et celles-là sont françaises. 6 Voulez-vous ces raisins-ci ou ceux-là?

EXERCISE III. 1 Est-ce que c'est votre livre ou celui de votre soeur? 2 Il a apporté notre addition et celle de nos amis. 3 Cette lettre et celle que j'ai reçue la semaine dernière. 4 Notre jardin est plus petit que celui de notre voisin. 5 Ces tableaux sont plus beaux que ceux que nous avons vus hier. 6 Est-ce que c'est votre voiture ou celle de votre frère?

EXERCISE IV. 1 Avez-vous lu cette histoire? 2 Pas encore, je lis celle-ci. 3 Lirez-vous celle que je lisais? 4 Lisez les instructions. 5 Lisons leur brochure. 6 Quel livre lisiez-vous? 7 Celui qu'il m'a prêté. 8 Je ne le lirais pas. 9 Je lirai celui qui est ici.

EXERCISE V. 1 Nous élirons un maire. 2 Il a été réélu notre député. 3 Je relisais sa lettre. 4 Nous ne relirons pas l'histoire. 5 Qui a été élu? 6 En le relisant. 7 Sans être élu.

EXERCISE I. 1 Vous a-t-il montré ce que nous avons trouvé? 2 Elle nous a donné ce qu'elle a acheté. 3 Ce que vous avez dit n'est pas vrai. 4 Il vous donnera tout ce que vous demandez. 5 Je sais ce qu'il a fait. 6 Ce n'est pas ce que j'ai vu. 7 Je ne sais pas ce qui est dans cette boite.

EXERCISE II. J'écris ce que vous dictez. 2 Pourquoi ne leur avez-vous pas écrit? 3 J'écrirai plusieurs lettres après le déjeuner. 4 Il écrivit son nom sur un morceau de papier. 5 N'écrivait-elle pas dans sa chambre?

EXERCISE III. 1 Avez-vous quelque chose pour lui? 2 Je l'ai reçu de vous. 3 Nous ne continuerons pas sans eux. 4 Qui écoutait? Elle. 5 Qui a acheté votre maison? Lui. 6 Qui a montré la ville à vos amis? Moi. 7 Parle-t-il d'elle? 8 Avez-vous reçu l'argent d'eux? 9 Elle n'est pas si âgée que lui. 10 Mon ami et moi. 11 Lui et elles.

EXERCISE IV. 1 Qui est là? C'est moi. 2 Ce n'était pas vous? Non, c'était elle. 3 Ce sera lui. 4 Ce n'est pas moi. 5 C'est votre frère. 6 Non, ce n'était pas lui. 7 Ce n'est pas eux? 8 C'est Michel. 9 C'était Jean? 10 C'est Marie?

EXERCISE V. 1 Cet argent est à moi. 2 Ces fleurs ne sont pas à vous; elles sont à elle. 3 Est-ce que ces places sont à nous? 4 Non, elles sont à eux. **5** Ce manteau est à ma femme. **6** Est-ce que ces enfants sont à Marie? **7** Est-ce que cette assiette est à moi? **8** Non, elle est à cet homme.

Exercise VI. **1** Il disait cela. **2** Ils le diront. **3** Je ne le dirais pas. **4** Que lui avez-vous dit? **5** Dites-lui ce que j'ai dit. **6** Vous ne dites pas ce qu'ils vous ont dit. **7** Je vous dirai quelque chose demain. **8** Dites-moi votre nom. **9** Il ne dit que oui. **10** Que disiez-vous tout a l'heure?

Key to Lesson 19

Exercise I. **1** Il ne comprend pas votre question. **2** Pourquoi n'avez-vous pas appris à nager? **3** Prenez garde. **4** Je ne l'entreprendrai pas. **5** Est-ce que cela vous surprend? *or* Cela vous surprend-il? **6** Prend-elle du sucre? **7** Je reprendrai mon livre. **8** Me comprenez-vous? **9** Qu'apprenez-vous, le français ou l'anglais? **10** A quelle heure prenez-vous votre bain? **11** Reprenez cet argent.

Exercise II. **1** C'était vraiment intéressant. **2** Ils ont écouté attentivement. **3** Nous marchions lentement. **4** Nous les voyons rarement. **5** Elle a répondu immédiatement. **6** Ecrivez-le soigneusement. **7** Heureusement il était là. **8** Il nous a dépassé (*better than* passé) rapidement.

Exercise III. **1** A-t-il dépensé autant que vous? **2** Combien de sucre avez-vous mis dans mon café? **3** Parlez-vous plus de langues que lui? **4** Je n'ai pas assez d'argent pour cela. **5** Elle a mis trop de sel dans la soupe. **6** Nous avons moins d'argent qu'eux. **7** Avez-vous beaucoup d'amis en France? **8** Donnez-moi un peu de pain. **9** Cela m'a donné beaucoup de peine. **10** Combien d'enfants ont-ils?

Exercise IV. **1** Nous envoyons un paquet à Paris. **2** Nous avez-vous envoyé les billets? **3** Je le renverrais tout de suite. **4** Envoyez-nous l'information aussitôt que possible. **5** Ne renvoyez pas les choses. **6** L'enverra-t-il par la poste?

Exercise V. **1** Elle parle bien le français. **2** Il porte toujours des lunettes. **3** J'ai souvent été là. **4** Nous avons reçu une lettre de lui hier. **5** Elle parle souvent de vous. **6** Avez-vous déjà mangé? **7** Est-ce que le facteur a été ici ce matin? **8** Ils l'ont envoyé par retour de courrier.

Exercise VI. **1** Il ne me l'a pas rendu. **2** Je ne les lui montrerai pas. **3** Nous ne la leur donnerons pas. **4** Envoyez-le-lui. **5** Nous l'ont-ils envoyé? **6** Prêtez-moi votre couteau. **7** Je l'ai prêté à votre ami, mais il ne me l'a pas rendu. **8** Le leur avez-vous envoyé? **9** Apportez-les-moi.

Key to Lesson 20

Exercise I. **1** Voici les photographies; envoyez-les-lui. **2** C'est mon adresse; ne la leur montrez pas. **3** Cette robe est à moi; ne la lui prêtez pas. **4** Est-ce que ce sont ses clefs? Rendez-les-lui.

EXERCISE II. 1 Que faites-vous? 2 Je fais ce que vous m'avez dit. 3 Vous faites toujours la même chose. 4 Qu'a-t-il fait ce matin? 5 Faisons autre chose. 6 Que faisait-il? 7 Avez-vous fait cela? 8 Je ne le ferai pas. 9 Feriez-vous cela? 10 Ces enfants font trop de bruit. 11 Faites-le tout de suite. 12 Combien de fautes avez-vous faites?

EXERCISE III. 1 Je reçois une lettre presque chaque jour *or* presque tous les jours. 2 Chacun des candidats a reçu un diplôme. 3 Vous recevrez une invitation. 4 N'a-t-il pas reçu l'argent que nous lui avons envoyé la semaine dernière? 5 Combien avez-vous reçu? 6 Ils ne recevront pas le paquet avant le jour après demain.

EXERCISE IV. 1 Combien vous dois-je? 2 Il me doit vingt francs. 3 Vous devez fermer la porte. 4 Dois-je payer cette addition? 5 Il doit le faire. 6 Vous devriez dire la vérité. 7 Ils ne lui doivent pas d'argent. 8 Vous ne devez pas lui écrire. 9 Ils ne doivent pas le voir.

EXERCISE V. 1 En voulez-vous? 2 Voici l'argent; j'en ai dépensé dix francs. 3 Il a apporté ses croquis; il m'en a montré deux. 4 Combien d'enfants a-t-elle? 5 Elle en a trois. 6 Quelle en est la couleur? 7 Quel en était le prix? 8 J'en ai déjà mangé la moitié.

EXERCISE VI. 1 Y avez-vous mis de l'eau? 2 Oui, j'y en ai mis. 3 Avez-vous été à Paris? 4 Oui, j'y ai été. 5 Avez-vous acheté des raisins? 6 Non, il n'y en a pas. 7 Avez-vous mis de l'huile dans la salade? 8 Non, j'y en ajouterai maintenant.

Key to Lesson 21

EXERCISE I. 1 Je ne bois pas de bière. 2 Ils ne boivent pas de vin. 3 Elle buvait son café. 4 Ne buvez pas ceci; ce n'est pas très bon. 5 Je n'en boirai pas. 6 En avez-vous bu? 7 Nous devrions boire du thé et du café.

EXERCISE II. 1 Toutes ces valises sont à moi. 2 Toute la maison est pleine de fumée. 3 Où sont vos amis? Sont-ils tous ici? 4 Tout est prêt. 5 Avez-vous tout trouvé? 6 Toute sa famille habite à Paris. 7 Ils ont perdu tout leur argent. 8 Toutes ces règles sont utiles. 9 Avez-vous lu toute l'histoire? 10 Est-ce que c'est tout?

EXERCISE III. 1 Il ne veut pas prendre l'avion. 2 Voulez-vous le chercher? 3 Elle ne voulait pas l'apprendre. 4 Je voudrais vous aider. 5 Ne voulait-il pas vous écouter? 6 Voulez-vous nous raconter une histoire? 7 Ils ne veulent pas nous voir. 8 Il voudra vous payer. 9 Ne veulent-ils pas nous aider?

EXERCISE IV. 1 Il ne boit rien. 2 Elle ne m'écoute jamais. 3 Ils n'en avaient plus. 4 Nous n'étions que trois. 5 Il n'est ni vieux ni jeune. 6 Je ne boirai plus. 7 Elle ne m'a jamais vu. 8 Il ne mange ni viande ni poisson.

EXERCISE V. 1 Je ne peux pas vous parler aujourd'hui. 2 Il a pu le faire tout de suite. 3 Je pourrais y être avant six heures. 4 Pourriez-vous y aller cet après-midi? 5 Ils ne peuvent pas boire ce thé parce-

qu'il est trop fort. 6 Nous ne pouvions pas comprendre sa question.
7 Je ne pourrai pas rendre les choses la semaine prochaine. 9 Ne
peuvent-ils pas venir?

EXERCISE VI. 1 Nous les rencontrons tous les jeudis. 2 Ils voient
leurs amis tous les six mois. 3 Tout le monde le disait. 4 Quelques-
uns de ses parents étaient ici. 5 Nous avons rencontré quelques-unes
des femmes. 6 J'ai dépensé quelques francs. 7 Quelqu'un a entendu
un bruit. Nous avons mangé quelques pommes et quelques poires.
9 N'a-t-il pas parlé à quelques-uns de ces hommes?

Key to Lesson 22

EXERCISE I. 1 Je le sais. 2 Nous savions toujours comment le
faire. 3 Vous le saurez demain. 4 Ne savez-vous pas où il habite?
5 Si je savais cela je serais riche. 6 Ne sait-elle pas son numéro de vol?
7 Il le savait, mais il l'a oublié. 8 Savez-vous conduire?

EXERCISE II. 1 A qui appartient ceci? 2 Cette page contient toute
l'information. 3 Sa femme tenait les fleurs. 4 Cette maison appartenait
à nos ancêtres. 5 Tenez ceci. 6 Ces boîtes ne contiennent rien.

EXERCISE III. 1 Il reviendra demain. 2 Venez ici. 3 Ils venaient
tous les jours. 4 Il vient de Paris. 5 D'où viennent-ils? 6 Je ne
viendrai pas seul. 7 Nous viendrions avec vous si nous avions le temps.
8 Il vint à la fin du mois dernier. 9 Cela vous conviendra-t-il?

EXERCISE IV. 1 Ils sont allés au cinéma. 2 Elle n'est pas entrée.
3 Est-ce que les filles sont parties? 4 Personne n'était venu. 5 Les
cars seront revenus. 6 Elle serait restée. 7 Etes-vous tombé? 8 Je
suis allé seul.

EXERCISE V. 1 Ils lisaient les journaux français. 2 L'église que
nous avons vue était très vieille. 3 Quelles belles fleurs! 4 Mes amis
n'étaient pas présents. 5 Il avait de grandes mains et une petite tête.
6 Achetez-moi des raisins verts. 7 Ces règles sont très difficiles à
comprendre.

Key to Lesson 23

EXERCISE I. 1 Où allez-vous? 2 Il allait au théâtre. 3 Nous irons
à Paris demain. 4 Pourquoi ne va-t-il pas avec vous? 5 N'ira-t-il
pas seul? 6 Allons ensemble. 7 N'allez pas dans la rue. 8 Vont-ils
aux bateaux? 9 J'irais si j'avais assez d'argent. 10 Nous allons com-
mencer. 11 Je ne vais pas l'acheter. 12 Elle n'allait pas le faire.

EXERCISE II. 1 Elle ne veut pas me parler. 2 Vous ne devriez pas
dire cela. 3 Nous nous laverons. 4 Les enfants ne s'amuseraient pas.
5 Ne devrions-nous pas les prévenir. 6 Ils ne viendraient pas sans nous
le dire (*better to say* sans nous en prévenir). 7 Ils ne voulaient pas venir
avec nous. 8 Je ne veux pas lui parler. 9 Dois-je y aller sans vous?
10 Elle devrait écouter ce que je dis. 11 Ils ne le trouveront pas à la
maison. 12 Il ne voulait pas s'excuser.

EXERCISE III. 1 Les chevaux courent. 2 Ne courez pas si vite. 3 Il courait tout le temps. 4 Courons après eux. 5 Pourquoi courez-vous? 6 Les garçons courront ce soir. 7 Je ne courrais pas si j'étais à votre place.

EXERCISE IV. 1 Nous ne nous sommes pas amusés. 2 Ils se seraient habillés. 3 Les garçons ne s'étaient pas lavés. 4 Je me suis trompé. 5 Ils se sont établis. 6 Il ne s'était pas dépêché. 7 Pourquoi ne s'est-elle pas habillée?

Key to Lesson 24

EXERCISE I. 1 Pourquoi riez-vous? 2 Il ne nous suivra pas. 3 Il ne suffisait pas. 4 Ne riez pas si fort. 5 Cela ne suffira pas. 6 Il rira s'il voit cela. 7 Vous a-t-il suivi?

EXERCISE II. 1 Ils se disputent tous les jours. 2 Vous vous reposez trop souvent. 3 Vous êtes-vous promené? 4 Nous nous sommes disputés avec le garçon. 5 Vous êtes-vous reposés? 6 Je me lèverai plus tôt demain matin. 7 Ils ne voulaient pas se battre. 8 Nous devons nous excuser.

EXERCISE III. 1 J'ai oublié de lui écrire. 2 Nous avons attendu à la gare pour les rencontrer. 3 J'ai regretté d'avoir parlé. 4 Il l'a dit pour vous rassurer. 5 Elle essaie (or essaye) de m'aider. 6 Ils étudient pour passer un examen. 7 Nous travaillons pour gagner de l'argent. 8 Il se souvient d'avoir écrit ceci.

EXERCISE IV. 1 Il apprend à nager. 2 N'allez-vous pas réserver des places? 3 Ils nous ont invités à venir avec eux. 4 Laissez-moi passer. 5 Nous devons y aller demain. 6 Ne pouvaient-ils pas vous aider? 7 Nous ne pouvions pas trouver un garage. 8 Aimez-vous danser? 9 N'avez-vous rien à faire? 10 Ils doivent l'essayer.

EXERCISE V. 1 Sentez-vous le courant d'air? 2 Elle ne se sent pas bien. 3 Pourquoi êtes-vous sortis sans moi? 4 Ils partiront avant six heures. 5 Votre femme est-elle sortie? 6 A quelle heure reviendra-t-elle? 7 Sortons ensemble. 8 Il ne dort pas bien. 9 Ne mentez pas. 10 Le repas était servi en haut.

EXERCISE VI. 1 Il va chez lui. 2 Elle sortait de chez le coiffeur. 3 Il envoie cette lettre en Allemagne. 3 Ne sont-ils pas à Paris? 5 Nous les avons rencontrés chez mon frère. 6 N'est-il pas chez lui? 7 Elle n'était pas chez elle; elle était chez sa mère. 8 Nous les avons rencontrés comme ils sortaient de chez eux.

Key to Lesson 25

EXERCISE I. 1 Ils commencent; nous ne commençons pas; 2 vous jugez, ils jugeaient; 3 nous achetons, il n'achète pas; 4 a-t-il mené? mènerez-vous? 5 il répétait, ne répète-t-il pas? 6 il ne vous payera pas, ne le payez pas; 7 Ils renouvelleront leur abonnement.

EXERCISE II. 1 Ouvrez-vous le magasin à huit heures? 2 Il souffre beaucoup. 3 Elle m'a offert un verre de vin. 4 Qu'avez-vous découvert? 5 Ouvrez la porte. 6 Ne couvrez pas cette assiette. 7 Vous a-t-il offert quelque chose? 8 J'ouvrirai les portes et les fenêtres.

EXERCISE III. 1 Il y a des personnes qui disent cela. 2 N'y a-t-il pas de places pour nous? 3 Il n'y aura rien à faire. 4 Y a-t-il un bureau de poste dans cette rue? 5 Il n'y avait pas de tableaux sur le mur. 6 Y a-t-il des souris dans votre cuisine? 7 N'y avait-il pas de cigarettes dans le paquet?

EXERCISE IV. 1 De quoi parlez-vous? 2 Les cartes avec lesquelles ils jouaient. 3 Il part avant cinq heures. 4 La personne à qui nous l'avons donné. 5 Nous étions ici avant vous. 6 La mer était devant nous. 7 L'homme de qui il parle. 8 Dans quelle valise l'avez-vous mis? 9 Il est venu lui-même.

EXERCISE V. 1 Ne le permettez-vous pas? 2 Il n'a rien promis. 3 Nous ne leur permettrons pas de le faire. 4 Pourquoi ont-ils omis ceci? 5 Ils nous ont promis de venir. 6 Ne vous permettrait-il pas d'y aller?

EXERCISE VI. 1 A qui est cette place? 2 Qu'est-ce que vous écrivez? 3 De qui est-il l'ami? 4 Qu'est-ce qui sent si fort? 5 Pourquoi se plaint-il? 6 Qu'est-ce qui vous amuse? 7 A qui sont ces vêtements? 8 Il ne craint rien. 9 Tout le monde le craignait. 10 Pourquoi vous êtes-vous plaint? 11 Qui peindra le tableau? 12 Pourquoi n'éteint-il pas la lumière?

EXERCISE VII. 1 On frappe à la porte. 2 On vous demande. 3 On parle de vous. 4 On aime à être chez soi. 5 On chantait dans la rue. 6 On dit qu'elle va mourir. 7 Si l'on demande votre adresse.

EXERCISE VIII. 1 Ces cigarettes sont meilleures que celles-là. 2 Elle écrit mieux que vous. 3 Il a acheté une livre et demie de beurre. 4 Son vin est le meilleur. 5 Il est pire qu'hier. 6 Elle mange moins chaque jour. 7 Il joue le mieux de tous.

Key to Lesson 26

EXERCISE I. 1 que je ferme, que tu fermes, qu'il ferme, que nous fermions, que vous fermiez, qu'ils ferment; que j'attende, que tu attendes, qu'il attende, que nous attendions, que vous attendiez, qu'ils attendent; que je remplisse, que tu remplisses, qu'il remplisse, que nous remplissions, que vous remplissiez, qu'ils remplissent. 2 parte*, partes, parte, partions, partiez, partent; écrive, écrives, écrive, écrivions, écriviez, écrivent; lise, lises, lise, lisions, lisiez, lisent. 3 sache, saches, sache, sachions, sachiez, sachent; voie, voies, voie, voyions, voyiez, voient; dise, dises, dise, disions, disiez, disent. 4 que je passe; 5 qu'il ne parle pas; 6 que nous perdions; 7 que vous ne rendiez pas; 8 qu'ils réussissent; 9 qu'elle finisse; 10 qu'il écrive; 11 qu'ils ne sachent pas; 12 que vous vendiez.

* For brevity, que and the PRONOUN are omitted from this point.

Exercise II. 1 aille, ailles, aille, allions, alliez, aillent; fasse, fasses, fasse, fassions, fassiez, fassent; boive, boives, boive, buvions, buviez, boivent; 2 puisse, puisses, puisse, puissions, puissiez, puissent; vienne, viennes, vienne, venions, veniez, viennent; 3 aie, aies, ait, ayons, ayez, aient, sois, sois, soit, soyons, soyez, soient; veuille, veuilles, veuille, voulions, vouliez, veuillent; 4 que je vienne; 5 qu'il ne puisse pas; 6 que nous voulions; 7 que vous ne teniez pas; 8 qu'ils n'aillent pas; 9 que nous revenions; 10 que vous ne receviez pas; 11 qu'ils le fassent.

Exercise III. 1 eusse, eusses, eût, eussions, eussiez, eussent; fusse, fusses, fût, fussions, fussiez, fussent; fermasse, fermasses, fermât, fermassions, fermassiez, fermassent; 2 attendisse, attendisses, attendît, attendissions, attendissiez, attendissent; remplisse, remplisses, remplît, remplissions, remplissiez, remplissent; lusse, lusses, lût, lussions, lussiez, lussent; 3 pusse, pusses, pût, pussions, pussiez, pussent; tinsse, tinsses, tînt, tinssions, tinssiez, tinssent; prisse, prisses, prît, prissions, prissiez, prissent. 4 que je respondisse; 5 qu'elle ne reussît pas; 6 qu'ils n'eussent pas; 7 qu'elle vînt; 8 que nous parlassions; 9 que vous fussiez; 10 qu'il ecrivît.

Exercise IV. 1 C'est la seule chose qu'il vende. 2 Le meilleur livre que j'aie jamais lu. 3 Le plus beau tableau qu'il ait peint. 4 Donnez-le au premier homme qui vienne. 5 Attendez jusqu'à ce que je sois prêt. 6 Bien qu'il soit riche, il n'est pas heureux. 7 Nous leur parlerons avant qu'ils l'aient fini. 8 Il est venu afin que nous puissions en parler.

Exercise V. 1 Croyez-vous qu'il soit à la maison? 2 Je ne crois pas qu'elle veuille danser. 3 Je ne pensais pas qu'il vînt. 4 Faut-il que nous partions? 5 N'est-il pas probable qu'il le voie? 6 Ne savez-vous pas qu'il y sera? 7 Il n'a pas dit qu'il pouvait le faire. 8 Est-il possible que l'argent soit à lui? (or le sien). 9 Je ne pense pas qu'il en prenne.

Exercise VI. 1 Nous regrettons qu'il ne nous ait pas trouvés. 2 Elle craint qu'il (ne) vienne. 3 Faut-il que nous attendions? 4 Je doutais qu'ils vinssent. 5 Je crains qu'il (ne) vous attende. 6 Nous craignions que nous ne vous vissions pas. 7 Nous voudrions qu'ils n'eussent pas commencé. 8 Je voudrais qu'elle ne fût pas ici.

Exercise VII. 1 Faut-il que vous le fassiez? 2 Il faudra que vous lui écriviez. 3 Il ne faudrait pas qu'il le finît. 4 Il faut que nous le sachions. 5 Il ne faut pas que nous payions ces droits. 6 Il ne fallait pas qu'ils parlassent.

Exercise VIII. 1 Veut-il qu'elle le lise? 2 Ils veulent que je lui parle. 3 Voudra-t-il que vous leur écriviez? 4 Elle veut que vous acceptiez ceci. 5 Ils ne voudront pas que nous le gardions. 6 Ne veut-il pas que nous y restions. 7 Nous ne voulons pas qu'ils nous entendent. 8 Vouliez-vous que je le fisse pour vous? 9 Voulez-vous que je le fasse pour lui? 10 Ne voulez-vous pas que nous y allions? 11 Ne voulez-vous pas que je le lui envoie? 12 Voulez-vous que nous le cherchions? 13 Voulez-vous que je ferme la fenêtre?